Central Banks as Economic Institutions

Cournot Centre for Economic Studies

Series Editor: Robert M. Solow, *Institute Professor Emeritus, Massachusetts Institute of Technology; President of the Cournot Centre for Economic Studies, Paris, France*

Conference Editor: Jean-Philippe Touffut, *Director of the Cournot Centre for Economic Studies, Paris, France*

Central Banks as Economic Institutions

Edited by

Jean-Philippe Touffut

Director of the Cournot Centre for Economic Studies, Paris, France

THE COURNOT CENTRE FOR ECONOMIC STUDIES SERIES

Edward Elgar

Cheltenham, UK • Northampton, MA, USA

Published by
Edward Elgar Publishing Limited
The Lypiatts
15 Lansdown Road
Cheltenham
Glos GL50 2JA
UK

Edward Elgar Publishing, Inc.
William Pratt House
9 Dewey Court
Northampton
Massachusetts 01060
USA

A catalogue record for this book
is available from the British Library

Library of Congress Control Number: 2008932891

ISBN 978 1 84844 108 8 (cased)
ISBN 978 1 84844 109 5 (paperback)

Printed and bound in Great Britain by MPG Books Ltd, Bodmin, Cornwall

Contents

Figures and tables

FIGURES

TABLES

Contributors

Patrick Artus is a Professor of Economics at the École Polytechnique and at the University of Paris 1 (Panthéon-Sorbonne), as well as Chief Economist at Natixis, the French investment bank. He is a member of the Conseil d'Analyse Économique reporting to the French Prime Minister, as well as a member of the Commission Économique de la Nation. His main fields of research are international economics and monetary policy.

Alan S. Blinder is a Professor of Economics at Princeton University and Co-Director of Princeton's Center for Economic Policy Studies, which he founded in 1990. He served as Vice Chairman of the Board of Governors of the Federal Reserve System from June 1994 to January 1996. He is a Trustee of the Russell Sage Foundation, a member of the Bretton Woods Committee and of the Bellagio Group and a former Governor of the American Stock Exchange. His main research fields are fiscal policy, monetary policy and the distribution of income.

Willem Buiter is a Professor of European Political Economy at the European Institute, London School of Economics and Political Science, and a Professor of Economics at the University of Amsterdam. He is a member of the European Central Bank (ECB) Shadow Council and chairs the Council of Economic Advisers of the Second Chamber of the Dutch Parliament. From 2000 to 2005, he was Chief Economist of the European Bank for Reconstruction and Development, and from 1997 to 2000 he served as external member of the Monetary Policy Committee of the Bank of England. His main research interests include monetary and fiscal policy, public finance, economic and political European integration, corporate governance and public goods.

Nazire Nergiz Dincer has been a Planning Expert at the State Planning Organization of Turkey since 1998. She was a Visiting Scholar at the University of California, Berkeley in 2005–06. Her research interests are central banking, exchange rate policy, inflation and exchange rate uncertainty and their effects on the economy, bank regulation and supervision, and the Turkish economy.

Barry Eichengreen is a Professor of Economics and Political Science at the University of California, Berkeley, a Research Associate of the National

Bureau of Economic Research (Cambridge, MA) and a Research Fellow of the Centre for Economic Policy Research (London, UK). He was Senior Policy Adviser at the International Monetary Fund from 1997 to 1998, and he is the convener of the Bellagio Group of academics and economic officials. His main research interests are international finance and monetary policy.

Benjamin M. Friedman is a Professor of Political Economy at Harvard University. He is an Adviser to the Federal Reserve Bank of New York and a member of the Brookings Panel on Economic Activity and the Council on Foreign Relations. Formerly an Adviser to the Congressional Budget Office, he has also worked with the Board of Governors of the Federal Reserve System, the Federal Reserve Bank of New York, and the Federal Reserve Bank of Boston. His main research interests are monetary economics, macroeconomics, and monetary and fiscal policy.

Carl-Ludwig Holtfrerich is a Professor of Economics and Economic History in the Department of Economics at the John F. Kennedy Institute of the Freie Universität in Berlin. A former Research Fellow at the Woodrow Wilson International Center for Scholars in Washington DC and the Center for European Studies at Harvard University, he has taught at the Johann Wolfgang-Goethe-Universität in Frankfurt/Main and at St. Antony's College, University of Oxford. As an economic historian, his main research focuses on economic policy in the United States and Canada.

Gerhard Illing is a Professor of Macroeconomics at the Ludwig Maximilian University of Munich and the Director of CESifo Economic Studies research centre. His main research interests include mechanism design of central banks, systemic risk and international financial architecture, asset markets and financial stability, and transparency and speculative attacks.

Otmar Issing is President of the Center for Financial Studies and Chairman of the Advisory Board of the House of Finance at the University of Frankfurt. He was a member of the executive board of the European Central Bank from June 1998 to May 2006. A former member of the board of the Bundesbank, he also served for many years on the Council of Economic Experts at the German Federal Ministry of Economics. Formerly a Professor of Economics at the University of Würzburg, his main research fields are monetary policy and the European Union.

Takatoshi Ito is a Professor of Economics at the Graduate School of Economics, University of Tokyo, and a member of the Japanese government's Council on Economic and Fiscal Policy. Formerly a Senior Adviser to the International Monetary Fund, he was Deputy Vice Minister for International Affairs at the Japanese Ministry of Finance from 1999 to 2001. His main research fields include international finance, open macroeconomics and the Japanese economy.

Stephen Morris is a Professor of Economics at Princeton University and the Editor of *Econometrica*. Formerly a Professor of Economics at Yale University, he has been a Visiting Scholar at several institutions, including the University of Cambridge, the London School of Economics and the International Monetary Fund. His main research interests are microeconomics and game theory.

André Orléan is a Director of Research at the CNRS (Centre National de la Recherche Scientifique) and a Director of Studies at the EHESS (École des Hautes Études en Sciences Sociales) in Paris. He is a member of the Advisory Committee of the AMF (Autorité des Marchés Financiers). His main research fields include monetary economics, finance, cognitive economics, and the economics of convention, a French heterodox movement of which he is a founding member.

Nouriel Roubini is a Professor of Economics at the Stern School of Business, New York University, and Co-Founder and Chairman of Roubini Global Economics LLC (www.rgemonitor.com), a web-based economic and geo-strategic information service and economic consultancy. He served on President Bill Clinton's Council of Economic Advisers, was a Senior Adviser to the Under Secretary for International Affairs, and was the Director of the Office of Policy Development and Review at the US Treasury Department. His main research interests are international macroeconomic issues, the economies of Europe and the United States, the Asian and global financial crises, emerging markets, and the reform of the international financial system and global economic imbalances.

Hyun Song Shin is a Professor of Economics at Princeton University affiliated with the Bendheim Center for Finance. He is a Fellow of the British Academy, the European Economic Association and the Econometric Society. His research interests include game theory and information economics with applications to financial stability and accounting.

Robert M. Solow is Institute Professor Emeritus at the Massachusetts Institute of Technology. In 1987, he was awarded the Nobel Memorial Prize in Economics for his contributions to economic growth theory. He is a Visiting Scholar at the Russell Sage Foundation, New York, where he is a member of the advisory committee for the Foundation's project on the incidence and quality of low-wage employment in Europe and the United States. Professor Solow is President of the Cournot Centre for Economic Studies.

Jean-Philippe Touffut is Co-Founder and Director of the Cournot Centre for Economic Studies.

Preface

This volume is one of a series arising from the conferences organized by the Cournot Centre for Economic Studies, Paris. These conferences explore contemporary issues in economics, with particular focus on Europe. Speakers, along with other participants and members of the audience, are drawn from backgrounds in academia, business, finance, labour unions, the media and national or multinational governmental and non-governmental agencies.

The specific texts presented here were delivered at the ninth conference of the Cournot Centre for Economic Studies held on 30 November and 1 December 2006.

Acknowledgements

I would like to thank all the participants at the Cournot Centre conference on central banking, especially Robert Solow, the chairman, who gave the conference the historical inspiration that tends to lack in purely economic debates. My warmest thanks to Therrese Goodlett, Anna Kaiser and Timothy Slind. From the organization of the conference to the preparation of the manuscript and the composition of the index, they have enabled this work to see the light of day under the best possible conditions. Special thanks also go to Richard Crabtree for translations. A film of the whole conference can be ordered on-line from the Cournot Centre at www. centrecournot.org.

About the series

Professor Robert M. Solow

The Cournot Centre for Economic Studies is an independent French-based research institute. It takes its name from the pioneering economist, mathematician and philosopher Antoine Augustin Cournot (1801–77).

Neither a think-tank nor a research bureau, the Centre enjoys the special independence of a catalyst. My old student dictionary (dated 1936) says that catalysis is the 'acceleration of a reaction produced by a substance, called the *catalyst*, which may be recovered practically unchanged at the end of the reaction'. The reaction we have in mind results from bringing together (a) an issue of economic policy that is currently being discussed and debated in Europe and (b) the relevant theoretical and empirical findings of serious economic research in universities, think-tanks and research bureaux. Acceleration is desirable because it is better that reaction occurs before minds are made up and decisions taken, not after. We hope that the Cournot Centre can be recovered practically unchanged and used again and again.

Notice that 'policy debate' is not exactly what we are trying to promote. To have a policy debate, you need not only knowledge and understanding, but also preferences, desires, values and goals. The trouble is that, in practice, the debaters often have only those things, and they invent or adopt only those 'findings' that are convenient. The Cournot Centre hopes to inject the findings of serious research at an early stage.

It is important to realize that this is not easy or straightforward. The analytical issues that underlie economic policy choices are usually complex. Economics is not an experimental science. The available data are scarce, and may not be exactly the relevant ones. Interpretations are therefore uncertain. Different studies, by uncommitted economists, may give different results. When those controversies exist, it is our hope that the Centre's conferences will discuss them. Live debate at that fundamental level is exactly what we are after.

There is also a problem of timing. Conferences have to be planned well in advance, so that authors can prepare careful and up-to-date texts. Then a publication lag is inevitable. The implication is that the Cournot Centre's conferences cannot take up very short-term issues of policy. Instead, a balancing act is required: we need issues that are short-term enough so that they are directly concerned with current policy, but long-term enough so that they remain directly relevant for a few years.

I used the words 'serious research' a moment ago. That sort of phrase is sometimes used to exclude unwelcome ideas, especially unfashionable ones. The Cournot Centre does not intend to impose narrow requirements of orthodoxy, but it does hope to impose high standards of attention to logic and respect for facts. It is because those standards are not always observed in debates about policy that an institution like the Cournot Centre has a role to play.

OTHER BOOKS IN THE COURNOT CENTRE SERIES

2007. *Augustin Cournot: Modelling Economics*
Edited by Jean-Philippe Touffut
Contributors: Robert J. Aumann, Alain Desrosières, Jean Magnan de Bornier, Thierry Martin, Glenn Shafer, Robert M. Solow, Bernard Walliser

2006. *Advancing Public Goods*
Edited by Jean-Philippe Touffut
Contributors: Patrick Artus, Avner Ben-Ner, Bernard Gazier, Xavier Greffe, Claude Henry, Philippe Herzog, Inge Kaul, Joseph E. Stiglitz

2005. *Corporate Governance Adrift: A Critique of Shareholder Value*
Michel Aglietta and Antoine Rebérioux

2004. *The Future of Economic Growth: As New Becomes Old*
Robert Boyer

2003. *Institutions, Innovation and Growth: Selected Economic Papers*
Edited by Jean-Philippe Touffut
Contributors: Philippe Aghion, Bruno Amable, with Pascal Petit, Timothy Bresnahan, Paul A. David, David Marsden, AnnaLee Saxenian, Günther Schmid, Robert M. Solow, Wolfgang Streeck, Jean-Philippe Touffut

Introduction

Jean-Philippe Touffut

Few institutions have spread as widely throughout the world as central banks have. With 18 in existence at the end of the nineteenth century, their numbers had grown to 173 by the beginning of the twenty-first century. Although the first central banks were government banks, they progressively incorporated functions that made them into the bank of banks of the twentieth century. The role they were assigned changed during the 1990s as they were gradually required to become more independent from government control. The transformation has affected the whole planet: since 1990, the central banks of 34 countries have adopted new statutes.

As the instruments of monetary policy have changed, so its management has evolved: today more importance is attached to the transparency of the Bank's short- and mid-term objectives, rather than intermediate targets, such as exchange rate stability, growth of the monetary mass or the level of nominal interest rates. It is difficult to separate monetary policy from the instruments used to pursue it and the legitimacy with which it operates. In fact, the strictly economic arguments and the arguments to be drawn from historical analysis are indistinguishable. This work originates from the conference organized at the end of 2006 by the Cournot Centre, the aim of which was precisely to account for the institutional construction of central banks over the last few decades. Current events since the date of the conference have kept these institutions constantly at the centre of the economic stage: the leading role they are credited with playing in the economy has been the object of many commentaries outside this field, which do not always show a clear understanding of the foundations of their actions and the limits within which they operate.

Times have changed since Walter Bagehot wrote, in 1874,[1] 'in ordinary times the Bank is only one of many lenders, whereas in a panic it is the sole lender'. The role of the central bank has never been limited to lending. It overlooks economic activity, a position it owes to its discourse as much as to its actions. Thus, the central bank organizes its public statements in a very precise manner. The declarations of the governors, often widely reported in the press, represent a few lines in the vast mass of information, often very dense, that the central bank issues in the form of statistics or studies. One particularity of central bank publications is that they are the object of crossed interpretations that may conflict to the point of contradicting the initial expression of their authors. They are also the object of expectations, which can go against the intention of the communication.

Whatever the contradiction affecting the central bank's utterances, its formulation does not call into question the legitimacy expressed. The declaration of a central banker must be interpreted, like any utterance, according to its context. Classic expressions such as 'there is a risk that inflation will rise over the short term' or 'the markets are right to expect a forthcoming rise in the interest rate'[2] share a particularity. They favour implicature over presupposition;[3,4] they express political sovereignty. With presupposition, responsibility for the implicit meaning of the message lies entirely with the speaker, whereas with implicature it lies entirely with the addressee. Central bankers do not adopt a discourse that is codified in its syntactical components, but one that depends on the context and is linked to the utterance; in other words, they can always take refuge behind the literalness of their statements.

The expression of the institution's independence reveals the mark of its autonomy in relation to its history. What the discourse of the central bank treats as given – all the arrangements that found its ahistoric universality – is the product of a long collective path dependence that has led to this seemingly natural fact.[5] The formulations of the central bank play a part in crediting economic agents with rational behaviour, sidestepping the question of the social conditions of access to this aptitude and the action required to render these conditions universal. The central bank is thus situated *a priori* in the sphere of market transactions. The countries that changed the statutes of their central banks during the 1990s had thus confirmed their conversion to this world of autonomous beliefs.

André Orléan explores the foundations, continuation and crises of this astonishing collective belief, in which the specific power of money is revealed. An explanation based on the legal enactment of the central bank's commitments proves to be unsatisfactory. Admittedly, the legal constraint does increase its credibility, given the heavy punishments incurred if it fails to honour its commitments, but, at best, it gives the central bank operational independence. Moreover, the legal constraints vary greatly from one country to another: in the United States, for example, the Federal Reserve Board has a triple mandate, whereas most of the other central banks have one main objective of price stability. A comparative analysis of the history of these institutions, corroborated by the study of two events described by André Orléan, shows that, fundamentally, money possesses its own power. This is, by definition, overlooked by the legalistic approach. The discrepancy between the constraints imposed by law and the historical grounding of the central bank is clearly exposed in the contribution by Carl Holtfrerich, devoted to the Reichsbank. From the establishment of the empire in 1871 to the introduction of the euro in 1999, the vicissitudes of the German central bank help to explain the foundations of the European Central Bank. The Reichsbank and then the Bundesbank were constantly subordinated to political objectives. Thus, Holtfrerich's analysis shows that the positions adopted by these institutions supported the promotion of a specific mercantilism, founded on exports. Restricting domestic demand, with the help of appropriate fiscal and monetary policies, makes it possible to keep imports and national inflation at a low level and to free productive resources in order to export more.

Benjamin Friedman's text raises the question of the relevance of central bankers' discourse on financial and non-financial economic activity. How should the policy objectives of a central bank be presented, internally, to the financial markets, or to the general public, as 'targets' of monetary policy? The questions of the transparency and accountability of the central bank bring into play all the representations of the institution in charge of public policy. Not only does monetary policy affect real economic results, such as production and employment, it is also, in practical terms, the only instrument available for pursuing public policy over the medium term. Policies must have objectives involving real results and dismiss the argument according to which monetary policy only has one independent instrument and should only concentrate on one sole economic aim.

If one judges the conformity of the central banks' discourses and recommendations to the results as presented by them over the last 15 years, 'monetary policy has been a great success', says Gerhard Illing in the introduction to his contribution. Their approach, inspired by the new neoclassical synthesis, would thus appear to be justified. This approach focuses on the commitment of central banks to exert an effective influence on long-term real interest rates through ensuring the credibility of its action on short-term interest rates and through communicating in advance information on the variations they envisage for future nominal interest rates. In this interpretation, the money supply only plays a marginal role. Part of the discourse is founded on the implementation of financial innovations, supposed to make the markets globally more efficient. These innovations may also generate problems of a more serious nature in the case of grave deterioration in the economic climate. During a period of crisis, the injection of liquidities by central banks can save the situation, but it can also amplify the problem: institutions that are already in debt, counting on intervention by the central banks in the event of a crisis, are encouraged to take even bigger risks. Upstream, the best policy consists in trying to prevent the formation of financial weaknesses, rather than undertaking to intervene, a costly commitment when facing the risk of financial collapse.

Problems of stability can conflict with the other objectives of the monetary authority. A central bank may hesitate to raise interest rates at the speed required for efficient stabilization of the economy. If there is a risk that a rate rise will endanger highly-indebted institutions, the central bank may find itself in an interest-rate trap: the problems of financial stability may oblige it to follow a trajectory of disproportionate gradualism. Along the same lines, during favourable periods, central banks may raise interest rates above the level required to deal with problems of stabilization, with the aim of giving themselves more room for manoeuvre when the climate worsens. Once again, the conditions of stability may be contradictory to an efficient policy of stabilization. The scenario developed in Illing's contribution is illustrated in the contemporary financial crisis that began in autumn 2007 and continues to unfold in summer 2008.

As Stephen Morris explained during the Cournot Centre conference, economists can no longer defend the idea of a dichotomy between the actions taken by the central bank, using the instruments at its disposal, and the play of economic agents, making their decisions independently. His contribution with Hyun Song Shin shows that it is in the grey area between the interpretations of both sides that decisions are shaped. Monetary policy endeavours to make up for failures in coordination: even if successful communication can reduce the weight of the direct instruments used by the central bank, such as the control of overnight interest rates, these instruments remain decisive during times of crisis. Morris and Shin point out that since the 1990s, central banks have had to master the art of coordinating expectations in the economy. When the policy of issuing information fails to coordinate expectations, the instruments are called to the rescue. Their impact can be as strong as its use is unforeseen. If the coordination of expectations is possible, then we have at our disposal a powerful and efficient instrument. This has been illustrated over the last 15 years by the successes achieved with greater transparency in communication by the central banks.

Transparency is the characteristic that most clearly differentiates today's central banks from those of the past. Over the last few years, this virtue has been extended to their objectives, procedures, principles, models and data. Is this a general trend? Is it likely to last? The chapter by Barry Eichengreen and Nazire Nergiz Dincer seeks to answer these questions. It shows that the trend is remarkably widespread. On the question of durability, it appears that the effects on the variability of inflation and production are positive. If the institutional systems that generate good results obtain public approval and support, there is every reason to believe that this trend towards transparency in monetary policy will endure.

A number of studies have already been conducted on this subject, but we know little about the real trends of transparency, their correlates and consequences. Theoretical research has opened up some useful prospects, but its implications are limited, to say the least. Eichengreen and Dincer make a new contribution by creating an index of transparency for central banks. This index takes into account the different components and dimensions of transparency, and it covers a greater number of countries, over a longer period of time, than any previous study. Analysis of the spread of transparency over space and time brings recent trends to light. In which countries, and for what reasons have central banks become more transparent? What effect does transparency have on the persistence of inflation and on the variability of inflation and production? By considering both the determinants and the effects of transparency, the authors use the analysis of determinants to identify instrumental variables to illustrate the correlation observed between the different results.

The next two contributions, revised at the beginning of 2007, give a special flavour to this collection of papers, for they give the recipe for the financial crisis that was to strike the world eight months later. Like Nouriel Roubini, Takatoshi Ito describes the origins of a smouldering crisis, needing no more than a spark to set it ablaze, although the source of the spark was still unknown. Thus, Ito examines the role of central banks, faced with the global disequilibria in finance that have appeared since 2003. He finds four characteristics to be particularly disquieting: the very heavy current account deficit of the United States, the large current account surpluses of China, other East Asian and oil-producing countries, the accumulation of currency reserves by these countries because of their resistance to currency appreciation, and substantial entries of capital into the United States, together with low world interest rates. Chief among the elements that make it impossible for this phenomenon to continue is the durability of consumption in the United States, sustained by real estate growth. (The author's intuition proved right.) This is one of the ten scenarios that Roubini puts forward in order to understand the saga of the crisis developing before his eyes. Each version, from the most reassuring to the most devastating, reveals a conception of the central bank as either the focal point of anticipations of economic activity, or the keystone of the system. Until very recently, central bank action was limited to predicting systemic crises, that is, crises that endangered the economy's financial structure. Central banks thus acted as lenders of last resort in order to save the few institutions which made up the framework. In March 2008, the injection of 29 billion US dollars by the US Federal Reserve Board to help bail out Bear Stearns Companies, a brokerage firm, was unprecedented. For the moment, it is impossible to tell if this is the beginning of a shift in central banks' responsibility to non-banking institutions. Indeed, the Federal Reserve Board has not lent money to a non-banking institution since the 1930s. When a central bank acts in favour of a company that is not subject to the same strict regulatory and supervisory framework as banks are, it places non-banking institutions on an equal footing with banks, but without the same rules on regulatory capital, liquidity ratios, compliance and disclosure standards, to name just a few. Does this widen the legitimacy of central banks? What political body can justify this shift?

At the international level, the G8 has not become the directorate of international monetary affairs as it had hoped at one time. No political body has succeeded in dealing with the politico-economic discordance whose determinants have overtaken the eight most powerful countries in the world. The round table with Patrick Artus, Alan Blinder, Willem Buiter and Otmar Issing, chaired by Robert Solow, brings into perspective the concerns of central banks. What should their objectives be? What instruments will they be able to use? What are the consequences and effects of globalization on monetary policy? These questions take on different aspects, according to the monetary authorities' perception of communication and transparency, and depending on their independence and accountability. From one region of the world to another, the current crisis reminds us that the responses of the central banks redefine their influence on economic activity and their political position.

NOTES

1. Bagehot (1874).
2. Statement by the governor of the European Central Bank, 1 February 2006.
3. In linguistics, an 'implicature' is anything that is inferred from an utterance, but that is not a condition for the truth of the utterance.
4. Without going too deeply into the semantic analysis of the discourse, it appears that these two phrases do not stand up to the test of syntactical behaviour, negation or interrogation, which completely change the statement.
5. The central bank is thus presented as an institution of the economy, as described by Pierre Bourdieu (2000, pp. 15–17).

REFERENCES

Bagehot, Walter (1874), *Lombard Street: A Description of the Money Market*, New York: Scribner, Armstrong.
Bourdieu, Pierre (2000), *Les structures sociales de l'économie*, Paris: Seuil.

1. Monetary beliefs and the power of central banks

André Orléan

INTRODUCTION

> If all money is fiduciary, as Simiand maintains, we still have to determine, at each stage in its evolution, the reasons for this collective trust. There is no task more imperative for economic historians than to discover its nature and measure its strength, society by society. This calls for a detailed analysis of the whole social atmosphere. (Marc Bloch in a review of François Simiand's, 'La monnaie réalité sociale')[1]

In a system with purely self-referential money, free of all the constraints of fixed rate convertibility, the central bank's commitment to maintaining the purchasing power of the unit of account plays a pivotal role. It is responsible both for sustaining the nominal anchorage and for stabilizing private price expectations. Modern theory rightly stresses the importance of this task and the difficulty of accomplishing it. One point is given particular attention: the disruptive influence of the government in power.[2] Before elections, the government is tempted to increase the money supply, to the detriment of price stability, so as to stimulate the economy and increase its chances of re-election. Within the framework of a model with rational expectations, private agents, perfectly aware of this inflationary expedient of the incumbent government, adapt their price expectations accordingly, so that the government's measures simply end up producing inflation, without stimulating production at all. To avoid this result, so prejudicial to everyone concerned, modern theory argues that the central bank should be independent in order to give credibility to its fight against inflation. By insulating the issuing institution from governmental pressure, independence allows it to evade the short-termist temptations of the government and concentrate on its objective of price stability. This widespread line of reasoning has led to the current international consensus to adopt inflation targeting as the monetary policy norm for an independent central bank. If proof were needed, we need look no further than the large number of central banks that have rewritten their statutes to this effect over the last

15 years. Michael King (2001) counted 34 central banks that had done just that between 1990 and 2001.

This analysis, however, tends to pass over the question of the forces capable of producing such independence, or, more accurately, in keeping with the 'Ulysses and the sirens' model (Elster, 1979), the question is answered by assuming that governments tie their own hands, that is, restrict their own authority. Is this a satisfactory answer? Leaving aside the question of whether such a scenario is desirable, I shall examine whether or not it is actually possible. More precisely, in what is the independence granted by the sovereign – the government – a *credible* obstacle to any of that sovereign's subsequent actions? What it has granted, is it not within its power to take away again? Put another way, how can central bank independence be made truly credible? This is the crux of the analysis, because without a credible commitment, it is easy to lapse into the contradictions of temporal incoherence.

In studying this question, the next section criticizes what I have called the 'legalistic illusion', the view that the legal enactment of commitments affords credible protection of the autonomy of the central bank against the encroachments of the government. This is not the case. Yet there is no doubt that central banks, at various moments in their rich history, have succeeded in resisting governmental pressure. To understand the nature of the forces that lead to such a result, in the subsequent two sections I shall study two episodes from the past in which the monetary authority succeeded in imposing its point of view: the end of the Herriot government in April 1925 and the policy of the Reichsbank after the autonomy law of May 1922. In both cases, the central bank prevailed, because it could rely on an extremely powerful and well-structured movement of opinion. What can be seen here, in these collective movements of opinion, is the specific power of money, what I have referred to elsewhere as the 'power of the multitude' (Lordon and Orléan, 2008). This monetary belief, which runs widely through the social body, has the power to constrain the government, which cannot oppose it without seriously undermining its own legitimacy. It is the very expression of that 'collective trust', of which Marc Bloch says that there is no task more important for economic historians than to 'discover its nature and measure its strength', calling for 'a detailed analysis of the whole social atmosphere'.[3] I shall return to this essential dimension of monetary reality in the conclusion, recalling that the central bank's authority, in other words its ability to preserve its independence, finds its most solid foundation in its capacity to be the faithful spokesperson of collective monetary beliefs. Focusing on legal independence, on the contrary, may prove to be highly counterproductive, if this aspect is raised to the status of objective *per se*.

THE LEGALISTIC ILLUSION

The most common way to tackle the question of credible commitment consists in having recourse to the judicial system. As Olivier Blanchard and Stanley Fischer put it, in their *Lectures on Macroeconomics*: 'The law, constitutional or less fundamental, is obviously one solution to the dynamic inconsistency problem' (1989, p. 600).

Legal enactment of a commitment significantly increases its credibility, because of the heavy penalties incurred if the commitment is not honoured. The 'legalistic conception', which views law as the principal source of credibility, is deduced from this. It is very present in the literature on central bank independence. Its most visible manifestation can be found in the importance attached to the statutes of central banks. Thus, for example, most of the indicators supposed to measure the independence of central banks are constructed by coding legal data, and especially their statutes. This legalistic conception has already been the object of numerous criticisms (Cukierman, 1994; Forder, 1996; King, 2001). It has been pointed out that a wide discrepancy can exist between *de jure* independence, as measured by these indicators, and *de facto* independence, as revealed by actual behaviour. Two explanations have been suggested for this: either the incompleteness of the law, which leaves open a wide area in which the rights and duties of each party remain undefined, or the structural existence of significant differences between the letter of the law and real-life practices. To these criticisms, which are equally valid for private individuals, I must add new ones, more essential in my opinion, because they are specific to the situation of interest here, where it is the government that must be constrained. The government, as the trustee of sovereignty, possesses not only a whole arsenal of means of exerting pressure, but also considerable prerogatives in legislative matters. At the very least, it retains the capacity to propose new laws. Thus, the aptitude of laws to subjugate the sovereign government credibly appears to be highly questionable. There is no shortage of examples where governments have contravened constitutional clauses without difficulty.

There is no indication, for example, that the enshrinement of dollar–peso parity in fundamental Argentine law presented any obstacle to its reconsideration by the government in December 2001. Likewise, although the constitutionality of the US Congress resolution of 5 June 1933, abrogating the gold clause, was called into question, it is clear that this raised no serious obstacle to its application. As the jurist Arthur Nussbaum wrote in 1934: 'The American Congress, like other legislatures, could not but attempt to mitigate by restriction of the gold clause the dangerous consequences of severe depreciation of the monetary unit. It can scarcely be believed that any constitution should make it impossible to meet so exigent a situation' (p. 64).

In the event of difficulties, it is the responsibility of the government to act to improve the situation, including by changing laws or interpreting them to suit its needs. In this, it is simply doing its job. On this point, I share the scepticism of Milton Friedman when he observed that historically, nearly all serious conflicts between the central bank and government have ended with the victory of the government over the bank:

> It seems to me highly dubious that the United States, or for that matter any other country, has in practice ever had an independent central bank in the fullest sense of the term. Even when central banks have supposedly been fully independent, they have exercised their independence only so long as there has been no real conflict between them and the rest of the government. Whenever there has been a serious conflict, as in time of war, between the interest of the fiscal authorities in raising funds and of the monetary authorities in maintaining convertibility into specie, the bank has almost invariably given way, rather than the fiscal authority. To judge by experience, even those central banks that have been nominally independent in the fullest sense of the term have in fact been closely linked to the executive authority. (1962, pp. 226–7)

As an illustration, some historians[4] have observed, in connection with the Banque de France, that the 1878–1913 period – so different from the period preceding it precisely because of the strong independence enjoyed by the Banque de France – can be explained entirely by the fact that, contrary to the periods before and after, the Treasury had no major needs. In other words, it would be wrong to think of this independence as the result of a shift in the balance of power in favour of the bank. In fact, the balance of power between the government and the central bank had not changed from previous years, but in the absence of any important issue facing the Treasury, successive governments had no need to impose their legitimacy and power (Blancheton, 2001, p. 75). It was a walk-over for the bank!

All these reflections lead me to abandon the legalistic illusion: the law is not capable of subordinating the democratic sovereign, for reasons pertaining to the very nature of democratic sovereignty. In this, I diverge from the interesting point of view proposed by Alex Cukierman, who also criticizes what he calls 'legal independence', or independence as enacted in the law, but solely to take into account countries where the legal rules are not respected. I adopt a different perspective here: even a government that respects the law can circumvent legal constraints, simply because it can change laws. This argument does not deny the pertinence of Cukierman's point of view, in so far as non-respect of the law can indeed constitute an additional tool in the hands of the incumbent government. The ability to get round legal constraints, however, is in no way limited to non-respect of laws. It is inscribed in the sovereignty itself and is perfectly compatible with democratic legality.

At this stage in the argument, some people may assert that although laws can of course be changed, this is a costly process for the government, which will therefore hesitate before embarking on such modifications, all the more so since the costs are likely to be high. I would agree absolutely. In a certain way, the analysis I propose can be presented as an attempt to evaluate the costs relating to legal amendments. What the following analyses will show is that the strategic costs – the costs that really matter – are essentially of a political nature. The correct evaluation of these costs therefore entails a detailed analysis of the socio-political balances of power. To put it simply, it is easy, at time t, to change laws that, at that given moment in time, no longer enjoy the support of public opinion. This political approach to costs contrasts with the naïve view that these costs are essentially of a legal nature, that is, costs relating to the 'technical' functioning of the judicial system. This idea appears in the work of Blanchard and Fischer, when they associate a decreasing scale of costs of change with the legal gradation from constitutional law through ordinary law to discretionary choice: 'Discretionary policies, such as monetary policy, can be changed at low cost; rules fixed by law, such as much of fiscal law, are changeable at greater costs; rules fixed by constitutional law, such as the rights of private property or interstate commerce, are in principle also changeable, but at yet greater cost' (1989, p. 600). It is easy to disprove this view: at certain times, a constitutional law can be changed much more quickly than a discretionary choice. Everything depends on the nature of public opinion at the moment in question, and thus I must reject the idea of objective legal costs.

Does this mean that legal independence has no meaning? We shall see that the answer is no, but not because law is a credible obstacle to a possible turnaround by the government. For this reason, the word 'independence' is not appropriate. It would be better to speak of 'operational autonomy',[5] a term that accentuates the intrinsic limits of what can be achieved. But what is this operational autonomy founded on? If it does not proceed from the law, what is its source? This raises the fundamental question of monetary power. According to the legalistic approach, money in itself has no power. It only has the powers vested in it by law. The only real power is that of the government. That is not my position. I believe that there is a specific monetary power, capable of constraining the government. To understand the nature and limits of this power, what better object of analysis than the case of a central bank taking on the government and winning? Such a case illustrates the nature of the forces mobilized by monetary power in the defence of its autonomy. My example is provided by the episode of the *Cartel des gauches* (the 'Coalition of the left'), examined by

Jean-Noël Jeanneney (1976, 1977), and the way it was thwarted by the 'wall of money'.

THE *CARTEL DES GAUCHES* AND THE WALL OF MONEY

The event examined here is the fall of the Herriot government on 10 April 1925, after 11 months in power. What is of interest is the fact that this fall was the direct result of decisions made by the Bank of France, particularly the public revelation, on that day, that the legal limit imposed on fiduciary circulation had been exceeded. We are thus dealing with a historical episode in which the central bank proved itself to be capable of constraining the government. Let us start by recalling the economic situation in France in 1924, when the *Cartel des gauches* won the general election of 11 May.

First, the monetary situation: forced circulation had been introduced on 5 August 1914: the gold standard was abandoned and a floating rate prevailed on the foreign exchange market. In addition, France had incurred massive debts of all forms to finance the war: long-term loans, short- or medium-term Treasury bills and direct advances from the Bank of France. On 11 November 1918, these direct advances reached 18 billion francs, about 10 per cent of total war expenses. To appreciate the scale of this figure, we can compare it to total fiduciary circulation before the war, which was less than 6 billion. Obviously, using the note-printing press to finance the Treasury automatically led to a large increase in banknote circulation, which exceeded 30 billion francs in 1918. The situation deteriorated even further after the Armistice, because of the size of public deficits over the 1919–24 period. Nevertheless, and this is a vital point in my analysis, the French completely believed not just in a necessary return to the gold standard, but in a return to the pre-First World War conditions of parity. There was a strongly established consensus within French society on this point,[6] among experts, politicians and the general public: everyone believed in the return to pre-war parity. For this reason, everyone was fiercely opposed to inflation, a term used at the time to refer not to price rises, but to an increase in the issue of paper money. It was clear to everyone that strong deflation would be a necessary step in the restoration of pre-war parity.[7]

In this situation, two monetary facts played an important role: first, the size of the direct advances to the Treasury from the Bank of France;[8] second, the total fiduciary circulation. These were both subject to legal limits. During the war and up until 1919, the ceilings were continually being raised according to the needs of the moment. In April 1919, the limit for direct advances was set at 27 billion francs; in September 1920, the legal limit for fiduciary circulation was raised to 41 billion francs. These extensions in the ceilings show the limitations of the legal guarantee, although they could be justified by the needs of the endangered homeland. After the war, however, the Bank of France started to resist. Let us examine this resistance, starting with the question of direct advances. Here, the sovereign government made full use of its executive and legislative powers. It started in 1919 by asking for the ceiling to be raised from 21 to 24 billion francs.

This was a significant event, in so far as the request could no longer be justified by the war effort. Nevertheless, the Bank of France did not believe it could oppose the request. When the finance minister, Louis-Lucien Klotz, asked for an additional advance of 3 billion francs in 1919, however, some of the regents of the bank, such as Edouard de Rothschild, argued for a pure and simple refusal (Blancheton, 2001, p. 187). After some legal vicissitudes, the bank reversed its opinion and agreed to the request, succeeding, nevertheless, in inserting a clause, in the agreement of 24 April 1919, stipulating the provisional character of the advance and its rapid repayment out of forthcoming Treasury revenue. Under Article 3 of the agreement, the Treasury undertook to deduct a sum from the next loan issue sufficient to pay off the advances provided for by the present agreement (ibid., p. 188). Thus, at the end of March 1920, on conclusion of the loan issue in question, the Bank of France turned to the government for repayment of its advances, in accordance with the undertakings made by the government.

The finance minister at the time, Frédéric François-Marsal, had to admit that the government was not in a position to honour its engagements. Bertrand Blancheton writes: 'The regents were in a state of shock: what influence could they have over monetary policy if the agreements they signed were not even applied?' (ibid., p. 188). And yet, having little alternative, they signed a new agreement, on 14 April 1920, again stipulating that the government undertook to repay the advance of 3 billion francs received in 1919 out of the revenue of the next loan issue. Moreover, the government declared that it would subsequently continue to pay back its debt to the issuing institution at the rate of at least 2 billion francs per year as from 1 January 1921. With the same causes producing the same effects, and despite the launch of a new loan issue in the autumn of 1920, the finance minister once again failed to meet his commitments; he did not pay back the 3 billion francs. But what could the General Council of the Bank of France do? They said they were 'once again deeply disappointed' (ibid., p. 189). In January 1921, Governor Antoine Robineau declared, before the Bank's shareholders: 'It is not without the deepest disappointment, as you cannot doubt, that your Council has twice had to yield to the inevitable in this way' (ibid., p. 189). Here, we can see the extent to which the central bank can be powerless against the will of government. Towards the end of 1921, the agreement was duly respected for the first time: 2 billion francs were paid back to the Treasury and the ceiling was brought down from 27 to 25 billion. In 1922, however, budgetary difficulties once more obliged the government to renege on its commitments; it paid back only 1 billion francs. The same thing happened in 1923, when only 800 million francs were repaid. The Bank of France was swindled once again. As we can see, the fact that a legal limit is set on direct advances does not constrain governmental action at all. The government can either change the ceiling through legislation, or quite simply breach it.

And yet, if we now turn our attention to the legal limit on fiduciary circulation, the situation is very different. Why? Because, unlike direct advances, this figure was the object of particular vigilance on the part of the public. This indicator played a central role in the way the public perceived the value of bank notes. It was even the preferred expression of this value, far more so than the gold reserve or the budget deficit (Perrot, 1955). The way the press concentrated its attention on the weekly balance sheet in which the Bank of France published this figure provides just one illustration. Any increase in fiduciary circulation provoked great disquiet among the French public, who were hypnotized by the fear of exceeding the legal limit of 41 billion francs. As Marguerite Perrot wrote in a book dedicated to public opinion in France: 'This figure of 41 billion, fixed by Parliament without any great concern for variations in national income or possible economic turbulence, suddenly takes on the status of a myth; it is the figure beyond which lies inflation' (ibid., p. 126). Because this figure was the object of strong collective emotional investment, it acquired a force[9] that the incumbent government was obliged to take into account. But that was not all. The consensus 'not to puncture the ceiling', to use the expression of the time, reached far beyond public opinion. It was shared by experts, both in the Treasury and the issuing institution, by politicians and by the government itself. Edouard Herriot, President of the Council, and his minister of finance, Étienne Clémentel, continually repeated, in every possible way, that they were fiercely opposed to any inflation. On 17 January 1925, for example, Herriot made this astonishing declaration to the Chamber of Deputies:

> Well, whatever happens, whatever the restrictions it entails, however heroic the obligations to which you may be compelled, even if, at certain moments, your personal situation, my dear colleagues, might suffer, I ask the whole Chamber to understand that everything must be subordinated to the necessity of putting a stop to the policy of loans and expedients. No inflation! Let us subordinate everything to that. (Quoted in Blancheton, 2001, p. 219)

As we can see, there was no hesitation about the use of superlatives. Herriot even declared that 'for some people, including himself, anti-inflationism is a religion'[10] (quoted in Jeanneney, 1976, p. 214). In the same vein, Robineau, the governor of the Bank of France, declared rashly that 'he would cut his wrists rather than sign a new note' (quoted in ibid., p. 214).

The strength of this collective belief can also be measured by the risks taken by the very few dissenting voices, such as Charles Rist when he criticized the dogma of deflation. On this subject, Jacques Rueff wrote:

> Those who have not experienced the problem of stabilization cannot appreciate the intellectual and moral courage, even personal risk, entailed by this declaration. . . . Mr. Colson, at the time vice-president of the Council of State, was threatened with dismissal, because, in a communication to the Academy of Moral and Political Sciences, he had indicated, very cautiously and with many reservations, but to the scandal of all his colleagues, that he wondered whether it was reasonable to pursue the return to post-War parity. (Quoted in Blancheton, 2001, p. 225)

In this situation, on the strength of such collective support, the Bank of France had the means to resist the government. By threatening to call public and political opinion to witness, it was putting forward the very credible menace of a collapse in confidence in the government, both in parliament and on the street, for such dogmas cannot be challenged with impunity. Obviously, what is at issue here is not the legal enactment of limits to fiduciary issue, but the existence of a monetary belief shared by the whole social structure, including the government itself. Consequently, when the ceiling was exceeded in 1925, the Council of the Bank of France could demand that the government bring the circulation back within the legal limit, and the government had no choice but to comply, leading to its fall. It has been said that Herriot trapped himself, because he presented himself as a defender of the ceiling, and could not, therefore, use political persuasion to weaken the common conviction and make the idea of exceeding the ceiling acceptable to a proportion of the population. He remained entirely the prisoner of the dogma.

It is also worth noting that the government did not sit idly by; it actively sought to avoid exceeding the limit. It resorted to a whole series of expedients to reduce the number of notes in circulation, such as intensifying the use of cheques,[11] instructing public treasurers to reduce their cash balances as far as possible, and introducing a special currency in Madagascar and the Sarre. When all of these measures proved to be inadequate, there remained the tactic of publishing falsified balance sheets, which was used up until the beginning of April 1925. Here, we can appreciate the scale of the resources available to the executive powers. It was the will of the Bank of France, supported by the trust of public opinion, that forced the government into admitting that the limit had been exceeded.

This episode gives us a different view of the monetary question to that proposed by the models of temporal inconsistency, in that it highlights, not the strategic component of behaviour, but, on the contrary, the weight of monetary convictions. The players, including the government, are moved essentially by beliefs. It is these shared beliefs that constitute the true source of monetary power. Through these beliefs, it is trust in the money that is being expressed. If the government cannot do just what it wants, this is not because of the constraints of law, but because it is faced by public opinion, which is ultimately the sovereign. Thus, it is public opinion that decides. Monetary belief affects all the different players. Contrary to the idea of the central bank being ruled by its conservative nature, this hypothesis leads us to explain the actions of the central bank in terms of the monetary belief that shapes the social body at any given moment. From this perspective, the example of German hyperinflation during the 1920s is particularly enlightening.

GERMAN HYPERINFLATION

Let us start by recalling, briefly, that at the end of the First World War, Germany was faced with the same problem as France, that is, a substantial public debt, of which a large part was monetized, but with the additional enormous burden of war reparations. This led to intense domestic debate about the best way to end inflation. To explain this controversy, the contrast between two theories of inflation – the quantitative theory and the balance of payments theory – provides a useful starting point. According to the quantitative theory, inflation was essentially of a monetary nature. Without the printing of bank notes, there could be no durable increase in prices. According to the balance of payments theory, it was the balance of payments deficit, caused by the war reparations, that was responsible for inflation through its action on the exchange rate. Two different policies ensued: the first focused on putting an end to the monetary financing of the public deficit, whereas the second considered solving the problem of reparations to be the absolute prerequisite to any serious monetary reform. Gerald Feldman, in his *opus magnum*, writes that 'the balance-of-payments theory of inflation . . . was the dominant, virtually "official" theory in German academic and political circles' (Feldman, 1993, p. 399). One of its most fervent propagators, in terms of both its theoretical foundations and its political implications was the nationalist deputy Karl Helfferich. This is how he described the chain of causalities:

> The depreciation of the German mark was caused by the excessive burdens thrust on to Germany and by the policy of violence adopted by France; the

increase of the prices of all imported goods was caused by the depreciation of the exchanges; then followed the general increase of internal prices and of wages, the increased need for means of circulation on the part of the public and of the State, greater demands on the Reichsbank by private business and the State and the increase of the paper mark issues. Contrary to the widely held conception, *not inflation* [meaning the creation of money – author's note] *but the depreciation of the mark was the beginning of this chain of cause and effect*; inflation is not the cause of the increase of prices and of the depreciation of the mark; but the depreciation of the mark is the cause of the increase of prices and of the paper mark issues. (Quoted in Bresciani-Turroni, 1968, p. 45)

It could not have been put more clearly. If we turn our attention now to the central bank, the Reichsbank, we can see that the situation was less clear-cut, as Carl-Ludwig Holtfrerich ably describes in his book (1986) on German inflation, which serves as our reference here. At least up until 1920, the Reichsbank considered, in keeping with quantitative theory, that the monetary financing of the public deficit was an important source of inflation. Consequently, it exerted pressure on the government to reform the tax system and reduce spending, just like in the French case. In 1921, however, the Reichsbank's attitude changed. This shift was linked to the question of reparations, which had now become the main focus of attention, since it was in early 1921 that the total sum and the required annual payments became known. These latter were set at 2 billion gold marks plus 26 per cent of the value of exports. Rudolf Havenstein, President of the Reichsbank, spoke out firmly: 'I consider the London offer and the obligations that arise from it to be impossible and unbearable for our economy and our finances and fateful, if not fatal, for our exchanges and our monetary system' (quoted in Feldman, 1993, p. 336). There followed a change in the priorities of the Reichsbank, which now considered modification of the reparations to be a prerequisite of monetary stabilization. The bank's position thus became ever more consistent with the balance of payments theory, if not in all its theoretical dimensions, then at least, and most importantly, in its conclusions as to the policy that should be pursued.

These convictions led the central bank to end its opposition to monetary financing of the state. This is illustrated, for instance, by Havenstein's request for suspension of the clause that legally limited note issue by requiring at least one-third of the circulation to be backed by mixed reserves. Although this clause had long since been circumvented, its suspension clearly expressed the Reichsbank's desire to have a completely free hand to monetize deficits.

It is astonishing that a central bank should act so 'out of character' as to adopt such lax, non-conservative policy. Should it be interpreted as a consequence of the statutory rules, which made the Reichsbank so closely dependent on the government that any attempt to oppose governmental decisions would be futile? This is exactly how the countries of the Entente analysed the situation. They believed that this statutory subordination to the government was the root cause of the laxist policy on the issuing of money. Consequently, they sought to change the situation by endowing the Reichsbank with independent status, hoping to obtain a more rigorous monetary policy. They took advantage of the discussions about a moratorium on reparations to impose this reform, in the form of the autonomy law of 26 May 1922 (Holtfrerich, 1988). This change in statute is interesting, because it allows us to observe empirically the influence of legal changes on the policy of the central bank. There was none.

From this standpoint, the reaction of Havenstein was exemplary. He violently contested the idea that the Reichsbank could have contributed in any way to the creation of artificial inflation. Once again, he insisted that inflation was the consequence of an imbalance in the balance of payments such that, even if the budget deficit had been corrected by a more efficient collection of taxes, 'the note presses will still be compelled to remain in motion' (quoted in Feldman, 1993, p. 403). In his opinion, it was imperative for the Reichsbank to discount Treasury bills. This was a perfectly autonomous, independent decision, for which Havenstein assumed full responsibility, declaring: 'neither the Reich Chancellor nor any Reich authority has ever put pressure on the Reichsbank Direction to grant credits to the Reich. Rather, we have always voluntarily decided to accept the Treasury bills offered by the Reich for discount' (quoted in ibid., pp. 403–4). It could not have been put better. The Governor had always acted in keeping with what he thought ought to be done, so that autonomy had absolutely no effect on his policy. This was not a question of law, but of conviction. Consequently, the modification of the statutes did not bring about any change in monetary policy. Explaining themselves on this point, the monetary authorities stressed that the central bank gave priority to national interests. If it had refused monetization, the economic, political and social consequences would have been devastating. Whence that rare example of an independent central banker not only pursuing a perfectly lax policy of note issue, but finding reason for great satisfaction in the increasing printing capacities of the Reichsbank. On 17 August 1922, for example, he declared triumphantly: 'The Reichsbank . . . today issues 20,000 billion marks of new money daily . . . Next week the bank will have increased this to 46,000 billion daily . . . In a few days we shall therefore be able to issue in one day two-thirds of the total circulation' (in Widdig, 2001, p. 44). It was this type of public speech, whose effects on the financial markets can easily be imagined, that raised serious doubts about Havenstein's capacity to fulfil his duties.[12] And yet it was simply the consequence of the way he perceived his priorities.

CONCLUSION

Monetary beliefs are much more than economic theories. They incorporate moral, social and political considerations: moral in that they are founded on a certain idea of the collective good and the values that make it up; social because they have in view the stability of hierarchies between different groups and classes; political, finally, because they must be taken into account in any strategic approach defining what ought to be done and how to do it. From this point of view, the French and German examples are unequivocal. If the Bank of France defended deflation, it did so for ethical reasons and a certain view of social stability. Likewise, the popularity of the balance of payments theory among the ruling classes in Germany is closely linked with their political rejection of the Treaty of Versailles. In addition, I have shown what an influential role these collective beliefs play through the emotional charge invested in them. They construct the references on which private and public players base their decisions.

These beliefs constitute an essential and neglected dimension of the monetary sphere. Neglected because the standard economic approaches are too inclined to reduce money exclusively to its role as an instrument used to facilitate exchange. And yet money is much more than a simple instrument. First and foremost, it is a bond. It is that which unites, that through which a community of shared destiny can form and grow stronger. The most visible expression of this unity lies in the monetary convictions that stitch the social fabric together. The power of money can be measured directly by the strength of the collective commitment to and belief in that money. Here we find, in a different form, the traditional idea of trust proposed by François Simiand, and then Marc Bloch. It is this trust in money that escapes political manipulation and confronts it. It is the true source of the power of central banks. It is this, and not their statutory independence, that central banks rely on to constrain government. This is a power that has nothing to do with legality, a power that derives entirely from the shared conviction of the economic players. As Charles Goodhart (1992) emphasized: 'An "independent" central bank will still need to maintain its elective and political supports by ensuring that a sufficient proportion of the population understands and accepts its objectives and actions' (p. 31). That is the essential point. We must not allow the call for statutory independence to eclipse this reality.

NOTES

1. In *Annales d'Histoire Économique et Sociale*, **VIII** (39), 31 May 1936, p. 307.
2. As Capie et al. observe (1994), this influence is even considered to be the essential cause of obstacles to the maintenance of price stability: 'The "time inconsistency" literature suggests that it has been the incentive structure (on central banks) rather than technical/operational limitations that has hindered the attainment of price stability' (pp. 35–6).
3. See the epigraph.
4. In particular, see the excellent book by Bertrand Blancheton (2001).
5. Blancheton (2001) develops this point.
6. The war reparations that Germany was supposed to pay played an important role in this belief. Lack of space prevents me from going into more detail on this point.
7. The model the experts had in mind was the restoration of the franc's gold parity after the war of 1870. The forced circulation of the franc was abolished once the advances to the Treasury had been repaid. See Blancheton (2001).
8. At the time, this was referred to as the 'Mouvement Général des Fonds' (General Movement of Funds). I shall stick with the modern term.
9. This episode provides an illustration of the theses expounded by Frédéric Lordon (2000) on the 'strength of simple ideas'.
10. We could multiply the declarations of the different protagonists: 'Whatever the cost, we must strive towards revaluation of the franc . . . in the same way as Great Britain, which dared to remain faithful to the doctrine of the pound returning to gold parity' (Herriot, quoted in Jeanneney, 1976, p. 222).
11. Which produced savings of at least 200 million notes (Blancheton, 2001, p. 210).
12. See what Lord D'Abernon had to say about him (Feldman, 1993, p. 715).

REFERENCES

Blanchard, Olivier J. and Stanley Fischer (1989), *Lectures on Macroeconomics*, Cambridge, MA and London: MIT Press.

Blancheton, Bertrand (2001), *Le Pape et l'Empereur. La Banque de France, la direction du Trésor et la politique monétaire de la France (1914–1928)*, Paris: Éditions Albin Michel, coll. 'Histoire de la Mission historique de la Banque de France'.

Bloch, Marc (1936), 'Compte rendu de "La monnaie réalité sociale"', Annales d'Histoire Économique et Sociale, **VIII** (39), 31 May, pp. 306–7

Bresciani-Turroni, Costantino (1968), *The Economics of Inflation. A Study of Currency Depreciation in Post-War Germany*, London: August M. Kelley, 1st Italian edition 1931, 1st English edition 1937.

Capie, Forest, Charles Goodhart, Stanley Fisher and Norbert Schnadt (eds) (1994), *The Future of Central Banking: The Tercentenary Symposium of the Bank of England*, Cambridge: Cambridge University Press.

Cukierman, Alex (1994), 'Central bank independence and monetary control', *Economic Journal*, **104** (427), pp. 1437–48.

Elster, Jon (1979), *Ulysses and the Sirens*, Cambridge: Cambridge University Press.

Feldman, Gerald (1993), *The Great Disorder. Politics, Economics, and Society in the German Inflation, 1914–1924*, Oxford and New York: Oxford University Press.

Forder, James (1996), 'On the assessment and implementation of "institutional" remedies', *Oxford Economic Papers*, **48** (1), pp. 39–51.

Friedman, Milton (1962), 'Should there be an independent monetary authority', in Leland B. Yeager (ed.), *In Search of a Monetary Constitution*, Cambridge, MA: Harvard University Press, pp. 219–43.

Goodhart, Charles (1922), 'Entretien', *Revue d'Économie Financière*, **22** (Autumn), pp. 31–5.

Holtfrerich, Carl-Ludwig (1986), *The German Inflation 1914–1923: Causes and Effects in International Perspective*, Berlin and New York: Walter de Gruyter.

Holtfrerich, Carl-Ludwig (1988), 'Relations between monetary authorities and governmental institutions: the case of Germany from the 19th century to the present', in Gianni Toniolo (ed.), *Central Banks' Independence in Historical Perspective*, Berlin and New York: Walter de Gruyter, pp. 105–59.

Jeanneney, Jean-Noël (1976), *François de Wendel en République. L'argent et le pouvoir 1914–1940*, Paris: Éditions du Seuil, coll. 'L'univers historique'.

Jeanneney, Jean-Noël (1977), *Leçon d'histoire pour une gauche au pouvoir. La faillite du Cartel (1924–1926)*, Paris: Éditions du Seuil, coll. 'Histoire Immédiate'.

King, Michael (2001), 'The politics of central bank independence', *Central Banking*, **XI** (3), February, pp. 50–57.

Lordon, Frédéric (2000), 'La force des idées simples. Misère épistémique des comportements économiques', *Politix*, **13** (52), pp. 183–209.

Lordon, Frédéric and André Orléan (2008), 'Genèse de l'État et genèse de la monnaie: le modèle de la *Potentia Multitudinis*', in Yves Citton and Frédéric Lordon (eds), *Spinoza et les sciences sociales*, Paris: Éditions Amsterdam, pp. 127–70.

Nussbaum, Arthur (1934), 'Comparative and international aspects of American gold cause abrogation', *Yale Law Journal*, **44** (1), pp. 53–89.

Perrot, Marguerite (1955), *La monnaie et l'opinion publique en France et en Angleterre de 1924 à 1936*, Paris: Armand Colin, Cahiers de la Fondation Nationale des Sciences Politiques.

Widdig, Bernd (2001), *Culture and Inflation in Weimar Germany*, Berkeley, CA, Los Angeles, CA and London: University of California Press.

2. Monetary policy in Germany since 1948: national tradition, international best practice or ideology?

Carl-Ludwig Holtfrerich

INTRODUCTION

The historicity of institutions limits the view that contemporary central bankers have of their goals and methods. The theoretical background, which justifies this statement, is the concept of path dependency. It pertains not only to the QWERTY keyboard of a typewriter,[1] but to institutions as well. More recently, research has devoted a lot of attention to the link between culture – for example, tradition – and economic institutions and outcomes.[2]

There is no important industrial country where monetary policy institutions and outcomes have been as varied as Germany's since the foundation of the *Deutsche Reich* in 1871: central bank control by and independence from the government; one open and one suppressed hyperinflation; the great deflation after 1873 and the even greater deflation from 1929 to 1932; two periods of foreign exchange controls (1914 to 1919 and, mostly in peacetime, 1931 to the mid-1950s); two currency reforms (1923–24 and 1948), or even four counting the introduction of the Deutschmark in former East Germany in 1990 and the introduction of the euro in 1999; and numerous central bank reforms. Compared to countries such as the United States, Switzerland and Sweden, and even the United Kingdom and France, this is quite a record. Germany's monetary policy history, until it ended with the creation of the European Central Bank (ECB) on 1 January 1999, is, therefore, one of the best cases from which to draw lessons on the development of central banks as economic institutions. This chapter focuses on the Bundesbank's history since 1948, and its determining influence on the institutional shape of the ECB, and draws on previous experiences with central banking in Germany.

The chapter will address the following questions:

- Was the Bundesbank's high degree of independence from the government the result of international learning from best practice or of other factors?
- Was the Bundesbank's record of relative price stability the result of national tradition, namely the trauma of the two cases of hyperinflation in Germany during the twentieth century, or of other considerations?
- Was the Bundesbank's concentration on the price-stability goal at the expense of the full-employment and economic-growth target after 1973 the result of its and of the German population's inflation fear, of a new policy assignment, of a new alignment with the financial sector instead of industry, or of ideology?
- Was the Bundesbank's determining influence on the institutional shape of the ECB the result of imposing – via its already established factual role as Europe's central bank – the national tradition of the Federal Republic of Germany on Europe, of international learning from best practice, or of ideology?

THE ORIGIN OF THE BUNDESBANK'S INDEPENDENCE

I will begin with an introduction to Germany's tradition regarding the government control/central bank independence question before the 1948 foundation of the Bank deutscher Länder, the forerunner of the Bundesbank (established in 1957).

When the Reichsbank – the German Reich's central bank – began operations on 1 January 1876, the law stipulated that the Chancellor was the head of the Reichsbank and that the President and Directorate had to follow his instructions. Although the bank's capital was largely private, the shareholders did not have the rights they would normally have had in a stock company. The Reichsbank was made a 'legal entity under public law', and its personnel were civil servants of the Reich. The Central Committee (*Zentralausschuss*), representing the private equity holders, was granted more access rights than the public to information about the conduct of the Reichsbank business and held advisory functions, especially concerning credit policy matters and in the appointment of members of the Directorate. In only one field was it equipped with real power: it had the right to veto any of the bank's business with the Reich or state treasuries conducted on conditions other than normal, for example, on a preferential basis. Government control of the Reichsbank was further accentuated by the fact that the Reich retained the right to terminate the activities of the bank or to nationalize it by purchasing its private capital shares at face value (Borchardt, 1976, pp. 15–16; Holtfrerich, 1988, pp. 108–10).

In fact, the Reichsbank Directorate was largely free of government interference until 1914.[3] The gold standard rules, which had been in place since 1871, restricted the autonomy of the Reichsbank to a much greater extent than its legal subordination to the Reich's Chancellor.

This changed fundamentally when Germany dropped the gold standard at the outbreak of the First World War. The government demanded from the Reichsbank practically unlimited lender-of-last-resort financing from the Reichsbank, first of war and then of postwar expenditures, until the end of hyperinflation in 1923. As one of the conditions of the reparations moratorium, however, the Allies demanded that the legal subordination of the bank to the Reich's Chancellor be terminated. This was done through the so-called autonomy law of 26 May 1922, put into effect by a government decree of 24 July 1922.[4] It is thus somewhat ironic that hyperinflation – according to Phillip Cagan's (1956) definition – began in Germany in July 1922. The Allies had expected that, having gained independence, the Reichsbank would use its newly acquired power to curb the rate of monetary expansion, even against the government's wishes (Holtfrerich, 1986, p. 168). This hope was also based on the fact that, at a meeting in London in October 1921, Reichsbank President Rudolf von Havenstein had demanded, and won, the support of the Governor of the Bank of England, Montagu Norman, to strengthen the Reichsbank's position *vis-à-vis* the government in a new banking law (Sayers, 1976, pp. 175–6). It is noteworthy, however, that in public discussions of the autonomy law of 1922, the independence of the Reichsbank was opposed, using the argument that it was alien to the German tradition (Singer, 1922, pp. 734–5).

When the Reichsbank was reorganized in connection with the Dawes Plan in 1924, it retained its independence from the German government, and the government's access to Reichsbank credit was strictly limited. Its new president, Hjalmar Horace Greeley Schacht (from December 1923 to March 1930), who enjoyed the full backing of the international financial world, was able to assert the power of the Reichsbank *vis-à-vis* the Weimar Republic's relatively unstable governments, especially by successfully demanding regulation of German capital imports, deficit reduction and public debt retirement. The Reichsbank under Schacht has even been called a *Nebenregierung*, a supplementary government, due to its successes in imposing its will on the regular government and the legislators, and thereby creating a state-within-the-state situation (Müller, 1973).

Nevertheless, when the Dawes Plan was fully implemented by law on 30 August 1924, Germany reintroduced the gold standard, this time as a gold exchange standard. The Reichsbank remained independent from the

German government, but was subject to foreign supervision for the duration of the Dawes Plan. This supervision lasted until March 1930, when the Dawes Plan was replaced by the Young Plan. Extensive powers had been granted to the note-issue commissioner, a foreigner, and to the General Council: only half of its members represented the private owners of the bank; the other half consisted of foreigners. In practice, however, the Reichsbank did not perceive foreign supervision in the same way as it did control by its own government. Rather, it strengthened the hand of Schacht in his dealings with the German government. It was, therefore, no coincidence that Schacht resigned when the Young Plan removed foreign supervision. As in the pre-1914 period, however, the constraints of the gold standard once again restricted the Reichsbank's room for manoeuvre, until the Reichsmark's convertibility ended with the introduction of foreign exchange controls in the wake of the banking crisis of July 1931. From then on, the Reichsbank was independent not only of the German government, but also of the gold standard rules and – with the exception of the right of the Bank for International Settlements (BIS) to participate in changes of the German central banking law – of foreign supervision.

In March 1933, Adolf Hitler, who had come to power on 30 January, reinstated Hjalmar Schacht as Reichsbank President. Schacht opened wide the credit resources of the bank in order to finance the government's large employment and rearmament measures, while – together with the government – further tightening Germany's foreign exchange controls. Formally, the bank enjoyed the same degree of independence from the government as since 1922. It supported the government's expansive fiscal policy voluntarily, as it had done during the hyperinflationary phase of 1922–23, immediately after it had been granted independence under Allied pressure. Its motive in both cases was patriotism and, in 1933, its determination to end deflation and economic depression.

A banking law of 27 October 1933 revised the institutional set-up of the Reichsbank somewhat. It mainly transferred the right to appoint and revoke the bank's President and Directorate members from the private owners of the bank (the Central Committee, which was abolished) to the Reich's President, and authorized the Reichsbank to trade in the open market with government fixed-interest securities and to make use of such securities as secondary cover for its note issue on an equal footing with commercial bills. The German government – in compliance with the Young Plan Treaty that created the BIS – had asked the BIS for the approval of these changes. This approval came on 9 October 1933, due in large part to the excellent reputation that Reichsbank President Hjalmar Schacht – present at the meeting of the Board of Directors of the BIS – enjoyed among his international colleagues.[5] It is worth noting that the delicate question of formal Reichsbank independence from the German government was not touched upon at this time. In the Reichstag, however, on 30 January 1937 – the fourth anniversary of Hitler's seizure of power and the day the infamous enabling law of 21 March 1933 was extended for another four years – Hitler announced that the government would resume unlimited sovereignty over the Reichsbank (Verhandlungen des Reichstags, 1938, p. 10). The announcement came after several other successful – in other words, without cost for Germany – breaches of the Versailles Treaty, and meant that Germany would no longer respect the right of the BIS to participate in changes to the German central banking law (Bayrhoffer, 1941, p. 94; Puhl, 1941, pp. 49–50). Eleven days later, not the Reichstag, but the Reich's government – authorized by the enabling law – passed a new Reichsbank Act accordingly. It stipulated – similar to the original Reichsbank law of 1875 – that the Directorate administer the bank, but that it be subordinate to the Führer and the Reich's Chancellor. This time, even Hjalmar Schacht, at the helm of the Reichsbank, approved enthusiastically of the loss of the central bank's independence (Schacht, 1937, pp. 137–9).

The Reichsbank remained subordinate to the government until the end of the Second World War. Schacht, along with all the members of the Directorate, opposed Hitler's unreserved exploitation of the bank's credit resources to finance the war effort. Their opposition led to the dismissal of Schacht and three of his colleagues on the Directorate in January 1939 (Hansmeyer and Caesar, 1976, pp. 380–85). This time, the hyperinflationary consequences of Hitler's limitless borrowing were made invisible by price controls and the nearly total rationing of goods.

At the end of the war, when Germany was divided into four occupation zones, the Reichsbank, with its head office in the Soviet Sector of Berlin, ceased to exist as a central bank for all of Germany. In line with their deconcentration policy, the Allies preferred to reorganize Germany as a decentralized federal state with a federalized central banking structure (Geisler, 1953, pp. 83–4; Wandel, 1980, pp. 59–62). The Reichsbank branch offices were initially kept in place only by the Western Allies. Their functions were reduced to banking supervision, processing cash deposits and disbursements, clearing cashless transactions and transmitting information and instructions from the military governments to credit institutions. The latter included blocking the accounts of politically unacceptable persons and institutions as well as implementing the military law that required them to report and surrender foreign currency holdings and other foreign assets (Buchheim, 1999, pp. 63–4). On the initiative of the United States, completely new institutions were founded by military government legislation around the turn of the year 1946–47 in the American and French zones, and, in February 1948, in the British zone (Distel, 2003, pp. 105, 133, 186).

These *Landeszentralbanken* (*Land* central banks) replaced what was left of the Reichsbank structure. The British joined in only after the United States agreed, in 1948, to the creation of the Bank deutscher Länder, based in Frankfurt, as the central bank of the *Land* central banks, again legislated by the three Western military governments.[6] This forerunner of the Bundesbank assumed regular central banking functions on 20 June 1948, when currency reform in the western zones of occupation made this possible. The federal structure of this system as a whole was now similar to the US Federal Reserve System. In contrast, the structure of the Reichsbank up to the end of the Second World War, as per German tradition, had been a centralized one, from the headquarters in Berlin down to the branch offices all over Germany, and had thus more closely resembled the Bank of England and the Banque de France.

What about the control–independence question? The government of each *Land* had provided the necessary capital for the 'legal entities under public law' and appointed the head personnel of the *Land* central banks and their respective presidents, who composed the *Zentralbankrat* (Central Bank Council) of the Bank deutscher Länder. Yet the new monetary policy institutions were subordinate neither to the government of their respective states (*Länder*), nor to the government of the Federal Republic of Germany after its foundation in 1949. In this sense they were independent. Nevertheless, the three Western powers had formed the Allied Bank Commission (ABC), comprising the heads of the finance divisions of the military governments and – after the foundation of the Federal Republic – of the high commissioners, in order to control the new central bank system. All important monetary policy decisions were subject to approval by the ABC. It was entitled to issue instructions to the Central Bank Council, which in turn controlled the bank's *Direktorium* (Executive Board), and when necessary to veto its decisions. It is symbolic that the seat of the ABC was the top floor of the headquarters of the Bank deutscher Länder in Frankfurt. In this sense, the bank was subject to government control, like the Banque de France since the nineteenth century (Plessis, 1985; Bouvier, 1988) and the Bank of England after it was nationalized in 1945, and unlike the US Federal Reserve System.

In practice, however, the ABC never used its veto power. Differences of opinion between the bank and the ABC were discussed and worked out before any formal decisions were made by the Central Bank Council. The President of the Executive Board, Wilhelm Vocke, with his diplomatic skills and persuasive manner, played a crucial role in this. Like the ABC, he favoured market-oriented as opposed to interventionist policy tools anyway (Holtfrerich, 1999, pp. 323–4). Furthermore, acting as a 'strong central banker' (in the Kenneth Rogoff sense today) he favoured above all the pursuit of price stability, which was the ABC's main interest. Vocke, however, aimed for price stability not for its own sake, but for a different reason, as we shall see later. As during the Weimar Republic, the Allies were strongly interested in currency stability and a solid reconstruction of the German economy in order to secure their interwar foreign investments in Germany (Deutsche Bundesbank, 1988, p. 104). Both the bank and the Allies agreed that the German government's access to the bank's credit had to be strictly limited.

The bank's freedom from interference by the West German government was overwhelmingly applauded by the German public. Only a few politicians and academic economists argued in favour of restricting the bank's autonomy in the first two years of the Federal Republic (Die Bundesbank, 1950). Already by 1951, the bank's independence was almost universally accepted as the future standard (Caesar, 1981, p. 202; Gaugenrieder, 1960, p. 4). This explains the outcome of the following legislative history of the first West German central banking act.

In August 1951, with the consent of the Allied Powers that were returning sovereign rights to Germany, the West German parliament enacted a significant change to their 1948 central banking law (*Bundesgesetzblatt*, 1951, p. 509). Finance Minister Fritz Schäffer was in charge of preparing central bank legislation, including a Bundesbank law requested by the West German constitution of 1949. It was evident in early 1951 that the Bundesbank law would not be enacted by the end of the year due to a number of differences of opinion and unsettled questions. Finance Minister Schäffer therefore prepared a small bill in March 1951 as a temporary measure for the intervening period. In it he simply transferred the controlling powers of the ABC over the Bank deutscher Länder to the federal government. The central bank was up in arms, protesting that it would receive instructions to supply whatever credit the government demanded. The ministers of the economy, Ludwig Erhard, and of justice, Thomas Dehler, who had not been previously consulted, were also opposed to government control of the central bank. The cabinet settled on a compromise. The ABC's instruction and veto power over monetary-policy decisions of the Central Bank Council were not transferred to the federal government, but were abolished. Instead, the central bank was obliged to support the general economic policy line of the government 'within the framework of its functions', in other words, only in so far as its measures did not conflict with securing currency stability. To integrate further the government's economic and the bank's monetary policies, the finance minister and the minister of the economy were entitled to participate in the meetings of the Central Bank Council and even to call for such a meeting. They had no voting rights, but were empowered to put forward motions. If one of them found that a decision of the Central Bank Council ran counter to the general economic policy line of the government, he had the right to suspend the decision, but only for eight days (Deutsche Bundesbank, 1988, pp. 98–108). These measures presented no real restriction on the independence of West Germany's central bank, an independence which has survived intact since August 1951. When, however, the law creating the Bundesbank – successor to the Bank deutscher Länder – was drafted in the 1950s, continued independence was far from certain. It became a matter of political controversy.

There were several clashes between the Adenauer government in Bonn and the Bank deutscher Länder in Frankfurt before the Bundesbank law was framed and finally enacted on 26 July 1957 (*Bundesgesetzblatt*, 1957, vol. I, pp. 745–55). After the outbreak of the Korean War on 25 June 1950, an economic boom had set in that threatened price stability in Germany as elsewhere in the Western world. The Central Bank Council was inclined to fight inflation not only by using administrative tools, such as raising its reserve requirements, but also by a hefty hike in the discount rate. The minister of the economy, with his overall market-oriented attitude, was in favour of this approach to the problem, but Chancellor Konrad Adenauer, concerned about the still high unemployment rate, and Finance Minister Fritz Schäffer, with a view to the interest costs of government debt, were against it. On Adenauer's insistence, the meeting of the Central Bank Council on this matter, as an exception, took place in the Chancellery in Bonn on 26 October 1950. The political objections in Bonn were of no avail, however. The discount rate was raised directly from 4 to 6 per cent (Holtfrerich, 1999, pp. 337–8), which was considered to be an unusually high rate at the time.

Adenauer also sharply attacked the bank's policy in public after it raised its discount rate incrementally from 3 per cent in August 1955 to 5.5 per cent on 18 May 1956, this time with the consent not only of Minister of the Economy Erhard, but also of Finance Minister Schäffer. Chancellor Adenauer, on the other hand, who was worried that this would cause lower economic growth and higher unemployment in the election year of 1957 and would trigger the withdrawal of election campaign support by German industry, which had also been opposed, distanced himself from this policy measure five days after the last rate hike at the annual meeting of the Federation of German Industries with the following remark: 'a heavy blow to the German economy has been struck, and it is the small ones who fall by the wayside, to be precise . . . the small industries, small farmers, and small craftsmen. . . . Up to now, I have not been convinced that such a measure was necessary. I am not even convinced that it will attain the desired effect'.[7]

This disagreement strengthened Adenauer in his conviction that he must get West Germany's central bank under government control and at all costs get rid of Wilhelm Vocke as its president. The law to convert the Bank deutscher Länder into the Deutsche Bundesbank, then in preparation at an increasing pace, offered an opportunity to do just that.[8] In addition, the Chancellor was now absolutely determined to move the seat of the central bank from Frankfurt to Cologne, a distance of only 30 kilometres from the capital, Bonn.[9] When a draft of the Bundesbank bill was discussed in the 143rd cabinet meeting of 11 July 1956, Adenauer expressed his view that 'in choosing the location [of the Bundesbank], it should be borne in mind that the activity of the bank should be guided by the correct spirit. Its current location has resulted in the Bank deutscher Länder leading a very separate life. The federal central bank must be sensitive to the political atmosphere as it, more than other institutions, has to take this into account'.[10] It even got to the point that Adenauer's financial adviser, the Cologne banker Robert Pferdmenges, offered a specific piece of real estate in Cologne to the government as the future seat of the Bundesbank. The German press reacted with harsh criticism of this threat to the independence of West Germany's central bank (Deutsche Bundesbank, 1988, pp. 134–7).

After Finance Minister Schäffer had been unsuccessful in achieving an accord for the Bundesbank law during the first parliamentary session from 1949 to 1953, the Ministry of the Economy, under Ludwig Erhard, became the prime mover in the preparation of the law after the 1953 elections. Even more than Chancellor Adenauer, Schäffer was opposed to the central bank's total independence from the government. The Weimar governments' bad experiences with the totally independent Reichsbank, under Hjalmar Schacht, from the end of 1923 to 1930, for example with the state-within-the-state situation (see above), made Schäffer anxious to secure a measure of government influence over monetary policy decisions. The first Bundesbank bill, drafted by his ministry in March 1950, did not stipulate the bank's independence. Instead, it provided for a Federal Committee for monetary and economic policy decisions working alongside the Bundesbank (somewhat similar to the French idea of a *gouvernement économique* for integrating and binding the ECB into general macroeconomic policy formulation; see below). If the government vetoed a monetary policy decision, the committee would have the last word. It was to consist of ten members, five appointed by the government and five by the Central Bank Council, and of a chairman, also appointed by the government. Decisions were to be made by majority vote of the members. In the case of a tie, the chairman would make the decision, which would be binding for the Central Bank Council (Bethusy-Huc, 1962, p. 95). This sort of government control over monetary policy met with fierce opposition from the central bank. Ludwig Erhard and Minister of Justice Thomas Dehler were also against the idea. The press was adamantly in favour of the central bank's independence and rejected Schäffer's proposal.

Erhard's new Bundesbank bill of 1 March 1956 did not propose this sort of institution, intended to emasculate West Germany's central bank by reducing its independence. But when it was discussed in the cabinet meeting of 11 July 1956, Chancellor Adenauer kept expressing his fear that an independent central bank would lead to a state-within-the-state situation and – together with a majority of his cabinet – considered the delegation of monetary policy powers to a politically independent institution as unconstitutional. Erhard held out against it.[11]

The guarantee of independence in the Bundesbank bill came under attack from leading representatives of German industry, such as Fritz Berg, the president of the Federation of German Industries. With reference to the disastrous monetary policies during the Great Depression, when the Reichsbank was totally independent, it was argued that 'in periods of crisis, the independence of the central bank must always end' (Deutsche Bundesbank, 1988, p. 131). This time, businessmen demanded influence over monetary policy by way of an advisory board attached to the Bundesbank, somewhat similar to the committee that had been proposed in the Schäffer bill (ibid., pp. 122–32). This was to no avail. Along with the controversy over the organizational structure – centralized or decentralized – and the power of appointment for the leading personnel, the issue remained a hot topic of debate in the media, which almost unanimously favoured independence, as well as in parliament and its respective committees, up to the enactment of the Bundesbank law. All attacks on the central bank's independence were in the end defeated.[12]

The Bundesbank law of 26 July 1957 largely reversed the decentralization of West Germany's central banking system (Stern, 1999, p. 113). The *Land* central banks retained their name, but were merged with the Bundesbank and became its main offices in each *Land*. In this respect the unbroken tradition of the Reichsbank was re-established. The law, however, explicitly guaranteed the bank's independence from instructions by the government. This was contrary to the German tradition and rather the result of demands that the Allied Powers had imposed on Germany after the First World War, from 1922 into the Hitler period, and then again after the Second World War.

In practice, however, the Bundesbank's room for manoeuvre was quite restricted by international capital flows, especially after the convertibility of the Deutschmark – *de facto* in 1955 – and of the other European currencies – as of 1 January 1959 – had been established, and as long as the

Deutschmark was tied into the Bretton Woods system of fixed exchange rates. During this period it was the government's and not the bank's responsibility to decide on the Deutschmark's parity. Therefore, the Bundesbank's independence even increased when floating exchange rates were introduced in a general manner in 1973.

Around this time the independence issue moved once again to the political forefront. The Great Coalition government of 1967 to 1969 introduced a new concept of economic policy based on the *Stabilitäts- und Wachtumsgesetz* (Act for the Promotion of Stability and Growth of the Economy) of May 1967, which the new minister of the economy, Karl Schiller, had initiated. It equipped the government with Keynesian fine-tuning policy instruments, similar to the 'new economics' concept introduced by the Kennedy administration in 1961 in the United States. The concept necessitated a stronger coordination of the government's fiscal policy with the bank's monetary policy. This led to new discussions about the bank's autonomy into the 1970s, when rising inflation rates added fuel to the fire. Some Social Democratic politicians (especially Herbert Ehrenberg; Ehrenberg, 1973, pp. 33–4, 197–200), State Secretary in the Labour Ministry 1971–72, vice speaker of his party in parliament 1974–76, and Labour Minister 1976–82), along with labour union leaders and academic economists, demanded legislative restrictions on the independence of the Bundesbank. Ehrenberg was never able to win majority support for this within his own party, let alone within the cabinet (Robert, 1978, p. 37; Caesar, 1981, pp. 199–200).

Moreover, with the turbulence of the foreign exchange market in the early 1970s, a change in the Bundesbank law was proposed. The purpose was to extend its range of monetary policy instruments. In late 1972, the Bundesbank itself had asked the government and legislators to empower it to demand minimum reserve requirements on commercial banks' assets in addition to those on their liabilities, as well as to stipulate maximum quotas for the extension of commercial bank credit. From the political side, however, it was planned to require the government's agreement for using these new instruments. The Social Democratic Party (SPD) insisted on this sort of two-key provision as the price for the extension of the Bundesbank's instruments. Neither the SPD's coalition partner, the Free Democrats, nor the Bundesbank were willing to pay this price, which would have been an inroad into the bank's autonomy. In 1973, having reached the stage of parliamentary bill, the project was finally dropped.[13]

On a more general level of academic and political discussion around the time of the switch to floating exchange rates in 1973, it was demanded that the bank's policy be subjected to the same set of economic policy goals (the 'magic' quadrangle: price stability, full employment, fair growth, and external balance) that the government had been obliged to pursue explicitly since the *Stabilitätsgesetz* of 1967, and/or that the bank be subjected to government instructions under certain conditions. It was argued that the bank's task, as defined in the Bundesbank law of 1957, namely to secure currency stability, would otherwise lead to policy clashes with the government. One would have to differentiate between the formulation of policy priorities and the realization of policy goals. The bank's independence should pertain to the realization of goals only, while the choice of policy priorities should be the sole responsibility of the government (Duwendag, 1973, pp. 13–52; Robert, 1978, pp. 36–77; Kaiser, 1980, pp. 64–79). None of these proposals met with serious interest in parliament. Central bank independence had become too much of a 'sacred cow' to be tampered with. Although a simple law could have restricted the Bundesbank's independence, it was regarded by the German public as though it had a constitutional rank. Discussions of the independence issue subsided thereafter.

In contrast to these ideas, in 1975, Friedrich von Schelling, formerly president of a *Land* central bank and thus a member of the Bundesbank's Central Bank Council, proposed a change to the Bundesbank law. The bank should be obliged to pursue price stability as its only policy goal. To be successful at this alone was difficult enough for monetary policy, he argued. To charge the bank with further tasks would strain the capabilities of its limited set of policy tools (Schelling, 1975). Schelling's proposal was in practice realized (see below on the 'new policy assignment') and eventually legally enshrined in the ECB's constitution (see below on the 'institutional shape of the ECB').

THE ROOT OF THE BUNDESBANK'S PRICE-STABILITY ORIENTATION

It has been claimed time and again that the Bundesbank's determined and comparatively successful fight for price stability is rooted in Germany's trauma from two periods of extreme inflation in the first half of the twentieth century. While in the United States the fear of another great depression led to the reorientation of economic policies towards a Keynesian approach in order to preserve full employment after the Second World War, it was supposedly the fear of inflation of the German population that prompted the West German central bank to pursue a rigorous anti-inflationary policy (Pierenkemper, 1998).

There is no doubt that the Germans were traumatized by inflation at the beginning of the second half of the twentieth century and that this helped make even rigorous anti-inflationary measures palatable to the German population. There were, however, other countries with a comparably good price-stability record that had not experienced runaway inflation before, such as Switzerland and the United States. Therefore, it is unlikely that the specific German inflation fear was the driving motive behind the central bank's determined fight for price stability.

I finally found the clue when I carried out an in-depth study of West Germany's monetary policy during the period of fixed exchange rates (Holtfrerich, 1999). It turned out that after the first trade and currency liberalization measures in the wake of the creation of the Organisation for European Economic Cooperation (OEEC) and the European Payments Union (EPU) as a condition for Marshall Plan aid, the government in Bonn and the central bank in Frankfurt chose and pursued a sort of mercantilist policy strategy. As protectionist tools could not be used in this period, when Germany itself was likely to profit from European and worldwide trade liberalization, a different way of achieving mercantilism, namely export surpluses, had to be found. The solution was to keep domestic demand restrained by monetary and fiscal policies, thus keeping imports and domestic inflation low and freeing production resources for more exports. This strategy was contingent on a system of fixed exchange rates, without a self-regulating gold standard including freedom of capital movements, in other words with scope for an autonomous monetary policy. The early Bretton Woods system, without fully convertible currencies and with restrictions on international capital movements, left countries the opportunity to gain in international competitiveness by realizing relatively more price stability at home than abroad.

The success of this German strategy of monetary mercantilism, as I call it, is evidenced by the substantial current account surpluses posted by West Germany between 1952 and the Deutschmark appreciation of 1961, and by the fact that average annual price increases (as measured by the GNP deflator) of 3.4 per cent in West Germany between 1950 and 1958 were considerably lower than those in the rest of the OEEC (5.5 per cent per annum) (Giersch et al., 1992, p. 109). The phenomenon of monetary mercantilism was documented in the 1959 annual report (p. 11) of the Deutscher Sparkassen- und Giroverband (German Association of Savings Banks, which is still one of the fiercest protagonists of price stability), republished during the Deutschmark-appreciation debate of 1960 under a different title. The report demanded that the 'monetary protectionism' of the Federal Republic be dropped in order to ensure domestic monetary stability.

Of even greater significance in the context of this chapter is the fact that this mercantilist approach had been conceived and planned by the Bank deutscher Länder, and in particular by the president of its executive board,

Wilhelm Vocke, as a long-term strategy for German monetary policy. Already in 1950, Alec K. Cairncross, in his capacity as EPU adviser, took note of 'Vocke's well-known deflationary inclinations' (Ludwig-Erhard-Stiftung, 1986, p. 208).[14] After the Deutschmark had been depreciated in a general exchange rate realignment in September 1949, the central bank's aim was to ensure that overall monetary policy was relatively restrictive. In 1950, Chancellor Adenauer expressed his dislike for the policy (see above), but Ludwig Erhard appreciated it and agreed with the strategy. At the Central Bank Council's meeting of 26 and 27 October 1949, Vocke had already argued in favour of 'keeping domestic affairs tight in order to strengthen exports' (Dickhaus, 1996, pp. 70, 114). The president of the Central Bank Council, Karl Bernard, held the same conviction. Nevertheless, the majority of the Central Bank Council was not yet convinced of the wisdom of such an export-oriented mercantilist strategy (Holtfrerich, 1999, p. 344).

A marked change occurred in the overall attitude of the Central Bank Council following the outbreak of the Korean War at the end of June 1950. Presidents Vocke and Bernard realized that this was the opportunity to implement their plan. Erhard, wholly in favour of the approach, wrote to Vocke on 2 August 1950:

> [A] great opportunity for the future of German exports has arisen out of the current situation. If, namely, through internal discipline we are able to maintain the price level to a greater extent than other countries, our export strength will increase in the long run and our currency will become stronger and more healthy, both internally and with respect to the dollar. (Ludwig-Erhard-Stiftung, 1986, p. 183)

On 17 May 1951, in the wake of the inflation of the first year of the Korean War, Vocke explained his monetary strategy to an interested audience of experts as follows:

> Of course, the high rates of inflation have been a cause of great concern to us, but, if you compare these with foreign price levels and with the rates of inflation in other countries, you will see, with satisfaction, that we have consistently remained below them. And that is our chance, that is decisive, for our currency and especially for our exports. Raising exports is vital for us, and this in turn depends on maintaining a relatively low price and wage level. . . . As I have said, keeping the price level below that in other countries is the focal point of our efforts at the central bank, and it is a success. That should be borne in mind by those who say to us: your restrictive measures are too tight, are no longer necessary. (Vocke, 1956, p. 56)

As early as 1955, Henry C. Wallich, in his famous 1955 study of the German economic resurgence, identified this mercantilist approach as

Germany's monetary policy strategy in the first half of the 1950s (Wallich, 1955, p. 80). Fiscal policy had also made decisive contributions to this mercantilist strategy, particularly after the crisis connected to the outbreak of the Korean War. These contributions came in the form of special concessions (Export Promotion Act of 1951) as well as of guarantees for export credits (Hermes guarantees) and in macroeconomic terms of repeatedly posting budget surpluses deposited at the central bank (these government reserves were called '*Juliusturm*'), which helped to dampen domestic demand. Beyond that, fiscal policy encouraged personal savings through tax breaks and other subsidies on a large scale, thus also dampening domestic consumption.[15] On top of this came the enormous contribution made by the public sector with its investment expenditure to the macroeconomic net savings ratio: 44 per cent of the total between 1948 and 1960 (Stolper and Roskamp, 1979, p. 388).

Following the outbreak of the German foreign exchange crisis in the wake of the foundation of the EPU on 1 July 1950, the EPU special credit that Germany received was – in IMF-like manner – tied to a package of conditions. These amounted to the pursuit of restrictive monetary and fiscal policy, in order to dampen domestic demand, and credit and tax policy measures for promoting exports. When the foreign exchange crisis peaked in February 1951, the Allied High Commission, in a memorandum to the Federal Government on 7 February 1951, demanded, among other things, that German economic policy be focused not merely verbally, but effectively, 'on stimulating exports' (as quoted in Holtfrerich, 1999, p. 346). Subsequently, the Western Allies would be unable to rid themselves of the spirits they had conjured up in making this demand. Not only the presidents of the Bank deutscher Länder, Vocke and Bernard, but also the majority of the Central Bank Council had recognized by now the value of the strategy of monetary (and fiscal) policy mercantilism, and pursued it, particularly after Germany's currency crisis immediately following the outbreak of the Korean War, not merely successfully, but in excess.

This export-oriented strategy of economic growth and development became, through path dependency, a German tradition, even when the necessary condition, fixed exchange rates, no longer existed following the demise of the Bretton Woods system. This is evidenced by the fact that since the outbreak of the new economy crisis in 2001, Germany's fiscal policy and the monetary policy of the ECB – the clone of the Bundesbank – have remained relatively restrictive, evidently expecting, particularly in Germany, that current account surpluses would prime the economy. In 2004 and 2005, Germany exhibited the highest current account surpluses ever (around 4 per cent of GDP) without any signs of improvement in its domestic economic performance. There has been much greater price and wage stability in Germany than abroad for more than ten years. What German economic policy makers have failed to take into account, however, is that, apart from the Eurozone, which suffers as a whole from the relatively restrictive monetary policy of the ECB, the necessary condition for the success of an export-oriented mercantilist policy, namely fixed exchange rates, no longer exists. They have not learned from best practices worldwide, especially from the economic performance of the United States, which for a long time has been enjoying relatively high economic growth, full employment, and relative price stability in tandem with considerable current account deficits. They have also not served the national interest, which for Germany would have meant avoiding the actual relative decline in per capita real national income, and for Europe the realization of the now failed goals of the 2000 Lisbon Strategy. German and European fiscal and monetary policy makers were trapped in traditional concepts without realizing that the necessary conditions for them no longer prevailed. The result was a path-dependent lock-in situation, which seems to be the price to be paid for a lack of pragmatism!

THE NEW POLICY ASSIGNMENT AND ALIGNMENT OF 1973–74

As long as the Deutschmark exchange rate was fixed, monetary policy could not concentrate solely on domestic price stability.[16] Under all circumstances, it had to care for the stability of the exchange rate, even at the price of domestic inflation. For most of the period up to the end of the Bretton Woods system in March 1973, the Federal Republic's monetary history displayed a conflict between stabilizing the Deutschmark's exchange rate and domestic price stability. When capital inflows necessitated lowering the discount rate, their liquidity-augmenting and, therefore, price-pushing effect demanded a rise in the discount rate. This dilemma was especially strong from 1956 to the first Deutschmark revaluation in March 1961 and again from 1968 to March 1973. The trouble was that during the Bretton Woods period, the government, not the Bundesbank, was responsible for changes to the Deutschmark's parity, and the two often disagreed on the issue.

While monetary policy was often incapable of preserving domestic price stability with the policy tools it had control over, fiscal policy assumed responsibility not only for promoting growth and employment, but also for ensuring price stability at times in which it was in danger. It restricted expenditure, increased taxes, and, to increase pressure on prices, lowered custom duties beyond what was required by international agreements.

Conversely, in making its decisions on monetary policy, the Bundesbank had a view not only of ensuring price stability, but also of output- and employment-related goals. Even the labour unions were at times cooperative with relative wage restraint in order to ease inflationary pressure. Thus the various institutional actors and instruments of economic policy assisted each other during the Bretton Woods period.

After 1973, a fundamental change occurred in the division of tasks between the institutions responsible for fiscal and monetary policy. David Marsh noted that the Bundesbank shifted its policy priority to maximizing domestic price stability 'only towards the end of the Bretton Woods system, when the commitment to steady exchange rates was necessarily downgraded' (Marsh, 1992, p. 37). On the other hand, it was observed that the government no longer wished 'to have its fiscal-policy scope restricted by virtue of an orientation towards monetary stability, and left the task of achieving price stability to the Bundesbank alone' (Woll and Vogl, 1976, p. 145).[17] From 1974, therefore, the Bundesbank adopted a monetarist approach to secure price stability. For example, it announced in advance its targeted growth rate of the money supply for the coming year, derived from the growth rate of the production potential plus the inflation rate, which was considered to be unavoidable. Fiscal policy since then has no longer shared responsibility for the price stability goal and has relaxed its efforts to contribute to it. The consequence was that after 25 years of keeping the public-debt-to-GDP ratio around 20 per cent, from 1974 on, this ratio steadily increased, reaching almost 68 per cent in 2005 (Holtfrerich, 2007, pp. 60–61).

Norbert Kloten coined the term 'new policy assignment' for what had happened immediately after the end of the Bretton Woods system in Germany (Kloten et al., 1985, pp. 392 and 395).[18] Henceforth, it was the sole responsibility of the Bundesbank to secure price stability, of the government to promote economic growth, and of the collective bargaining partners to care for full employment by setting the price of labour. In my view, this compartmentalization of economic policy responsibilities – contrary, by the way, to the practice in the United States and many other countries outside the Eurozone with much better economic performances than that of Germany – was a fundamental mistake and explains much of the unemployment problem that has been faced in Germany and Europe over the last decades. This sort of policy assignment was implemented by the European Union when the responsibility for monetary policy was transferred from the national central banks to the ECB at the start of 1999 (Kösters, 2003, p. 484).

The shift of the Bundesbank to the more restrictive monetarist policy concept can be explained from another perspective: a new alignment with interest groups. From the start, the goal of the West German central bank's monetary policy had been mercantilist, namely to create export surpluses, and thus export-led growth. This had made it a natural ally of German industry, particularly to its most influential organization, the Federation of German Industries, which fought for the interests of the large export-oriented companies more than for the industries supplying the domestic market. This alliance was bound to break down when the Bretton Woods system, with generally undervalued exchange rates of the Deutschmark, ended. With floating exchange rates in place, restrictions on international capital movements lost their justification and were largely removed world-wide. This freeing of international capital movements was the beginning of what we today call 'globalization'. It is well known that after 1973, the volume of international capital movements exploded and departed from its prior, relatively stable relation to the expansion of world trade. It became essential, therefore, to take the interests of the internationally active financial sector of the economy into account, especially for a central bank in by then one of the strongest economies of the world. Unlike German industry up until 1973, the financial sector's interest was not in a relative undervaluation of the Deutschmark, but rather in making the Deutschmark attractive to foreign investors by displaying its strength on the foreign exchange market. A relatively restrictive monetarist policy cre-ating expectations of an appreciation of the Deutschmark – what German industry had always tried to prevent – would serve its interest best. That the Bundesbank, with its monetarist policy, served this interest up to the creation of the ECB is demonstrated by the fact that Germany joined the European Economic Monetary Union (EMU) with an overvalued exchange rate that it has been trying to correct for years through relative wage restraint and more price stability at home than in the other Eurozone countries.

The price of serving the financial sector's interests through monetary policy has been the slowing of German economic growth and a spectacu-lar increase in unemployment since 1973. It remains to be seen whether there will be a new alignment of the ECB's monetary policy aimed at cor-recting the course that led to this impasse.

THE BUNDESBANK'S INFLUENCE ON THE INSTITUTIONAL SHAPE OF THE ECB

The Bundesbank's influence on the institutional shape of the ECB can hardly be overestimated. For all practical purposes, the two appear to be clones, or twin sisters.[19] The Bundesbank played a crucial role during the negotiations leading up to the Maastricht Treaty of February 1992, which set the roadmap for creating the ECB and its design as well as the criteria for membership in the EMU. Throughout the process of discussions and negotiations from 1988 on, EU central banks in general, and the Bundesbank in particular, played a very powerful role: the creation of EMU was decoupled from the creation of the political union, especially after the decline of communism in Eastern Europe, the fall of the Berlin Wall and German unification had made the strengthening of West European integration an urgent matter. Practically speaking, therefore, the foreign ministers and other cabinet members, except the finance ministers, played only a minor part in the process. The heads of state, however, came in at crucial junctures and demanded compromise and kept the ball rolling, not least by imposing deadlines for progress on negotiations. They often did this by appealing to Europeans' emotions, pointing out the centrality of the project for securing peace in Europe after its disastrous history in the first half of the twentieth century. But in essence, the questions around the realization of EMU remained technocratic, a matter for experts and much too complicated in its details for the heads of state and for the electorate in EU member countries to engage in, unlike issues of domestic and foreign policy. It strengthened the elite dominance that had characterized the European integration process since its beginnings and transferred 'power within elites, especially in favour of central bankers, by entrenching monetary and fiscal-policy rules' (Dyson and Featherstone, 1999, p. 747).[20]

European Community President Jacques Delors, in particular, in accordance with Chancellor Helmut Kohl in Germany, brought the powerful Committee of European Community (EC) Central Bank Governors into a prominent role in the planning of EMU and the ECB 'as a means of binding-in the respective central bank governors, obliging them to take responsibility for EMU, and linking their credibility to the initiative' (ibid., p. 773). Its role, however, was restricted to supplying an answer to the question of 'how', not 'whether', EMU should be constructed. Other bodies occupied with EMU planning were ECOFIN, composed of finance and economy ministers and their officials, and the EC Monetary Committee, composed of finance ministry officials and their central bank counterparts.

As to the launch of the EMU process, the French and Italian finance ministers had criticized the constraints and asymmetries of the existing European Monetary System (EMS) and asked for reforms at the start of 1988, when the realization of the EC single market programme was under way, including complete freedom of capital movements. At this moment, it was Germany's foreign minister, Hans-Dietrich Genscher, who was the first to propose the establishment of an ECB, thus bypassing his colleague in the Ministry of Finance, Gerhard Stoltenberg, who disagreed with the proposal.

EC President Delors and Chancellor Kohl, together with President François Mitterrand, a 'European of the heart', adopted Genscher's proposal and worked for the EMU idea to be launched officially at the Hanover European Council in June 1988. With Mitterrand's enthusiastic support, the project was agreed on, and the Delors Committee was set up to study how EMU could be achieved. The presidents of all EC central banks were members, constituting the majority *vis-à-vis* few outside experts, namely Commissioner Frans Andriessen, Alexandre Lamfalussy of the BIS, Miguel Boyer to represent the new EC member of Southern European countries including Spain, and the Dane Niels Thygesen as a reputed expert. In April 1989, this committee issued the Delors Report. Significantly, the report was signed by all EC central bank governors, including Great Britain's, much to the displeasure of Prime Minister Margaret Thatcher and her cabinet members. They strongly opposed EMU before political unification, and such unification, they declared, would not happen in their lifetime. The British influence was marginalized from then on, but the Delors Report became a blueprint for EMU. It already outlined three stages for implementing EMU as well as other provisions that were later retained in the Maastricht Treaty.

In the search for the optimal organizational structure of the ECB, Germany's negotiating partners proposed the Bundesbank as a model. With its relatively greater success in achieving price stability in Germany than other important EC central banks had attained in their countries, with its credibility and reputation as a strong central bank, and with the Deutschmark already having assumed the role of a leading and anchor currency within the EMS, the Bundesbank's structure served as a blueprint for the institutional set-up of the ECB. This was especially so since best practice was agreed on by all sides as a guiding principle. Indeed, after the fall of the Berlin Wall and German unification, most EC members desired a speedy agreement on EMU in order to bind the enhanced economic power of Germany irreversibly into the European integration process and to curb its sovereign monetary power in favour of a supranational institution. In terms of sovereignty over monetary policy, Germany – with its key currency role in Europe – had to give up more than all its other partners. This, as well as the fact that a majority of the German population was opposed to the idea of giving up the Deutschmark, put Germany in a strong negotiating position and provided the basis for its power over outcomes of the EMU process (Moravcsik, 1999). The resistance of the German population to giving up the Deutschmark was a weighty argument on the German side for shaping the ECB like the Bundesbank. The German public was accustomed to having more confidence in its central bank than in its government. Designing the structure of the ECB according to the Bundesbank model would allow the ECB to capitalize on the Bundesbank's reputation and credibility and would help to convince the public that the European currency would be at least as stable as the Deutschmark.

The EMS that had been in place since 1979, binding the foreign exchange rates of the then European Economic Community (EEC) closely together, had already worked as a transfer mechanism for the Bundesbank's concept of 'sound money' from Germany to its EMS partners (Marcussen, 1998). Thus, it needed little discussion to arrive at the conclusion that 'sound money' should also be the basic objective of the ECB. As Germany's central bank was, in terms of price stability, the most successful and the most independent of all the EC central banks, the German side, especially the Bundesbank, demanded an at least equally independent status for the ECB and for its member central banks and was able to win the consent of all the others, whose central banks had traditionally not been free of government control.[21] In fact, the ECB was made even more independent than the Bundesbank had been: the German government possessed a suspending veto power over Bundesbank decisions for two weeks and, in principle, it could change the Bundesbank's statute and power by a simple law. No one has any veto power over decisions of the ECB governing council, and a change of the ECB's statute and power requires not simply a majority vote in parliament, as in the case of the Bundesbank, but a unanimous EU-wide treaty that would be almost impossible to bring about.

On the insistence of the Bundesbank, the Maastricht Treaty finally contained strict convergence criteria for monetary and fiscal developments in the member states, on whose fulfilment the access to the final stage of EMU depended. The Treaty, however, contained no provision for fixing responsibility for demand-management policies, including income policy, which would gain in importance. With the exchange rate tool forever gone, wages would have to bear an even greater burden of adjustment in cases of supply and demand shocks and structural divergence. Such Keynesian elements of economic policy had been fought by the Bundesbank ever since it had adopted a monetarist, in other words supply-side, line, which had been recommended by the German Council of Economic Advisers (*Sachverständigenrat*) (Sievert, 2003, pp. 36–40). After President Mitterrand's failed attempt at an expansionary Keynesian policy to combat unemployment and sluggish growth in France in the early 1980s, demand management was perceived to be discredited by almost all sides participating in the negotiation process for the Maastricht Treaty.

France, together with Germany in a leadership position during the EMU negotiations, was sceptical that the neo-liberal monetarist approach to EMU according to the Bundesbank's model would suffice to keep the European economy on a dynamic growth track. The French government and EC President Jacques Delors originally worked for a European *gouvernement économique*, meaning a less independent ECB and more scope for cushioning supply and demand shocks by making provisions for a concerted financing of investment on credit that would not be counted against the 3 per cent deficit maximum, perhaps concerted income-policy measures of the member states, and close coordination between the use of such instruments and the ECB's monetary policy. Today French political leaders, irrespective of their party affiliation, continue to push the idea more than ever.

At the time of the EMU negotiations, the French wanted the centralization not only of monetary policy, but of the other economic policy fields as well. The conservative monetarist ideology of the Bundesbank and of most other central banks, however, rendered these efforts ineffective. Instead, in order to ensure that fiscal policies of the member states could not escape their commitment to strict discipline, the 'no bail-out' clause was added to the other rules containing the conduct of fiscal policy (maximum budget deficits, public debt, and so forth). On the other hand, further supply-side elements, such as the principle of labour market and wage flexibility (requested from the British and German sides), and a commitment to privatization, did not find their way into the Treaty: one did not want to arouse the opposition of the European public against the agenda by including too many neo-liberal elements.

On the issues of transparency and accountability, the Maastricht Treaty, like the Bundesbank law, remained largely silent. For example, the question of the form the minutes of the governing council's meetings were to take (verbatim or simply summarizing results, with or without dissenting votes) and whether they should be published – as with the Federal Reserve – or not, was left open.

Constructing the ECB on the Bundesbank model, and thus transferring the monetarist legacy from the latter to the former, was a mistake in two main respects.

First, transferring the Bundesbank model meant that only an isolated element of the broader German model of 'organized capitalism' was adopted at the European level. The other, practically non-transferable, elements were not, such as the legal framework of regulation for industrial relations; the structure of corporate governance involving banks and employees in decision making; the collective-bargaining system based on the idea of social partnership; the dual system in vocational education and training; and the role of house banks in providing industrial financing for the corporate giants:

> These elements reflected a commitment, and institutional capability, to support social solidarity and an attitude of 'long-termism' in industry. At the heart of the German model was a complex, interwoven set of institutional arrangements for safeguarding consensus around the market model by managing and

ameliorating the effects of its functioning. It was a framework of 'burden-sharing' for the Bundesbank in its pursuit of price stability, not least in respect of the system of collective bargaining and its success in containing and reducing labour unit costs. . . . Hence an isolated aspect of the German model – an ECB modelled on the Bundesbank – could not be expected to operate in the same way. (Dyson and Featherstone, 1999, pp. 794–5)

Second, as developments in Germany since 1974 have demonstrated (Holtfrerich, 2007, pp. 105, 230–49), the 'real' effects of a stringent monetarist policy have been underestimated, hence its depressing impact on economic activity and employment formerly in Germany and now – in addition to the straitjacket of the Maastricht fiscal criteria – in the Eurozone. Moreover, as Federal Reserve Chairman Ben Bernanke informed the central bankers assembled at the ECB in Frankfurt on 9 and 10 November 2006, the closest the Federal Reserve ever came to a 'monetarist experiment' was the brief period of disinflation from October 1979 to 1982, when Paul Volcker was chairman. Because the underlying assumption of a stable relationship between monetary aggregates and other nominal variables, namely inflation and nominal output growth, did not turn out to be true, monetarism has 'not played a central role in the formulation of U.S. monetary policy since that time' (Bernanke, 2006). Formal growth rate targets for the money supply M1 were discontinued in 1987 when Alan Greenspan took over the chairmanship. Setting target ranges for the broader money supply M2 and other aggregates was stopped altogether after the statutory requirement for reporting such ranges, according to the Humphrey–Hawkins Act of 1977, lapsed in 2000. Bernanke concluded that 'a heavy reliance on monetary aggregates as a guide to policy would seem to be unwise in the U.S. context'. This was certainly meant to be cautious advice to ECB central bankers to drop monetarism in their policy formulation, too.

At the same conference, Michael Woodford of Columbia University, a leading monetary theorist, was more outspoken. In his formally elegant and empirically rich paper, he came to the conclusion that a successful fight against inflation could be pursued without regard for monetary aggregates. He urged the ECB to drop this pillar of its monetary policy, as it would only create confusion (Woodford, 2006).

CONCLUSION

We can now answer the four questions asked in the introduction.

The Bundesbank's high degree of independence from the German government was not originally the result of learning from best practice. Its forerunner, the Bank deutscher Länder, was designed and created by the

Western Allies' military governments. A Western German government did not yet exist. The bank was subjected to close supervision by the Allies, which, like the Reich's chancellor in the German tradition, reserved the right to give instructions for monetary policy decisions. They exercised this right not to misuse the bank's credit resources for the benefit of their governments, but to block the road to renewed inflation in Germany. When Allied supervision ended in 1951, the bank's independence from the now existing German government remained – despite the contrary German tradition – although some German politicians proposed otherwise. It was kept intact precisely for the same purpose that the Allies had had in mind, namely to secure price stability. In the process of framing the Bundesbank law of 1957, independence was again questioned with reference to the German tradition. Meanwhile, best practice in Germany – as in the United States – spoke so much in favour of preserving independence that its opponents in government and parliament were unable to garner enough support to end it. The same was true in 1973 when the worldwide change from fixed to floating exchange rates triggered a new debate on the Bundesbank's independent status.

The Bundesbank's steady focus on the price-stability goal and its outstanding relative success in preserving price stability have often been attributed to Germany's trauma of having lived through two hyperinflation periods during the first half of the twentieth century. The trauma may have helped to make the restrictive measures of the Bundesbank acceptable to the German public, but this policy line was actually pursued for a different purpose. In a fixed exchange rate system, more price stability at home than abroad proved to be a useful tool for increasing Germany's international competitiveness, producing export surpluses and following a strategy of export-led growth. I have termed this policy line 'monetary mercantilism'.

After the end of the Bretton Woods system in 1973, which had tamed the Bundesbank's power over monetary policy due to its obligation to defend the fixed exchange rate of the Deutschmark, the bank's capacity to control monetary developments for the sake of securing price stability actually increased, in line with the predictions of the Mundell–Fleming model. In 1974, after the German government had embarked on a social spending spree in 1970, the Bundesbank adopted monetarism as its new policy concept. This was earlier than any other central bank. It stuck to the policy concept until it lost its power over monetary policy to the ECB in 1999, in other words much longer than other important central banks, such as the Federal Reserve or the Bank of England. Monetarism was very successful in terms of price stability, but, due to its underestimated real effects, worked like a brake on Germany's economic growth and employment. In 1974, a new policy assignment was effectuated between the different authorities of economic policy. From then on, the Bundesbank concentrated on the price-stability goal, the government was responsible for economic growth, and the task of securing full employment was handed over to the collective bargaining partners. The different authorities no longer shared responsibility for all three goals and terminated their prior coordination of monetary, fiscal and wage-setting policies. This sort of policy assignment was adopted by the European Union when the ECB began operations. It embodies the ideology of neo-liberalism that has spread around the world, even into third-world countries, and found expression in the agenda of the Washington Consensus, summarized by John Williamson in 1990 (Williamson, 1990). A new alignment of monetary policy with the interest of the financial instead of the industrial sector in 'sound money' also played a role.

What about the roots of the Bundesbank's determining influence on the institutional shape of the ECB? The Bundesbank model was certainly not imposed on the other European partners against their will. Germany was, however, in a stronger bargaining position than the others. This explains why the German government and the Bundesbank were able to win the assent of all their partners to the principle of ECB independence and to a change in their central banks' statutes accordingly. It also explains why France, the second strongest player in the Maastricht negotiation process, was not successful with its demand for a *gouvernement économique* with more centralization of economic-policy powers than just the monetary one. Best practice, none the less, played a big role. The Bundesbank model, with its success story in hardening the German, and within the EMS, most other European currencies, was recognized by the non-Germans as best practice and, therefore, acceptable. The ideology of sound money and fiscal prudence, along with the neo-liberal agenda as laid down in the Washington Consensus, also played a role. With Keynesianism allegedly discredited, the monetarist stance of the Bundesbank has become widely accepted in Europe.

NOTES

1. This refers to Paul A. David's 1985 article, 'Clio and the economics of QWERTY', which appeared in the *American Economic Review*, **75**(2), Papers and Proceedings of the Ninety-Seventh Annual Meeting of the American Economic Association (May, 1985), pp. 332–7.
2. See Greif (1994), Guiso et al. (2005, 2006), and Tabellini (2006).
3. Only two cases are known in which Bismarck gave instructions to the Reichsbank Directorate. In December 1880, he ordered the bank to raise its discount rate and to restrict its lombard credit. In 1887, for foreign-policy reasons, he instructed the bank to stop lombarding Russian bonds. The Directorate complied in both cases (Holtfrerich, 1988, p. 112).

4. This point is also discussed by André Orléan in his contribution to this volume; see Chapter 1.
5. BIS Archive, 'Minutes of the thirty-fifth meeting of the Board of Directors of the Bank for International Settlements held in Basle on 9th October 1933 at 10 a.m.' [file: BIS Board] and verbatim protocol, 'Discussions relating to the contemplated modification of the Reichsbank law' [file: 7.18 (4), box/folder: HUL 4 – vol. VI 13]. I am greatly indebted to the BIS chief archivist, Piet Clement, for mailing me copies of these documents on 14 November 2006.
6. For more on the creation of this postwar West German central banking system, see Distel (2003).
7. Translated from Deutsche Bundesbank (1988, p. 116). See also Koerfer (1987, p. 117).
8. See Hentschel (1988) for more on the legislative history of this law.
9. Adenauer had first demanded this during the 110th cabinet meeting in 1955. See Kahlenberg (1997), 110th cabinet meeting on 21 December 1955, TOP F. For further discussions of this issue, see Kahlenberg (1998), 113th cabinet meeting on 18 January 1956, TOP C; 118th cabinet meeting on 8 February 1956, TOP B; and 143rd cabinet meeting on 11 July 1956, TOP 3.
10. Translated from Kahlenberg (1998), 143rd cabinet meeting on 11 July 1956.
11. Kahlenberg (1998), 143rd cabinet meeting on 11 July 1956.
12. The role of these and later such conflicts between the Bundesbank and the West German government in securing the bank's independence as well as its credibility and reputation is analysed in a theoretical framework by Berger (1997) and by Berger and de Haan (1999).
13. Robert covers this issue extensively (1978, pp. 105–55).
14. His 1950 report on the German economy is reprinted in Ludwig-Erhard-Stiftung (1986).
15. For more details, see Holtfrerich (1999, p. 346, n. 115).
16. The following draws on Holtfrerich (1999, pp. 362–96).
17. See also Robert (1978, pp. 24–25).
18. See also Kloten et al. (1980, pp. 77–9). For the new assignment of economic policy roles, see also Fels et al. (1971), Starbatty (1984) and Tomann (1997, pp. 64–6).
19. Why this is so has been formally analysed by Debrun (2001). For a test of the hypothesis as to the conduct of monetary policy, see Smant (2002).
20. If not otherwise noted, I rely on this source for the following. For insiders' reflections on the negotiation process, see Pöhl (1996, 2003) and Köhler and Kees (1996).
21. See Dehay (2001) for a comparison of the lack of political union when the Bundesbank's forerunner, the Bank deutscher Länder, took up its function in 1948 and when the ECB took responsibility for monetary policy in 1999.

REFERENCES

Bayrhoffer, Walther (1941), 'Die alte und die neue Reichsbank', in *Deutsche Geldpolitik. Schriften der Akademie für Deutsches Recht*, Gruppe Wirtschaftswissenschaft, (4), Berlin: Duncker & Humblot, pp. 87–102.
Berger, Helge (1997), 'The Bundesbank's path to independence: evidence from the 1950s', *Public Choice*, **93**, pp. 427–53.
Berger, Helge and Jakob de Haan (1999), 'A state within the state? An event study on the Bundesbank (1948–1973)', *Scottish Journal of Political Economy*, **46**, pp. 17–39.
Bernanke, Ben S. (2006), 'Monetary aggregates and monetary policy at the Federal Reserve: a historical perspective', Remarks at the Fourth ECB Central Banking Conference, Frankfurt, Germany, 10 November, http://www.federalreserve.gov/boarddocs/Speeches/2006/20061110/default.htm, 20 November 2006.

Bethusy-Huc, Viola Gräfin von (1962), *Demokratie und Interessenpolitik*, Wiesbaden: Franz Steiner.

Borchardt, Knut (1976), 'Währung und Wirtschaft', in Deutsche Bundesbank (ed.), *Währung und Wirtschaft in Deutschland 1876–1975*, Frankfurt am Main: Fritz Knapp, pp. 3–55.

Bouvier, Jean (1988), 'The Banque de France and the state from 1850 to the present day', in Gianni Toniolo (ed.), *Central Banks' Independence in Historical Perspective*, Berlin/New York: Walter de Gruyter, pp. 73–104.

Buchheim, Christoph (1999), 'The establishment of the Bank deutscher Länder and the West German currency reform', in Deutsche Bundesbank (ed.), *Fifty Years of the Deutsche Mark: Central Bank and the Currency in Germany since 1948*, Oxford: Oxford University Press, pp. 55–100.

Bundesgesetzblatt [Federal Law Gazette], various years.

Caesar, Rolf (1981), *Der Handlungsspielraum von Notenbanken. Theoretische Analyse und internationaler Vergleich*, Baden-Baden: Nomos.

Cagan, Phillip (1956), 'The monetary dynamics of hyperinflation', in Milton Friedman (ed.), *Studies in the Quantity Theory of Money*, Chicago, IL: University of Chicago Press, pp. 25–117.

David, Paul A. (1985), 'Clio and the economics of QWERTY', *American Economic Review*, **75** (2), Papers and Proceedings of the Ninety-Seventh Annual Meeting of the American Economic Association, May, pp. 332–7.

Debrun, Xavier (2001), 'Bargaining over EMU vs. EMS: why might the ECB be the twin sister of the Bundesbank?', *Economic Journal*, **111**, pp. 566–90.

Dehay, Éric (2001), 'L'independence de la Banque centrale: de la Bundesbank à la Banque centrale européenne', in Bernd Zielinski and Michel Kauffmann (eds), *France-Allemagne. Les défis de l'euro. Des politiques économiques entre traditions nationales et intégration*, Asnières: PIA, pp. 185–211.

Deutsche Bundesbank (1988), *30 Jahre Deutsche Bundesbank. Die Entstehung des Bundesbankgesetzes vom 26. Juli 1957*, Dokumentation einer Ausstellung, Frankfurt am Main: Deutsche Bundesbank.

Deutscher Sparkassen- und Giroverband [German Association of Savings Banks] (1960), originally published in *Jahresbericht* [Annual Report] *1959*, Bonn.

Dickhaus, Monika (1996), *Die Bundesbank im westeuropäischen Wiederaufbau. Die internationale Währungspolitik der Bundesrepublik Deutschland 1948 bis 1958*, Munich: Oldenbourg.

Die Bundesbank (1950), *Aufbau und Aufgaben: Bericht über eine Aussprache führender Sachverständiger*, Frankfurt am Main: Fritz Knapp.

Distel, Joachim (2003), *Die Errichtung des westdeutschen Zentralbanksystems mit der Bank deutscher Länder*, Tübingen: Mohr.

Duwendag, Dieter (ed.) (1973), *Macht und Ohnmacht der Bundesbank*, Frankfurt am Main: Athenaeum.

Dyson, Kenneth and Kevin Featherstone (1999), *The Road to Maastricht. Negotiating Economic and Monetary Union*, Oxford: Oxford University Press.

Ehrenberg, Herbert (1973), *Zwischen Marx und Markt. Konturen einer infrastrukturorientierten und verteilungswirksamen Wirtschaftspolitik*, Frankfurt am Main: Societätsverlag.

Fels, Gerhard, Herbert Giersch, Hubertus Müller-Groeling and Klaus-Dieter Schmidt (1971), 'Neue Rollenverteilung in der Konjunkturpolitik', *Die Weltwirtschaft*, **1**, pp. 5–8.

Gaugenrieder, Carl A. (1960), 'Die rechtliche Stellung der deutschen Zentralnotenbank im Staatsgefüge in Geschichte und Gegenwart', Doctoral Dissertation, Universität Würzburg.

Geisler, Rolf P. (1953), *Notenbankverfassung und Notenbankentwicklung in den USA und Westdeutschland*, Berlin: Duncker & Humblot.

Giersch, Herbert, Karl-Heinz Paqué and Holger Schmieding (1992), *The Fading Miracle: Four Decades of Market Economy in Germany*, Cambridge: Cambridge University Press.

Greif, Avner (1994), 'Cultural beliefs and the organization of society: a historical and theoretical reflection on collectivist and individual societies', *Journal of Political Economy*, **102**, pp. 912–50.

Guiso, Luigi, Paola Sapienza and Luigi Zingales (2005), 'Cultural biases in economic exchange', version May 2005, http://www.kellogg.northwestern.edu/faculty/sapienza/htm/cultural_biases.pdf, 9 October 2006.

Guiso, Luigi, Paola Sapienza and Luigi Zingales (2006), 'Does culture affect economic outcomes?', *Journal of Economic Perspectives*, **20**, pp. 23–48.

Hansmeyer, Karl-Heinrich and Rolf Caesar (1976), 'Kriegswirtschaft und Inflation (1936–1948)', in Deutsche Bundesbank (ed.), *Währung und Wirtschaft in Deutschland 1876–1975*, Frankfurt am Main: Fritz Knapp, pp. 367–429.

Hentschel, Volker (1988), 'Die Entstehung des Bundesbankgesetzes 1949–1957. Politische Kontroversen und Konflikte', *Bankhistorisches Archiv*, **14**, pp. 3–31, 79–115.

Holtfrerich, Carl-Ludwig (1986), *The German Inflation 1914–1923: Causes and Effects in International Perspective*, Berlin/New York: Walter de Gruyter.

Holtfrerich, Carl-Ludwig (1988), 'Relations between monetary authorities and governmental institutions: the case of Germany from the 19th century to the present', in Gianni Toniolo (ed.), *Central Banks' Independence in Historical Perspective*, Berlin/New York: Walter de Gruyter, pp. 105–59.

Holtfrerich, Carl-Ludwig (1999), 'Monetary policy under fixed exchange rates (1948–1970)', in Deutsche Bundesbank (ed.), *Fifty Years of the Deutsche Mark: Central Bank and the Currency in Germany since 1948*, Oxford: Oxford University Press, pp. 307–401.

Holtfrerich, Carl-Ludwig (2007), *Wo sind die Jobs? Eine Streitschrift für mehr Arbeit*, Munich: Deutsche Verlags-Anstalt.

Kahlenberg, Friedrich P. (ed. for the Bundesarchiv) (1997), *Die Kabinettsprotokolle der Bundesregierung, vol. 8: Die Kabinettsprotokolle 1955*, Munich: Oldenbourg, http://www.bundesarchiv.de/kabinettsprotokolle/web/index.jps, 31 January 2007.

Kahlenberg, Friedrich P. (ed. for the Bundesarchiv) (1998), *Die Kabinettsprotokolle der Bundesregierung, vol. 9: Die Kabinettsprotokolle 1956*, Munich: Oldenbourg, http://www.bundesarchiv.de/kabinettsprotokolle/web/index.jps, 31 January 2007.

Kaiser, Rolf H. (1980), *Bundesbankautonomie. Möglichkeiten und Grenzen einer unabhängigen Politik*, Frankfurt am Main: R.G. Fischer.

Kloten, Norbert, Hans-J. Barth, Karl-Heinz Ketterer and Rainer Vollmer (1980), *Zur Entwicklung des Geldwertes in Deutschland. Fakten und Bestimmungsgründe*, Tübingen: Mohr.

Kloten, Norbert, Karl-Heinz Ketterer and Rainer Vollmer (1985), 'West Germany's stabilization performance', in Leon Lindberg and Charles S. Maier (eds), *The Politics of Inflation and Economic Stagnation*, Washington, DC: Brookings Institution Press, pp. 353–402.

Koerfer, Daniel (1987), *Kampf ums Kanzleramt. Erhard und Adenauer*, Stuttgart: Deutsche Verlags-Anstalt.

Köhler, Horst and Andreas Kees (1996), 'Die Verhandlungen zur Europäischen Wirtschafts- und Währungsunion', in Theo Waigel (ed.), *Unsere Zukunft heißt Europa. Der Weg zur Wirtschafts- und Währungsunion*, Düsseldorf: ECON, pp. 145–74.

Kösters, Wim (2003), 'The monetary and economic policy coordination in the third stage of the EMU: the risk of asymmetric shocks', in Jean-Victor Louis and Assimakis P. Komninos (eds), *The Euro: Law, Politics, Economics*, London: British Institute of International and Comparative Law, pp. 483–6.

Ludwig-Erhard-Stiftung (ed.) (1986), *Die Korea-Krise als ordnungspolitische Herausforderung der deutschen Wirtschaftspolitik. Texte und Dokumente*, Stuttgart: Fischer.

Marcussen, Martin (1998), 'Ideas and elites: Danish macroeconomic policy discourse in the EMU process', PhD thesis, University of Aalborg.

Marsh, David (1992), *Die Bundesbank. Geschäfte mit der Macht*, Munich: Bertelsmann.

Moravcsik, Andrew (1999), *The Choice for Europe: Social Purpose and State Power from Messina to Maastricht*, London: University College London Press.

Müller, Helmut (1973), *Die Zentralbank – eine Nebenregierung. Reichsbankpräsident Hjalmar Schacht als Politiker der Weimarer Republik*, Opladen: Westdeutscher Verlag.

Pierenkemper, Toni (1998), 'Die Angst der Deutschen vor der Inflation oder: kann man aus der Geschichte lernen?', *Jahrbuch für Wirtschaftsgeschichte*, 1998 (1), pp. 59–84.

Plessis, Alain (1985), *Le concours de la Banque de France à l'économie, 1842–1914. États, Fiscalités, Économies*, Paris: Sorbonne.

Pöhl, Karl Otto (1996), 'Der Delors–Bericht und das Statut einer Europäischen Zentralbank', in Theo Waigel (ed.), *Unsere Zukunft heißt Europa. Der Weg zur Wirtschafts- und Währungsunion*, Düsseldorf: ECON, pp. 193–209.

Pöhl, Karl Otto (2003), 'Die Bundesbank und die Europäische Währungsunion', in Wilhelm Hankel, Karl Albrecht Schachtschneider and Joachim Starbatty (eds), *Der Ökonom als Politiker – Europa, Geld und die soziale Frage*, Stuttgart: Lucius & Lucius, pp. 455–62.

Puhl, Emil (1941), 'Die Wiederherstellung der deutschen Währungshoheit', *Deutsche Geldpolitik. Schriften der Akademie für Deutsches Recht, Gruppe Wirtschaftswissenschaft*, **4**, Berlin: Duncker & Humblot, pp. 35–50.

Robert, Rüdiger (1978), *Die Unabhängigkeit der Bundesbank. Analyse und Materialien*, Kronberg/Taunus: Athenäum.

Sayers, Richard S. (1976), *The Bank of England 1891–1944*, vol. 1, Cambridge: Cambridge University Press.

Schacht, Hjalmar (1937), 'Die Wiederherstellung der deutschen Währungshoheit', *Zeitschrift der Akademie für Deutsches Recht*, **4**, pp. 137–9.

Schelling, Friedrich von (1975), *Die Bundesbank in der Inflation. Plädoyer für eine neue Geldverfassung*, Frankfurt am Main: Fritz Knapp.

Sievert, Olaf (2003), 'Vom Keynesianismus zur Angebotspolitik', in Sachverständigenrat zur Begutachtung der gesamtwirtschaftlichen Entwicklung (ed.), *Vierzig Jahre Sachverständigenrat 1963–2003*, Wiesbaden: Statistisches Bundesamt, pp. 34–46.

Singer, Kurt (1922), 'Die Autonomie der Reichsbank', *Wirtschaftsdienst*, **7**, pp. 734–5.
Smant, David J.C. (2002), 'Has the European Central Bank followed a Bundesbank policy? Evidence from the early years', *Kredit und Kapital*, **35**, pp. 327–43.
Starbatty, Joachim (1984), 'Zur Rollenverteilung in der Konjunkturpolitik', *Ordo – Jahrbuch für die Ordnung von Wirtschaft und Gesellschaft*, **35**, pp. 151–66.
Stern, Klaus (1999), 'The note-issuing bank within the state structure', in Deutsche Bundesbank (ed.), *Fifty Years of the Deutsche Mark: Central Bank and the Currency in Germany since 1948*, Oxford: Oxford University Press, pp. 103–64.
Stolper, Wolfgang E. and Karl W. Roskamp (1979), 'Planning a free economy: Germany 1945–1960', *Zeitschrift für die gesamte Staatswissenschaft*, **135**, pp. 374–404.
Tabellini, Guido (2006), 'Culture and institutions: economic development in the regions of Europe', version May 2006, http://www.sscnet.ucla.edu/06S/econ11-1/zhang/regions_may06%5B1%5D.pdf#search=%22culture%20and%20institutions%3A%20economic%20development%22, 9 October 2006.
Tomann, Horst (1997), *Stabilitätspolitik. Theorie, Strategie und europäische Perspektive*, Berlin: Springer.
Verhandlungen des Reichstags (1938), *III. Wahlperiode 1936*, **459**, Berlin: Reichsdruckerei.
Vocke, Wilhelm (1956), *Gesundes Geld. Gesammelte Reden und Aufsätze zur Währungspolitik*, Frankfurt am Main: Fritz Knapp.
Wallich, Henry C. (1955), *Triebkräfte des deutschen Wiederaufstiegs*, Frankfurt am Main: Fritz Knapp.
Wandel, Eckard (1980), *Die Entstehung der Bank deutscher Länder und die deutsche Währungsreform 1948*, Frankfurt am Main: Fritz Knapp.
Williamson, John (1990), 'What Washington means by policy reform', in John Williamson (ed.), *Latin American Adjustment: How Much Has Happened?*, Washington, DC: Institute for International Economics, pp. 7–20.
Woll, Artur and Gerald Vogl (1976), *Geldpolitik*, Stuttgart: Gustav Fischer.
Woodford, Michael (2006), 'How important is money in the conduct of monetary policy?', Paper prepared for the Fourth ECB Central Banking Conference, Frankfurt, Germany, 9–10 November, http://www.columbia.edu/~mw2230/moneyconf-final.pdf, 20 November 2006.

3. What objectives for monetary policy?

Benjamin M. Friedman

INTRODUCTION

The overflow crowd packed into the House of Representatives' largest hearing room fell into a hush as the chairman of the Federal Reserve Board, Mr F. Milton, made his entrance and took a seat at the witness table, accompanied by the vice chairman, Mr L. Robert, and the Federal Reserve System's chief economist, Mr P. Edward. The US economy had been spiralling downward for ten months. With 26 million people out of work, unemployment had reached 17 per cent of the labour force. Industrial production had declined 23 per cent from the previous peak. Both corporate bankruptcies and home mortgage defaults were running at record rates for the post-World War Two period. Of the nation's 7000 commercial banks in operation a year earlier, 1429 had failed.

The chairman of the House Banking Committee, Mr P. Wright (D, Tex.), called the hearing to order, welcomed the three witnesses, and sombrely invited Mr Milton to present his opening remarks.

'Thank you, Mr Chairman,' Mr Milton began. 'I am pleased to report that during the past year US monetary policy has been outstandingly successful. Overall inflation has again been exactly 1.0 per cent, and prices other than for food and energy have risen by just 0.9 per cent. My colleagues and I are here to accept this committee's congratulations and those of the American people.'

Such a situation is, of course, unthinkable. The purpose of any economic policy is to advance a nation's economic well-being, meaning the prosperity of its citizens and the vitality of the institutions through which they participate in economic activity, both in the present and for the future. Whether working men and women are able to make a living, whether the businesses that they own and at which they work can earn a profit and invest adequately for future growth, and whether the banks and other financial institutions on which both individuals and businesses rely can survive in the face of the risk taking that is central to their reason for existing, are all fundamental aspects of that well-being. Experience shows that rising (or falling) prices can and sometimes do undermine the efficient functioning of economic activity, so that price stability is a key desideratum in just this regard. But price stability is instrumental, valued not for itself but for how it enhances an economy's capacity to achieve those goals that, even if they are not genuinely primary from the perspective of basic human concerns, are at least instrumental at a higher level. The idea that economic policy should pursue price stability as a means of promoting more fundamental economic well-being, either now or in the future, is not grounds for pursuing price stability at the expense, much less to the exclusion, of that more fundamental economic well-being.

If monetary policy were unable to exert influence over real outcomes in any more direct way, but were able none the less to influence the evolution of prices, then – from the perspective of how to conduct monetary policy, though not more generally – promoting fundamental economic well-being and pursuing price stability would amount to the same objective. But today the debate over whether monetary policy is 'neutral' with respect to real economic outcomes seems largely an episode from the discipline's past, perhaps worth recalling for whatever insights into subsidiary matters it may have provided along the way, but not a serious challenge on the core question that was at issue. Few economists, and certainly few business people, market investors, or even ordinary citizens who concern themselves with economic affairs, believe that actions taken by the central bank have no impact on output, or employment, or asset values. Hence it is not legitimate to duck the question of whether and how monetary policy *should* seek to affect real outcomes by subsuming that question within the larger one of whether monetary policy *can* do so. Both theory and evidence indicate that, in a world such as the one today's advanced industrialized and post-industrial economies occupy, monetary policy can affect output, employment and other quantitative aspects of non-financial economic activity over at least some significant period. The relevant question is in what way it should seek to do so.

Two closely related questions frame the core of this debate. First, merely pointing to generic 'real outcomes' does not constitute a constructive normative position either. Individual citizens are, and have a right to be, concerned with many facets of the economic environment in which they live: their income levels, their employment prospects, their ability to start a business or borrow to purchase a new home, just to name a few. From an aggregate perspective, further aspects of an economy's actual and prospective situation are plausibly of concern to public policy makers: the levels of production and employment in relation to 'full-employment' benchmarks, the economy's international balances, its investment rate, among others. Even when these disparate measures of economic activity are positively correlated (which they are not under all circumstances), the relationships are far from perfect. Hence some view of which real objectives policy makers should be seeking to achieve – along with price stability – is important.

Second, the Tinbergen principle, relating the number of independent objectives any economic policy can achieve to the number of independent instruments it has to deploy, is especially pertinent in any discussion on monetary policy (Tinbergen, 1952, 1966). Technical non-essentials aside, monetary policy consists in setting a single instrument: either the quantity of liabilities the central bank has outstanding or the rate of return eligible market participants pay to hold those liabilities as their assets. (Except for coincidence, policy makers cannot set both the quantity and the rate of return if the market is to clear.) Hence even if there is agreement on which real outcomes monetary policy should properly seek to influence – and even if all real outcomes of interest in this regard are perfectly correlated – there remains the problem that even a single real objective, together with that of stable prices, raises the fundamental tension to which Tinbergen pointed when the policy maker is setting only one true instrument.

The purpose of this chapter is to explore the set of practical issues that central banks in the modern world face as a consequence of the intersection of these two intertwined sets of considerations. The chapter begins by asking which aspects of non-financial and financial economic activity are properly of concern to monetary policy makers. (In effect, the issue here is just why the fictional House Banking Committee hearing portrayed above is such an absurdity.) Next, the chapter turns to the operational issue of what policy objectives the central bank should articulate, either in its internal analysis or in its communication with higher authorities, as well as financial market participants and the general public, as 'targets' of monetary policy. Here the key considerations at issue include matters of transparency and of accountability of the central bank as a public policy-making institution. The chapter then digresses to consider a class of representations of how the economy functions in which some (though not all) of the matters under discussion here take on a different – specifically, a simpler – character. The chapter concludes by assembling the various propositions advanced into a set of positive principles for the conduct of monetary policy.

OBJECTIVES FOR MONETARY POLICY BEYOND PRICE STABILITY

It is straightforward that aspects of economic activity like aggregate output and employment are matters of direct concern for public policy. National income mostly varies in pace with national output, and so aggregate output represents the total economic gain accruing to a nation's citizens. The balance between aggregate employment and a nation's labour force indicates the availability of work for those citizens able and willing to seek it.

Further, each of these aspects of real economic activity, while of concern in itself, also matters for the evolution of prices. Greater employment in relation to the available supply of labour requires firms to compete harder for workers and therefore to increase wages. If wages increase faster than productivity, per unit costs of production rise and firms must either raise product prices or narrow their profit margins. Greater aggregate output in relation to an economy's capacities likewise increases production costs, even apart from wage costs, and again requires firms to increase prices or reduce margins. Neither measure is complete even within its own sphere – the total economic gain accruing to all of a nation's citizens says nothing about how that gain is distributed among them, and neither the increase in employment nor the unemployment rate says anything about whether the jobs being created deliver a satisfactory income and decent working conditions – but both are none the less central to any plausible set of policy objectives describing what an economy is supposed to achieve for those it serves. Further, monetary policy has the demonstrated capacity to influence both.

The composition of economic activity also matters as soon as the purview of policy becomes forward looking. At any point in time, individuals' economic well-being hinges largely on how much they are consuming. But both individuals and the economy in the aggregate have reason to consume less than all of current production in order to invest in future productive capacity. To the extent that such forward-looking expenditures involve debt financing (or, equivalently, to the extent that required equity returns vary with interest rates), monetary policy has the ability to affect the willingness and ability to undertake productive investment – indeed, judging from historical experience, it has greater ability to affect the pace of investment than of consumption.

It does not necessarily follow, however, that the economy's investment rate, whether for new factories and equipment and office buildings or for new housing, is a plausible independent objective for monetary policy. Monetary policy actions (say, variations in whatever interest rate the central bank is setting) that affect investment also affect aggregate output and employment. Tinbergen's principle applies, and, with a single instrument, only by coincidence would the policy action consistent with the optimally desired investment rate be identical to that consistent with the optimally desired levels of aggregate output and employment. Only in conjunction with some other policy instrument, most obviously fiscal policy, is it plausible to entertain distinct policy objectives with respect to both aggregate output and the investment–consumption mix within that aggregate.

The same argument applies to the economy's international imbalance. There are ample cogent reasons for policy makers to be concerned with the relationship between a nation's exports and its imports (and, in parallel, between its capital outflows and capital inflows). An excess of imports over exports represents the net transfer of goods and services from a nation's trading partners, and, in parallel, the net transfer of production and employment to those trading partners; even if the nation as a whole is better off on account of the additional absorption of goods and services, the jobs and sales thereby forgone are nevertheless real losses for specific groups of workers and firms. An excess of imports over exports also means that a nation is borrowing from foreign lenders, and transferring claims on its assets to foreign owners, at a greater rate than it is lending to foreign borrowers and accumulating assets abroad. Over time the accumulation of an ever larger overall net debtor position requires the devotion of an increasing share of national income to servicing the resulting obligations. In the meantime, if the required increase in foreign holdings outpaces the increase in foreign demand for assets denominated in the nation's currency, its exchange rate will decline with consequent implications for its domestic asset markets. Here too, however, the monetary policy actions that affect the relationship of imports and exports are the same as the monetary policy actions that affect aggregate output and employment. Only in conjunction with a second policy instrument, again most obviously fiscal policy (as in Robert Mundell and Marcus Fleming's classic model), is it plausible for the central bank to entertain independent objectives with respect to the nation's foreign trade and investment balance.

Monetary policy makers also have both practical and historical reasons for seeking to maintain the vitality of financial institutions and the functioning of financial markets. The US Federal Reserve System was created as a direct response to a series of banking crises (in 1901, 1907 and 1913, and also before that in the nineteenth century) that not only shut down much of the nation's financial system, but spilled over to impair the nonfinancial economy as well. The visible sign of that motivation was the new central bank's charge to 'provide an elastic currency'. More recently, the 'Asian financial crisis' of the late 1990s (which was not limited to Asian countries) again showed how the impairment of a country's banking system interrupts the credit creation process, destroys asset values, and otherwise impedes the ability of households and firms to carry out their ordinary economic affairs – as, for that matter, happened in the United States and many other countries besides during the depression of the 1930s.

Unlike considerations such as investment rates and export–import balances, however, it is unclear what efficacy monetary policy *per se* has with respect to financial soundness. In this case more-specialized policy instruments like bank capital requirements, or prudential regulation and supervision, or margin requirements on the purchase and holding of specific assets, are what mostly matter. To be sure, at times when banks or other highly leveraged institutions are holding precarious asset positions, ordinary variation in interest rates can affect the health of their balance sheets or, for some, even their survival. But such considerations mostly lie outside the ordinary purview of monetary policy.

Finally, in recent years both central bankers and students of monetary policy have asked increasingly whether asset prices should be a specific focus of concern for monetary policy. Japan's experience since 1989, the point at which equity and real estate prices in that country peaked sharply, has been a particular spur to ideas along such lines, but developments in the United States – the rapid gains in equity prices during the latter half of the 1990s, and subsequently the rise in home prices since 2000 – have raised this question as well. As former Federal Reserve Chairman Alan Greenspan put one version of the argument, in principle, either sudden increases or sudden declines in asset prices can exert unwanted effects on non-financial economic activity, but in practice sudden increases are rarely seen; hence the concern of the central bank is to avoid sudden declines (Greenspan, 1999). The harder question to which this proposition gives rise is whether monetary policy should simply accept whatever asset price increases occur and then act to prevent sudden declines – this was a familiar interpretation of the Federal Reserve's actions during the late 1990s (what many market participants called the 'Greenspan put') – or, instead, proactively resist what it perceives as unwarranted asset-price increases to begin with. (The second strategy clearly involves the need to identify, as it is occurring, when an increase in asset prices becomes excessive.) Either way, however, it is clear that what matters for purposes of monetary policy is not asset prices *per se*, but the prospect that asset prices may exert an impact on more basic aspects of economic activity, like output or investment, that are properly objects of monetary policy concern.

In sum, despite the potentially wide range of aspects of real economic activity that routinely enter the ongoing public discussion of monetary policy, in the absence of coordination with some independent policy instrument, most importantly fiscal policy, the aggregate levels of output and employment, and of each in relation to the corresponding 'full-employment' benchmark, represent much of what it is plausible to expect monetary policy to seek to achieve among legitimate real economic objectives. Output and employment may be metaphors for a longer list of real economic considerations, but in the context of monetary policy their metaphorical content is less than is often assumed. For purposes of the routine conduct of monetary policy, output and employment – along with stable prices – are the heart of the matter.

MULTIPLE POLICY OBJECTIVES AND MULTIPLE POLICY TARGETS

Even so, the Tinbergen principle immediately implies a problem: two objectives, price stability and output/employment (three if output and employment are sufficiently imperfectly related to constitute independent objectives), but only one instrument. Even apart from the inability to predict future economic developments in a setting in which the influence of policy is subject to time lags, monetary policy cannot be expected to achieve desired paths for both prices and real outcomes. Barring some special coincidence – and this is the subject of discussion in the next section – the best that a policy with only one instrument can achieve is to keep the economy on the path that represents the optimal compromise between the two objectives. Considerations of uncertainty only make matters more difficult.

In recent years many central banks have addressed this tension between multiple objectives and their unitary monetary policy instrument by resorting to 'inflation targeting'. In current usage of the term, the two essential components of an inflation targeting strategy for conducting monetary policy are (i) the clear public statement of what rate of price increase policy makers are seeking to achieve over some medium- to long-run horizon, in practice typically stated in terms of a target range, and (ii) the formulation, in internal central bank discussion as well as statements to the public, of the economic trajectory intended to follow from the chosen monetary policy in terms of the implied path for inflation. In principle, as many advocates of inflation targeting have emphasized (see, for example, an early statement by Mervyn King, 1997), inflation targeting need not imply that the chosen inflation rate is policy makers' sole objective. The Tinbergen principle dictates that, apart from situations of degeneracy and analogous mathematical pathologies, the number of economic variables sufficient to express the economic trajectory sought by any economic policy equals the number of independent instrument variables policy makers are using. Hence with only one instrument – again, either a short-term interest rate or the quantity of central bank liabilities – monetary policy makers can describe their intended economic trajectory with only one variable. The analytical appeal of doing so by means of inflation (or prices), rather than some real variable like output or employment, rests on the presumption that, in the long run, monetary policy actually is neutral with respect to those real outcomes, which ultimately depend only on factors such as endowments, preferences and technologies. Hence by choosing inflation for this purpose, policy makers are focusing on a variable that monetary policy can influence over not just the medium horizon but the long run as well. (Of course, as the discussion below elaborates, in practice the appeal of choosing inflation for this purpose may be something other than analytical.)[1]

This implication of the Tinbergen principle is most explicit in the inflation targeting framework developed by Lars Svensson, in which policy makers frame their decision in terms of how rapidly to bring inflation back to the desired rate after some departure from it (Svensson, 1997). Given policy objectives for both inflation and output/employment, the length of the interval over which policy makers should optimally seek to return inflation to the publicly declared target range depends on the weight that they place on their inflation objective relative to that on their output/employment objective. For a given short-run cost of disinflation in terms of unemployment and forgone output, the greater the weight on real outcomes is, the more slowly policy makers would optimally seek to return inflation to the target range, and vice versa.

Advocates of inflation targeting, both within central banks and among academic researchers, frequently ground the argument in favour of this way of conducting monetary policy in considerations of transparency and accountability: telling the public which single variable to associate with monetary policy, and also the numerical target at which the central bank is aiming for that variable, makes clear what policy makers are trying to achieve. When the aim of policy is well known and the results straightforward to monitor, it is also possible for both higher authorities and the public to hold policy makers accountable for their success or failure. Transparency of the central bank's policy is presumably helpful in that it reduces the uncertainty that financial market participants, as well as households and firms more generally, face in carrying out their respective economic plans, thereby making the economy as a whole more efficient. Further, especially when the objective is low and stable inflation, transparency of that particular objective also helps to anchor the public's inflation expectations, thereby reducing the real economic costs associated with combating any unexpected increase under circumstances (such as are commonly assumed in today's 'New Keynesian' economic framework; see, for example, Clarida et al., 1999) in which price-setting behaviour at any point in time depends not only on the level of real economic activity relative to full-employment benchmarks, but also on expectations of future inflation. Accountability of policy makers for the efficacy of their decisions and actions is plainly part of what constitutes effective democracy.

The argument for the greater transparency of the inflation targeting strategy fails, however – and with it the argument for the greater resulting accountability of monetary policy – when policy makers have objectives for real economic outcomes. According to the Tinbergen principle, describing the intended economic trajectory in terms of inflation alone need not imply that policy makers have no other objectives, but nor does it preclude such a univariate objective. The essential question is whether monetary policy makers have objectives for output and employment, or not.

If they do, then inflation targeting is more likely to undermine transparency of monetary policy than to promote it. The chief reason is that under inflation targeting, policy makers normally reveal to the public only one of their multiple objectives: that for inflation. If the public knew (and were able to use) the economic model on which policy makers rely in evaluating potential actions, the public could infer what path for output, or employment, or any other variable of interest would be expected to accompany the targeted inflation trajectory. (It could also work out the path for interest rates that the central bank planned to follow.) Few central banks disclose this information, however, including those that follow inflation targeting strategies. To make the matter yet more difficult, when policy is set by consensus among a committee of decision makers – as is the case at the Federal Reserve, the European Central Bank, and many other central banks – those decision makers often do not agree on a single economic model anyway. Nor do inflation targeting central banks quantify for the public (or, normally, even for themselves) the relative importance that they attach to their objectives for inflation and for real economic outcomes.

Indeed, many inflation targeting central banks at least appear to go to some effort *not* to reveal such aspects of their policy making to the public. An increasingly common practice, for example, following the initial lead of the Bank of England, is to issue at regular intervals a detailed monetary policy report, but to call it an 'Inflation Report' – as if inflation were the only aspect of economic activity of concern to monetary policy. Similarly, some inflation targeting central banks, in the public explanation that they provide of the rationale underlying their monetary policy strategy, avoid any reference to the possibility of tension, even in the short run, between their inflation objective and any real outcome.[2] In light of the favourable effect on short-run inflation–output trade-offs that ensues from keeping expectations of future inflation anchored at a low level (see again the standard New Keynesian representation of price-setting behaviour), the incentive for policy makers to downplay or even conceal their objectives for real economic outcomes is clear. (In parallel, Kenneth Rogoff (1985) famously argued for choosing central bankers known to place less weight on real outcomes, relative to inflation, than the general public.) But doing so hardly contributes to the transparency of their policy.

The same considerations undermine the argument for inflation targeting on the grounds of promoting the accountability of monetary policy. If policy makers have objectives for both inflation and real outcomes, but disclose only their inflation objective, then higher authorities as well as the general body politic can hold them accountable in an explicit way at most for their success or failure in meeting their inflation objective; for the rest they must rely on inference and guesswork. To be sure, in a situation like that of the fictional House Banking Committee hearing described above, real economic outcomes are so obviously at variance with any reasonable set of objectives that everyone would understand that the central bank had failed to execute its responsibilities. But then no such occurrence has developed, in the United States or any other economically advanced country, since before World War Two. The debate over the accountability of monetary policy revolves around failures that are more difficult to identify and measure.

The other possibility, of course, is that policy makers may not have objectives for real outcomes, but instead may actually direct their policy solely towards the achievement of the stated rate of inflation. The logic of the Tinbergen principle implies that an inflation-targeting central bank is not necessarily concerned with inflation alone, but it certainly does not imply that this cannot be the case. If it is, then an inflation targeting policy is fully transparent, and the standard consequences argued for accountability obtain as well. In this situation, however, monetary policy makers would be abdicating their responsibility for seeking, within the capacities of the instrument at their disposal, to achieve economic conditions in the interests of the public whom they supposedly serve, including individuals, businesses and financial firms. In the extreme, they would indeed fit the fictional caricature offered above.

Indeed, one interpretation of the movement towards inflation targeting among so many of the world's central banks (and, perhaps even more so, among academic researchers who advocate this policy rubric) is that this is precisely the state of policy making that inflation targeting is intended to bring about over time. A plausible consequence of constraining the discussion of monetary policy to be carried out entirely in terms of an optimal inflation trajectory is that, in time, objectives for real outcomes will atrophy, or even disappear from policy makers' purview altogether. This eventuality may ensue not only because the language and analytical framework within which discussion takes place naturally shapes what is discussed, but also because – exactly as the argument for accountability implies – policy makers inevitably take more seriously those aspects of their responsibilities for which they expect to be held accountable. Disclosing only the inflation objective, when in fact policy makers have objectives for inflation as well as real economic outcomes, biases the relative importance that they will attach to these respective objectives by fostering their accountability for inflation and not for real outcomes. In time, the objectives for real outcomes will devolve into a rhetorical fiction.

MIGHT MULTIPLE OBJECTIVES 'COINCIDE'?

As the arguments made above acknowledge, only by coincidence would the monetary policy actions that optimally steer inflation along the path sought by policy makers be identical in all circumstances to the policy actions that optimally achieve the path sought for output and employment. The crucial issue is disturbances that affect the economy's ability to produce goods and services at any given price. Because monetary policy works primarily by influencing the demand for goods and services, it is, at least in principle, able to offset a disturbance that spurs households or firms or even the government to buy either more or less than would be consistent with keeping the aggregate economy on the optimally desired path – for example, a military conflict that increases the government's need for ordnance and personnel, or a shortfall of profits that dampens firms' ability to undertake new investment. By contrast, in the face of shock to aggregate supply – say, an increase in the price paid to import oil or some other essential intermediate good, or a widespread decline in the productivity of industry (due perhaps to the need to protect workers, customers and facilities from potential terrorist attacks) – nothing that monetary policy can do is sufficient to restore the economy to its previous position.

Even so, as Olivier Blanchard and Jordi Gali (2005) have recently emphasized, a currently standard representation of aggregate supply behaviour does imply a coincidence (a 'divine coincidence', as they call it) between the monetary policy that would be optimal with respect to inflation alone and the policy that would be optimal with respect to output and employment alone. To recall, the standard New Keynesian Phillips curve expresses inflation at any point in time as the sum of a term depending on the relationship of current output to the corresponding full-employment benchmark and (typically with a coefficient based on the rate by which price-setting firms discount future profits, and therefore close to unity in the short run) the rate of inflation expected in the future.[3] If firms making price-setting decisions expect zero inflation in the future, current inflation therefore depends only on the current level of output compared to full-employment output; and, by definition, at full employment current inflation is zero. This property of the price-setting model immediately implies that – apart from the inflationary implications that follow from expected future inflation – there is no tension between the objective of keeping inflation at zero (or any other designated rate) and the objective of keeping output at full employment.

The real cost of disinflation can be large in this model, but none the less it is strictly a matter of what is needed to bring inflation *expectations* back in line with whatever is the optimally desired inflation rate.[4] Similarly, the rate at which an inflation targeting central bank should optimally seek to return inflation to the desired rate in Svensson's model, once some disturbance has resulted in either faster or slower actual inflation, is again merely a matter of what it takes to bring inflation expectations back into line. (This underlying logic makes it easy to see why anchoring expectations of future inflation is so important in any model based on this representation of aggregate supply – and, in parallel, why the recent literature of monetary policy has placed so much emphasis on the 'management of expectations'.[5])

Repeated empirical findings, however, indicate that in fact inflation exhibits more persistence over time than can plausibly be attributed to the sluggish movement of strictly forward-looking expectations.[6] Standard models based on costs of price adjustment (Gregory Mankiw, John Taylor, Julio Rotemberg–Michael Woodford, and others), as well as models based on infrequent opportunities for price adjustment (Guillermo Calvo, John Taylor, and others) imply that what should be 'sticky' is prices, not inflation. But the empirical observation is that *inflation* is what exhibits persistence. Explaining this persistence, in the sense of providing a theoretically coherent model that would give rise to it, has therefore emerged as a major focus of research on the inflation process.

One major strand in this line of research focuses on 'real rigidities', meaning not just the familiar impedimenta to perfect flexibility of prices and/or wages, but the attempt by price or wage setters to hold fixed one or another relationship in real terms.[7] Willem Buiter and Iain Jewitt (1981), for example, posited that wage setters, operating in the context of staggered contracts, attempt to maintain relative relationships between the *real* wages of workers in their firm and in other firms over the life of each contract being established. As Jeff Fuhrer and George Moore (1995) have shown, in contrast to the more conventional contracting models based on nominal rigidities, which in the end relate a two-sided average of the *price level* to the difference between actual and full-employment output, when this concern for relative real wages is a factor in wage-setting behaviour what is related to that real difference is a two-sided average of the *inflation rate*. Hence inflation in effect depends on its own past, and so the model is capable of delivering persistence of inflation consistent with commonly observed patterns.

As Blanchard and Gali (2005) have argued, however, such real wage-setting behaviour – or, for that matter, any comparable form of real rigidity – also severs the 'coincidence' by which, in the presence of a disturbance affecting aggregate supply, maintaining output equal to the welfare relevant full-employment level delivers zero inflation apart from whatever inflation is expected to prevail in the future. In effect, the real wage rigidity renders the relationship between the output level that represents full employment from the perspective of standard economic welfare considerations and the output level that results in any given desired inflation rate no longer invariant to the usual kinds of aggregate supply shocks. Hence monetary policy faces a trade-off in the short run between an output goal and an inflation goal for reasons that are wholly apart from the usual matter of inflation expectations. Given the persistence that this real rigidity imparts to the inflation process, the 'short run' for this purpose may well be of non-trivial duration; indeed, the available empirical evidence suggests that it may be quite long. (In addition, as in any standard model, to the extent that households and firms expect that policy makers will respond in such a situation by allowing inflation to exceed the desired level, the usual problem of inflation expectations emerges as well.)

The resulting trade-off gives policy makers yet another reason to have objectives with respect to not just inflation but real outcomes as well. It is then no longer true that, if only expectations of future inflation can be 'managed', doing what is optimal from the standpoint of price stability automatically means doing what is optimal from the standpoint of output, or employment, or whatever else may be on policy makers' list of real economic desiderata. Moreover, to the extent that, in an economy with real rigidities, objectives with respect to real outcomes thereby take on a higher level of analytical importance, the standard arguments on grounds of transparency and accountability mean that it is all the more important for the central bank to be open about what those objectives are.

SUMMARY OF CONCLUSIONS

In brief, the prescriptive conclusions of this chapter's inquiry into the appropriate objectives for monetary policy are as follows.

- In a world in which monetary policy not only can affect real economic outcomes like output and employment but, moreover, constitutes for practical purposes the principal available instrument of public policy capable of doing so over medium-run horizons corresponding to typical business fluctuations, policy makers cannot escape responsibility for having objectives with respect to real outcomes. The familiar argument that monetary policy has but one independent instrument and therefore must entertain only one economic objective is fallacious. While the relative weighting that policy makers give to real objectives and to the goal of price stability is of course subject to debate, it is inappropriate for monetary policy to pursue price stability (or any given designated rate of price increase) to the exclusion of concern for output or employment or other aspects of real economic activity.

- In the absence of effective coordination with fiscal policy, or some other comparable policy instrument, under ordinary circumstances it is implausible for the real objectives of monetary policy to extend beyond aggregate measures like output and employment. Matters of composition like the relative magnitudes of consumption and investment, or the economy's international balance, are in principle valid objects of concern; but only in coordination with fiscal policy can monetary policy seek to achieve such objectives.

- Asset prices can be important sources of information about future trends in inflation or real economic activity, or both, and monetary policy makers should take that information into account in deciding on their actions. But monetary policy should not elevate the level of asset prices, or movements of asset prices, to an independent objective to be pursued on its own account.

- As long as monetary policy makers do have objectives with respect to real economic outcomes, policy should not be organized along the lines of explicitly targeting inflation unless it also, in parallel, explicitly targets output or employment or some other stated real objective. To maintain objectives for both inflation and real outcomes, but publicly announce a desired target range and intended trajectory for inflation only, undermines the transparency of monetary policy. Organizing monetary policy in this way also therefore undermines policy makers' accountability for their actions.

- The possibility of real rigidities in economic behaviour, such as a concern for relative real wages in the wage-setting process – as seem to be implied by the repeatedly observed persistence of inflation – makes the case for having real economic objectives of monetary policy even stronger. When economic behaviour includes real rigidities, the level of output or employment that represents full employment from the standpoint of considerations of economic welfare need not be identical to the level that results in price stability (apart from non-zero inflation expectations) in the presence of disturbances to aggregate supply. Hence there is a trade-off between price stability and real objectives even apart from the need to induce price and wage setters to expect in the future the rate of inflation that monetary policy is seeking to achieve.

NOTES

1. This argument has also been made in Friedman (2004).
2. A good example is the Bank of Canada, which states the rationale for its policy as follows: 'Inflation control is not an end to itself; it is the means by which monetary policy contributes to solid economic performance. Low inflation allows the economy to function more effectively. This contributes to better economic growth over time and works to moderate cyclical fluctuations in output and employment'.
3. Such a formulation emerges from any of a number of underlying representations of the price-setting process, including Calvo's random opportunities for a firm to change prices, Rotemberg and Woodford's quadratic costs of price adjustment, and Taylor's staggered contracts; see Roberts (1995).
4. With the parameter values assumed by Blanchard and Gali (importantly including a real discount rate of 1 per cent – or, equivalently in a growing economy, 1 per cent above the real growth rate), the real cost of each percentage point of disinflation is a *permanent* output loss of 0.05 per cent, with present value equal to 5 per cent of output. For the US economy in 2006, this translates into a present-value real cost of more than 650 billion dollars for each percentage point of disinflation.
5. See, for example, Eggertsson and Woodford (2003).
6. Svensson's model (see again his 1997 paper) implicitly recognized this problem by allowing inflation to depend directly on lagged inflation.
7. An alternative approach is to take explicit account of imperfections in the information on which price or wage setters base their decisions; see, for example, Mankiw and Reis (2002).

REFERENCES

Blanchard, Olivier and Jordi Gali (2005), 'Real wage rigidities and the New Keynesian model', NBER Working Paper 11806 (November), National Bureau of Economic Research, Cambridge, MA.

Buiter, Willem and Iain Jewitt (1981), 'Staggered wage setting with real relativities: variations on a theme of Taylor', *The Manchester School*, **49** (September), pp. 211–28.

Clarida, Richard, Jordi Gali and Mark Gertler (1999), 'The science of monetary policy', *Journal of Economic Literature*, **37** (December), pp. 1661–707.

Eggertsson, Gauti B. and Michael Woodford (2003), 'The zero bound on interest rates and optimal monetary policy', *Brookings Papers on Economic Activity*, **1**, pp. 139–211.

Friedman, Benjamin M. (2004), 'Why the Federal Reserve should not adopt inflation targeting', *International Finance*, **7** (Spring), pp. 129–36.

Fuhrer, Jeff and George Moore (1995), 'Inflation persistence', *Quarterly Journal of Economics*, **110** (February), pp. 127–59.

Greenspan, Alan (1999), untitled remarks, in *New Challenges for Monetary Policy*, proceedings of a symposium sponsored by the Federal Reserve Bank of Kansas City at Jackson Hole, WY, 26–28 August.

King, Mervyn (1997), 'Changes in U.K. monetary policy: rules and discretion in practice', *Journal of Monetary Economics*, **39** (June), pp. 81–97.

Mankiw, N. Gregory and Ricardo Reis (2002), 'Sticky information versus sticky prices: a proposal to replace the new Keynesian Phillips curve', *Quarterly Journal of Economics*, **117** (November), pp. 1295–328.

Roberts, John M. (1995), 'New Keynesian economics and the Phillips curve', *Journal of Money, Credit and Banking*, **27** (November), pp. 975–84.

Rogoff, Kenneth (1985), 'The optimal degree of commitment to a monetary target', *Quarterly Journal of Economics*, **100** (November), pp. 1169–89.

Svensson, Lars E.O. (1997), 'Inflation forecast targeting: implementing and monitoring inflation targets', *European Economic Review*, **41** (June), pp. 1111–46.

Tinbergen, Jan (1952), *On the Theory of Economic Policy*, Amsterdam: North-Holland.

Tinbergen, Jan (1966), *Economic Policy: Principles and Design*, Amsterdam: North-Holland.

4. Financial stability and monetary policy: a framework

Gerhard Illing[1]

INTRODUCTION

Monetary policy has been a great success over the past 15 years: worldwide, inflation has been reduced steadily, and output volatility seems to be well under control. The performance of central banks in fighting inflation has been stunningly impressive. Whereas for a long time they were accused of suffering from dynamic inconsistency (the temptation to give in to incentives to carry out surprise inflation), the credibility of central banks now seems to be at its highest level ever. Following the advice of modern macroeconomic theory, which provides a sound welfare theoretical framework for price stability, most modern central banks try to stabilize the price level by steering aggregate demand via changes in nominal and real interest rates, respectively. The 'New Neoclassical Synthesis' (Woodford, 2003) provides a well-established framework for this approach to monetary policy, pointing out the crucial role of commitment in order to effectively influence long-term real interest rates by signalling the intended path of nominal rates in advance. According to prominent proponents of this framework, such as Woodford, money supply does not play a significant role.

Just at a time when central banking practices seem to be converging with theory, there is increasing concern among practitioners that an excessively generous provision of liquidity contributes to excessive asset-price movements (increases in equity and housing prices), endangering financial stability. The fear that loose monetary policy contributes to a rise in asset prices with the risk of a serious breakdown of financial institutions, following a collapse of these asset prices later on, poses a new challenge for monetary policy. This chapter tries to sketch a macro framework to help think about how concerns for financial stability may affect monetary policy. As an extension of recent work by Hyun Song Shin (2008), it provides a stylized model as a base for understanding the relationship between monetary policy and financial stability. The model demonstrates that recent financial innovations may have made financial markets generally more efficient, but they are likely to result in more drastic failures if things go really wrong. Public provision of liquidity by central banks in periods of financial distress can prevent inefficient liquidation, but it may also aggravate the problem, as relying on support in times of financial distress will encourage leveraged institutions to engage in even greater risks.

Over the last two decades, a surge of innovations in the theory of finance and unprecedented growth in information technologies have expanded dramatically the ability of the financial sector to spread risk. One might conjecture that the evolution towards more efficient and globally integrated financial markets makes the world a safer place. Recent trends in financial innovation – the substantial expansion of access to consumer credit, the capacity for homeowners to borrow against the equity on their homes, and the greater use of financial instruments for transferring and mitigating risk – seem to be moving financial intermediation closer to the neoclassical paradigm of smooth and frictionless markets as modelled a long time ago in the Arrow–Debreu paradigm.

Even though recent advances in information technology have enlarged the scope for risk sharing and have thus contributed towards smoothing and absorbing real shocks in normal times, there is a crucial difference with the paradigm of frictionless markets: incentive problems, prevalent in intertemporal delegation, prevent the implementation of standard contingent contracts. It is well known that the threat of inefficient liquidation present in standard debt contracts may provide an adequate incentive scheme in the presence of asymmetric information. The use of debt contracts that allow for inefficient liquidation in the case of specific events gives incentives to report correct information about the true state of the world. More generally, a fragile capital structure is meant to encourage a conservative attitude towards risk (see Diamond and Rajan, 2005). Informational frictions also motivate the use of high-powered contracts. Managers rewarded by performance-related payments have an incentive to engage in a high leverage ratio, even if this runs the risk of overemphasizing short-term concerns. When paid according to performance, managers may partake in herding behaviour.

Debt contracts provide powerful amplification mechanisms: changes in current or expected monetary policy, by affecting asset values, have a direct impact on the balance sheets of financial institutions. The change in balance-sheet conditions leads to responses that aggravate the initial impact on asset prices. It is well known that balance-sheet effects may aggravate fluctuations in the economy. High asset prices raise the value of collateral, and thus lower the cost of financing additional investment. This financial accelerator may cause pro-cyclical feedback effects. More efficient instruments for assessing the market value of financial claims allow for a much speedier transmission of asset-price movements into balance sheets, resulting in stronger feedback effects. In itself, this need not be a matter of concern: monetary policy could comfortably use more powerful transmission mechanisms. As long as the central bank is aware of amplified responses, it can dampen volatility efficiently. By fine-tuning interest rate movements, amplification effects are smoothed, allowing for effective stabilization policy.

The key problem is asymmetry, which is crucial: under certain conditions, a fall in asset prices, by forcing inefficient liquidation and resulting in the breakdown of key financial institutions, may have dramatic repercussions for the whole economy. Thus, there is the danger that, beyond a given threshold, the virtuous cycle will turn into a vicious cycle, running the risk of a financial meltdown. The recent trend towards securitization seems, at first sight, to get around some of these problems by shifting risk towards long-term investment institutions with highly diversified portfolios. Risk should then be passed on to those best able to cope with it, reducing the need for inefficient liquidation. It turns out, however, that exactly those highly leveraged institutions issuing these securitized papers usually increase their exposure to systemic risk (for empirical evidence, see Franke and Krahnen, 2005). It seems that, motivated by incentive concerns, the riskiest portion of the transactions initiated by leveraged financial intermediaries will not be diversified away.

Under normal conditions, these incentive mechanisms help to implement a smoother, more efficient allocation of risk. They work as powerful disciplinary devices in the presence of idiosyncratic risk. In contrast, in the face of aggregate shocks, there are good reasons to try to prevent inefficient liquidation by providing sufficient public liquidity: as long as these shocks cannot be diversified and are not subject to moral hazard concerns, injection of liquidity works as a public good (see Holmström and Tirole, 1998; Goodhart and Illing, 2002). The simple distinction between idiosyncratic and aggregate risk, however, becomes blurred in the context of fire sales: when the stability of large leveraged institutions is at stake, the disciplinary device of default, by triggering fire sales, might result in a financial meltdown.

The non-linearities involved in times of crisis are likely to motivate asymmetric reactions of monetary policy. Private agents, anticipating such an asymmetric response, may be encouraged to take excessive risks, thus building up stronger imbalances, and thus aggravating the underlying asymmetry (see Illing, 2004; Cao and Illing, 2008). In order to prevent excessive risk taking, the central bank may be inclined to commit itself to not following an asymmetric policy. In view of the social costs involved in times of financial crisis, such a commitment hardly seems credible. Thus, the issue of dynamic inconsistency for central banks comes back in a new context, now based on concerns of financial stability. The problem is not that firms will build up excessively high individual leverage positions, but rather that leverage will exhibit a high systemic component: managers have strong incentives to engage in similar trading strategies, creating high systemic risk exposure for events of small probability.

Given the non-linearities, the optimal second-best policy is likely to be characterized by trying to prevent the building up of financial fragility rather than engaging in an extremely costly commitment not to intervene when faced with the risk of a financial meltdown. Additional instruments, such as the prudent regulation of financial markets, may help to implement a policy closer to the first-best outcome. Analysing these issues thoroughly would require a careful modelling of the non-linearities involved in a dynamic context. This chapter takes a first step in that direction by attempting to sketch a framework for a tractable macro approach that takes into account systemic risk and that focuses (see the third section) on the conditions that characterize the asymmetry between booms and busts.

The next section presents the model of amplifier effects as developed by Shin (2008). It essentially models a highly stylized specification of a bank's balance-sheet channel. The incentive of bank managers to maintain a minimum level of leverage can create positive feedback between asset prices and lending. The market value of a bank's loans is a function of the price of the underlying asset. A higher market value improves the bank's balance sheet. Attempting to restore leverage, the bank is willing to expand its deposits in order to increase its lending. Increased lending to the young drives up the price of the underlying asset. In that way, an initial increase in the market value of loans will be reinforced by feedback mechanisms. Given that fundamental price, creditworthiness and the level of debt are interrelated, a lower interest rate that drives up the market value of loans will result in a property boom.

As argued by Shin, capital adequacy requirements have the reverse effect on the way down: the incentive to maintain a minimum level of capital adequacy creates a feedback mechanism between falling asset prices and reduced lending. The attempt to liquidate assets in order to fulfil some preset equity ratio drives down asset prices, reducing the market value of loans. This may in turn reinforce the fall in asset prices. In that sense, as Shin suggests, 'asset price booms . . . and slumps . . . can be seen as mirror images of each other' (ibid., p. 4).

Despite the formal equivalence of the mechanism, there are, nevertheless, important differences on the way up and on the way down in an economy with market imperfections. Defaulting forces inefficient liquidations. In the stylized model considered here (a pure endowment economy), this is captured by a redirection of assets that have a much lower valuation towards agents. In a more general model with endogenous production, forced liquidation will also have repercussions for real production.

The aim of this text is to characterize the conditions of asymmetric effects and analyse their implications for monetary policy. The third section presents the key criteria for financial fragility: (a) the extent of debt exposure, in particular of financial intermediaries; (b) the degree of illiquidity; and (c) the nature of contracts (fixed nominal claims). It shows that if the required capital adequacy ratio is less than the inverse of the desired leverage ratio plus one, bank equity provides a cushion against small shocks to the economy. As long as only a small share of mortgage holders defaults, losses will be absorbed by the erosion of bank equity. For large shocks, however, banks are forced to liquidate assets in order to restore capital adequacy. With assets being illiquid, fire sales may wipe out a bank's capital and lead to a breakdown in financial intermediation.

To some extent, new financial instruments, such as securitization, mitigate the asymmetry of the effects: losses arising from the default of mortgage holders simply drive down the market value of the securitized loans held by pension funds. As long as this fall in market value does not affect the solvency of leveraged institutions, risks are spread more widely, no longer being concentrated in the banking sector. Due to problems of asymmetric information, however, the issuing institutions, being highly leveraged – be they banks, hedge funds or Freddie Macs (Federal Home Loan Mortgage Corporation) – usually retain the riskiest tranches of the loans they initiate. Thus at some point, when low event risks materialize, fund managers will be forced to minimize losses by selling bad loans. The trigger mechanism of fire sales is thus bound to set in again, but even more forcefully.

AMPLIFYING EFFECTS ON CREDIT-CONSTRAINED MARKETS

In a frictionless neoclassical world with a well-functioning, complete set of markets, shocks to the fundamental system are dampened by smooth price adjustments. In contrast, in an economy with imperfect markets, amplifying rather than dampening effects may prevail.

Recent innovations seem to have made financial markets more efficient. One might conjecture that, finally, reality is beginning to resemble the perfect world designed by the theory of complete markets. Even though this intuition may hold true for quiet periods, some features suggest that in some circumstances, just the opposite may be true: smoother markets may create endogenous volatility. The underlying reason, pointed out by Shin (2008), is fairly simple: more efficient instruments for assessing the market value of financial claims allow for a much speedier transmission of asset-price movements into balance sheets. In an economy with market imperfections, balance sheets work as an incentive device. Stronger fluctuations in balance sheets may create feedback effects, amplifying changes in asset prices. These amplifications can, under some conditions, endanger systemic financial stability.

Let us first consider how the value of assets is determined in a credit-constrained economy with interconnected markets. What is the impact of exogenous shocks to the value of loans? Since agents' balance sheets are interconnected, the value of claims against one agent depends on the value of his or her claims against the others, creating endogenous counterparty risk. The default of one party may create contagion effects via spillovers on the balance sheets of others. With a network of interlinkages, the net exposure of the system is hard to assess. Recent work attempts to simulate domino effects on the interbank market. Usually, these simulations exhibit relatively little contagion (Upper and Worms, 2004; Eichberger and Summer, 2005). Such simulations neglect an important feedback effect: the market value of illiquid assets depends on the selling pressure created by debt exposure; fire sales will dampen the price of the fundamental asset, creating externalities.

The market value of mortgage loans L_i held by agent i depends both on the face value of these loans, the nominal debt D_i, and the market value of the agent's assets A_i. The market value of his or her assets is a function of the price of the underlying asset P and of the uncertainty in endowments w required to repay the loans. It also depends on the value of i's claims against other agents in the economy, which again depends on the value of those agents' claims against others, and so on. Let us write the system of mutual claims in a shortcut as L. Thus, we can write $A_i = A_i(L, P, w)$ and $L_i = f[D_i, A_i(L, P, w)]$.

Aggregating across all agents, we get:

$$L = f[D, A(L, P, w)].$$

In the financial system as a whole, the set of claims of all agents against each other cancels out. As shown by Shin (2008), under fairly general conditions the evaluation of debt in an interconnected system can be related to the value of the underlying fundamental assets in a straightforward way. Applying tools from lattice theory, as in Eisenberg and Noe (2001), it can be shown that there exists a unique profile of debt prices for a given interlinkage of debt. Thus, there is a unique fixed point $L(D, P, w)$.

Since the total value of claims against the others cancels out against the total value of obligations to the others, the equity value of the whole financial system depends entirely on the assets that are under no obligation to any other investor. If the fundamental value is unchanged, the equity value of the whole system is constant. Using a comparative static result from Milgrom and Roberts (1994), it is simple to show that the equity value of the whole financial system increases with an increase in the value of fundamentals. Using this result, analysing feedback effects caused by exogenous shocks in a simple stylized macro model is straightforward.

Following Shin (2008), let us consider an economy with residential property as the only real asset. There are young and old households in the economy. All agents are assumed to be risk neutral. Due to agency problems, however, risky wage income is uninsurable. Thus, young households are credit constrained: they can hold residential housing stock only if financed by borrowing from banks. Mortgages require collateral. The assets of young households consist of their property, while the mortgage loans to banks are their liabilities. The difference is their net worth.

Old households are assumed to have no liabilities. Their net worth consists of holding property and deposits (short-term claims) at banks. They also own bank equity. Starting from an initial distribution of property between young and old, there is an upward-sloping supply curve of the old for selling property. Housing being an illiquid market, owners are willing to buy additional housing only at much lower prices than they are willing to sell. This endowment effect arises naturally from asymmetric information: if the owner of the house has an informational advantage concerning the characteristics and quality of the property, potential buyers, fearing adverse selection, are prepared to buy only at a discount (for a formalization of this, see Illing, 1992). Thus, there is a kink in the net supply curve of the old at the endowment point (Figure 4.1). The fact that housing is an illiquid market, the resale value being much lower, is a key driving force in creating asymmetric effects.

For simplicity, all the old are assumed to have a lower willingness to pay for housing than the young (due to the fact that the non-contractable consumption value of owning property is higher for those with a longer life span). Thus, in the absence of credit imperfections, a transfer of all property from the old to the young would be efficient. Since the young are credit constrained, however, they can buy housing only against collateral. Due to credit constraints, banks' willingness to lend is based not only on the expected ability of the young to service debt payments (their expected future cash flow), but also on the value of property P. If, for some reason, there is an increase in the price of property, banks are willing to engage more strongly in selling mortgages, the value of collateral D being higher.

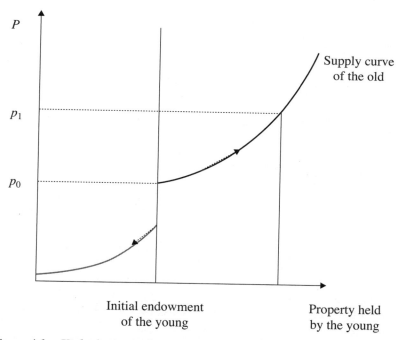

Figure 4.1 Kinked net supply curve of property

With this increased value in collateral, more young are in a position to buy more housing against mortgages, shifting effective demand upwards. Note that the induced transfer of housing from the old to the young is not, as claimed by Shin (2005), simply a redistribution effect – a shift *within* the Edgeworth box. Since the young have a higher willingness to pay for housing, this movement results in a Pareto improvement in a credit-constrained economy. Thus, rising asset prices may result in a more efficient allocation of the housing stock. The key point, however, is that, when bad shocks occur, not only will this improvement in the allocation of housing be reversed, but the economy may even end up with a much worse allocation of the housing stock (see next section).

Let us now consider more closely the banking sector, intermediating between the old and the young. Banks sell mortgage loans to the young, loans financed by deposits from the old. Let L be the market value of loans. Loans being collateralized, the market value L is increasing in the price of property P (see $L(P)$ in Figure 4.2). $L(P)$ is strictly concave since the market value cannot exceed the face value of the loan. The objective of bank managers is to maximize the rate of return on the equity of their shareholders (the old). When the market value of loans L goes up, the equity-to-debt

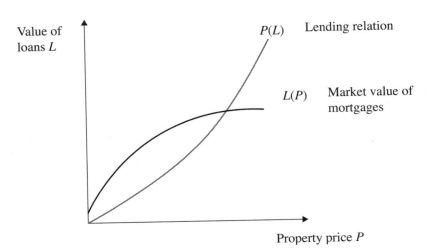

Figure 4.2   Feedback between the market value of loans and property prices

ratio is improving, thus reducing the leverage position of the bank. With an improved balance sheet, bank managers are willing to increase the provision of loans to the young. This will be true in particular if managers, being responsive to short-term incentives, attempt to restore their initial leverage position. Thus, the amount of credit provided – the face value of debt – is rising in the market value of loans $D(L)$. The induced higher effective demand of the young drives up housing prices P. Higher housing prices raise the market value of loans. Again, balance sheets improve and leverage is thus reduced, starting the cycle again. The balance-sheet channel results in a positive feedback, represented by the upward-sloping curve $P(L)$ in Figure 4.2. Market equilibrium is represented by the intersection of the $P(L)$ and the $L(P)$ curves.

Two features are the key driving forces for the positive feedback mechanisms presented.

1. Higher property prices raise the market value of loans $L(P)$. In an economy where balance sheets are evaluated according to market prices, this is immediately reflected in a higher net worth for the bank. Even under accounting rules relying on historic values, the improved balance sheet of the bank will be reflected in rising share prices.
2. The higher net worth induces banks to increase lending in order to extract higher profits. This drives up property prices, captured by the relation $P(L)$.

The $P(L)$ curve has a linear shape when bank managers, being responsive to short-term incentives, try to keep a constant leverage position. In that case, amplifier effects are particularly strong. More generally, managers will also take into account the increasing risk of default in their lending decisions, and thus use part of the improved balance position to increase precautionary liquidity holdings. In Figure 4.2, $P(L)$ is drawn as a concave function in the relevant range. For a given risk of wage income, a borrower's default risk is increasing in the face value of debt D. Household i is able to pay back its outstanding debt in the final period only if $D_i(1 + r)$ $\leq w_i$. The higher the property price P, the higher the debt exposure of the marginal buyer, dampening the bank's incentive to increase lending even further. Thus, for large enough L, increasing the default risk of marginal borrowers makes the curve steeper. The willingness to increase lending is lower the higher the bank's fragility (its exposure to the risk of its borrowers going bankrupt). When deciding on lending policy, however, each bank ignores the externality imposed on the economy by its own lending decisions (the impact of its own lending on the property price P). In particular, when assessing its own liquidity position, it does not take into account that by holding additional liquidity it confers positive externalities on other leveraged institutions. Taking this into account would reduce the risk of a fire sale in the case of a liquidity drain (see below).

The stage is now set to analyse the transmission mechanism of monetary policy in this stylized economy. Obviously, the positive feedback described above works as a powerful amplification mechanism. Consider a reduction in nominal interest rates. Since bank assets (collateralized mortgages) are of longer duration than their liabilities (deposits), the market value of mortgage values rises by more than the value of deposits when interest rates are falling. The $L(P)$ curve is shifted upwards (as in Figure 4.3). Thus, the net worth of the banking sector is raised, the leverage reduced. Banks respond to the increase in net worth by extending mortgage lending to the young, which drives up the price of housing, which in turn triggers the amplification mechanism sketched above.

Capital adequacy requirements create reverse effects when asset prices fall. Thus, a tighter monetary policy results in an amplified fall in housing prices. Higher interest rates reduce the market value of loans. Some of the mortgage holders may be driven into default. As long as the solvency constraint is satisfied for all banks, their net worth will only be partly eroded. At some point, however, when shocks are large enough, the capital adequacy constraint becomes binding for a subset of banks. In that case, raising new equity would be extremely costly. Realistically, the bank is then forced to sell part of its property holdings in order to regain solvency. Now the reverse mechanism sets in: the attempt to liquidate assets in order to

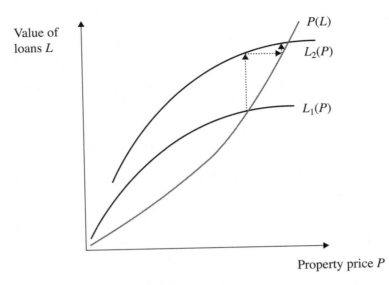

Figure 4.3   Amplification of lower interest rates

fulfil some predetermined equity ratio drives down asset prices, reducing the market value of loans even further. Concerted selling pressure leads to an endogenous downward response of the price of the fundamental asset. Thus, it may reinforce the fall in asset prices.

The incentive to maintain a minimum level of capital adequacy again creates a feedback mechanism between falling asset prices and reduced lending. In that sense, following Shin (2008), asset-price booms and busts can indeed be seen as 'mirror images'. Despite the formal equivalence of these mechanisms, there are, however, important asymmetries on the way up and down in an economy with market imperfections: defaulting forces inefficient liquidations. Note that the higher the initial increase in asset prices, the higher will be the initial debt exposure of the young, and thus the more likely the scenario of default. The next section analyses the impact of these asymmetries.

ASYMMETRIES BETWEEN BOOMS AND BUSTS

As discussed in the previous section, capital adequacy requirements can create amplifier effects equivalent to the propagation of lending booms via leverage, but in the reverse direction. Nevertheless, the impact on the whole economy may be dramatically different due to costly liquidation. In the

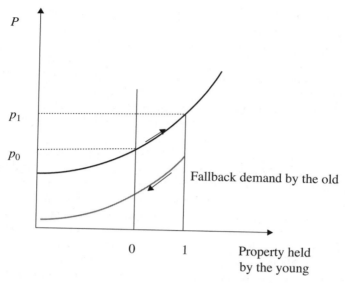

Figure 4.4   Asymmetries between booms and busts

stylized model considered here (a pure endowment economy), illiquidity is illustrated by a kink in the net supply curve of the old (see Figure 4.1): they are only willing to buy back housing from the young at much lower prices than they are willing to sell.

Let us now analyse the impact of tightening monetary policy after an extended period of low interest rates. Assume that an initially lax monetary policy contributed to a property boom, increasing the amount of property held by the young from point 0 to 1, as shown in Figure 4.4. Due to the higher collateral value of property as a result of lower interest rates, the young were able to increase their debt exposure. Being credit constrained, even the proportion of those already endowed with housing can take advantage of lower interest rates both by refinancing (in the absence of pre-payment penalties) and by using the increased value of collateral for mortgage equity withdrawals. In a credit-constrained economy, the increase in property prices allows for a better smoothing of intertemporal consumption for the young holding property.[2] The face value of aggregate debt exposure $D(1 + r)$ of the young is bound to increase despite low interest rates. Debt exposure is heterogeneous among the young: the marginal buyers of property, paying the highest prices, are those most heavily indebted.

When paying back the credit in the final period, a young agent i can amortize his or her mortgage only if his or her wage income w_i is sufficient to cover the debt obligations, including interest payments: $D_i(1+r) \leq w_i$. Wage income being stochastic for a given realization of aggregate wage income, some proportion of the young population may be forced to default. To simplify, if we assume that wage income is perfectly correlated among all young, those with the highest debt exposure will default first. Tightening monetary policy will accelerate defaulting, because it raises the burden of those agents with adjustable-rate mortgages; higher interest rates, by dampening the economy, may also trigger a negative wage shock.

As long as only a small share of mortgage holders defaults, a bank's losses will be absorbed by the erosion of bank equity (driving down the market value of loans). Bank equity provides a cushion against small shocks to the economy as long as the inverse of the desired leverage ratio plus one exceeds the required capital adequacy ratio. The solvency constraint requires that the ratio of equity to market value remains above an imposed threshold value: $(L - DP)/L = E/L > e^*$ (with DP being banks' debt exposure (deposits of the old) and $E = L - DP$ as the market value of equity). Due to incentive mechanisms, the debt-to-equity ratio is likely to be kept above a given threshold value (minimum leverage): $DP/E > l^*$, provided that $e^* < e < 1/(1 + l^*)$ shocks can be absorbed by fluctuations in bank equity.

The situation is different for sufficiently large shocks, however: the market value of loans falls to the point that the capital adequacy ratio is violated. Now banks are forced to liquidate assets in order to restore their capital adequacy ratio. With assets being illiquid, this can be done only at a discount: the fallback price at which some old are willing to buy back property is below the market price (compare with Figure 4.4).

The dashed curve in Figure 4.5 represents for all property prices P the amount of property a distressed bank has to sell in order to fulfil capital adequacy requirements. If property prices fall dramatically, all of the bank's assets have to be liquidated. At the initial property price P_1, distressed banks are forced to sell a positive amount of property in order to fulfil the required ratio r^* (see Figure 4.5). The attempt to liquidate property results in a steep fall in property prices, reducing the market value of loans even further. Banks are then forced to sell even more property in order to restore capital adequacy; property prices fall even further, and a vicious cycle sets in. Rather than coming back to the point the economy started at, price P_0, the fire sales forced by defaults may result in a dramatic reallocation towards agents who have a much lower valuation of these assets.[3] They may wipe out all of a bank's capital, leading to a complete breakdown in financial intermediation.

Several elements are required for triggering such a fire sale.

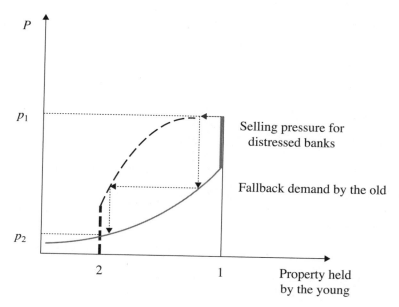

Figure 4.5 Fire sales by distressed banks

1. The higher the debt exposure, the more fragile the economy. The initial boom in property prices creates high debt exposure for marginal buyers. Similarly, mortgage equity withdrawals increase fragility, even though they allow for a smoother consumption path.
2. Even though fixed-rate mortgages can mitigate the negative impact, rising interest rates are likely to make the economy more fragile.
3. The key driving force is none the less the leverage of financial institutions. The higher the desired leverage, the lower the cushion available to financial intermediaries for absorbing shocks. The higher the leverage ratio, the more property-distressed banks are forced to sell. As Figure 4.6 illustrates, the selling pressure for sound banks with low leverage is negligible. In such a case, no equilibrium with forced liquidation exists.
4. Furthermore, the less liquid the assets are (the steeper the fall in property prices required to give the old incentives to buy back property), the stronger the amplification effect.
5. Finally, a crucial part of the story is the nature of financial contracts: the old put (part of) their income from selling property into bank deposits with fixed nominal claims. If, instead, they would hold their claims as equity shares of the bank, they would share proportionally

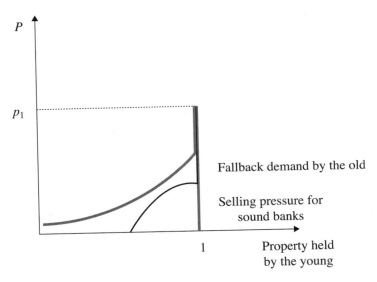

Figure 4.6   The case of sound banks

the losses in market value of defaulted loans, rather than triggering a fire sale with inefficient liquidation.

New financial instruments, such as securitization, appear to be clever instruments for mimicking such an efficient way of sharing risk between old and young. Securitized assets are held by pension funds instead of banks. Losses arising from the default of mortgage holders simply drive down the market value of securitized loans held by pension funds. When the old hold contributed rather than defined-benefit claims against the pension funds, they participate directly in the market risk of loans. Thus, securitization reduces the need for inefficient liquidation. Fluctuations in asset prices are passed through to the final claimants in the economy (the old).

In view of this argument, it seems that institutions like Fannie Mae (Federal National Mortgage Association) and Freddie Mac, by transforming risks into securities, help to limit the risk of fire sales. When banks retain only the first loss piece and sell the senior tranches exhibiting extreme risk, securitization allows for idiosyncratic risks to be separated from systemic ones, with extreme risks being borne by the holders of the senior tranches. Securitization could thus be an effective way to index debt contracts against macro shocks. The problem, however, is that these highly leveraged institutions usually increase their exposure to systemic risk. They seem to hold the riskiest tranches of the loans they initiate (Franke and Krahnen, 2005).

Thus, in the case of serious aggregate shocks, the economy will be made even more fragile: as soon as managers try to minimize their losses by selling bad loans, fire sales will be triggered. So again, at some point the trigger mechanism of fire sales is bound to set in, but in this case even more forcefully.

The arguments presented in this section suggest that recent trends in financial innovations have to be evaluated carefully. On average, at least for small shocks, they allow for a relaxation of the frictions imposed in a credit-constrained economy, and thus contribute to a more efficient allocation. In the case of severe negative shocks, these financial innovations may accelerate the need for fire sales, with disastrous repercussions for the whole economy. There is thus the danger that, beyond a certain threshold, the virtuous cycle turns into a vicious one, creating the risk of a financial meltdown. The non-linearities involved suggest that monetary policy should intervene to prevent such undesirable events, but they are likely to trigger asymmetric reactions: given the high social costs involved in a systemic crisis, there is a strong incentive to lower interest rates whenever there is an imminent risk of fire sales, whereas there seems to be no reason to tighten monetary policy when asset prices are rising.

Private agents, anticipating such an asymmetric response, will be encouraged to take excessive risks, thus building up greater imbalances, and thus aggravating the underlying asymmetry. Monetary policy works like a put option, encouraging banks to provide excessive lending even if aggregate debt exposure is already high. Figure 4.7 illustrates this effect: as long as

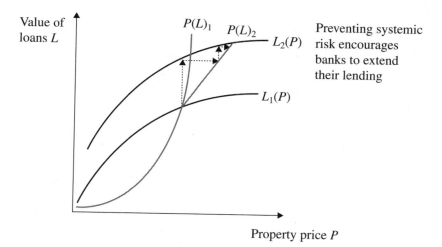

Figure 4.7   Asymmetric monetary policy as a put option

monetary policy does not intervene, banks will be reluctant to lend to borrowers with a high debt exposure in view of the implicit default risk. The inverse of the $P(L)$ curve will thus be rather inelastic (see the curve $P(L)_1$). In that case, fragile economies are not characterized by powerful amplifier effects; even a strong increase in market value will have hardly any impact on property prices. If, instead, monetary policy is expected to come to the rescue in systemic crises, banks can safely discount the default risk implied by increased lending. Thus, whenever monetary policy reacts asymmetrically, the inverse of the $L(P)$ curve is more elastic (as $P(L)_2$ in Figure 4.7), resulting in the strong amplifier effects described above, even when the economy is very fragile.

CONCLUSION

One has to be careful when evaluating the welfare implications of the increased fragility created as illustrated in this chapter. As long as central banks are able to steer the economy efficiently in times of aggregate crises, there should be no real reason for concern. After all, an injection of public liquidity in the face of aggregate shocks may work as a public good. The fire sale externality outlined above suggests that private agents have insufficient incentives to provide the adequate level of liquidity: none of the agents takes into account the positive externalities conferred on others by holding additional liquidity. Furthermore, for private institutions, there is no incentive to step in as an efficient provider of liquidity in emergency cases. As shown by Allen and Gale (2005), since holding liquidity involves an opportunity cost, and the suppliers of liquidity can only recoup this cost by buying assets at fire-sale prices in some states of the world, the private provision of liquidity by arbitrageurs will be inadequate to ensure asset-price stability. If the central bank, by injecting aggregate liquidity in emergency cases, is just compensating for this market failure, the perceived increase in fragility is not real; the higher risks incurred might actually be welfare improving.

There are two problems with such a complacent view. First, the simple distinction between idiosyncratic and aggregate risk is no longer clear-cut in the context of fire sales. If liquidity is provided whenever the stability of large leveraged institutions is at stake, the default mechanism cannot be an effective incentive device to discipline excessive individual risk taking by managers. The problem is not that firms will try to build up excessively high individual leverage positions, but rather that leverage will exhibit a high systemic component: managers have strong incentives to engage in similar trading strategies creating high systemic risk exposure for small probability events (for an explicit model, see Cao and Illing, 2008).

Second, stability concerns may conflict with other policy objectives of the central bank. In view of financial stability issues, a central bank may hesitate to raise interest rates at a pace required to stabilize the economy efficiently (this trade-off has been modelled by Sauer, 2007). If raising rates runs the risk of endangering highly leveraged institutions, the central bank might be caught in an interest-rate trap: concerns about financial stability may force the central bank to follow a path of disproportional gradualism. The policy of the Federal Reserve in 2004 might be seen as an instructive example (see Illing, 2005). Encouraged by the Federal Reserve's public commitment to follow an extended period of calm policy – as witnessed by statements such as 'policy accommodation can be maintained for a considerable period' – many institutions worldwide built up similar leveraged positions during 2003. The extremely cautious Federal Reserve policy,[4] whose monetary stance has been tightening since 2004, suggests that the implementation of a sufficient increase in interest rates may have been delayed until the most precarious leveraged positions had been unwound. In the presence of incomplete knowledge, central banks may be inclined to act cautiously. Given the asymmetries involved, they are likely to prefer to err on the side of caution rather than run the risk of a fire sale. In the same vein, during good periods, they may tend to raise interest rates above the level needed to address stabilization concerns, thus aiming to have enough ammunition when things get worse. Again, stability concerns may conflict with efficient stabilization policy.

In view of these risks, the central bank may be inclined to commit itself to not following an asymmetric policy. Given the high social costs involved in times of financial crisis, however, such a commitment hardly seems credible. Taking into account the non-linearities involved, optimal second-best policy is likely to be characterized by trying to prevent financial fragility from building up rather than engaging in an extremely costly commitment not to intervene when faced with the risk of a financial meltdown. Procyclical liquidity requirements could mitigate spillovers, and thus help to correct these externalities. To analyse this intuition, an extended model that allows for endogenous risk taking is required, but will be left to future research.

NOTES

1. I wish to thank Frank Heinemann, Stephan Sauer and the participants of the Cournot Centre Conference, 'Central Banks as Economic Institutions', held on 30 November and 1 December 2006, for constructive suggestions.
2. In general, when there is heterogeneity among the young with respect to the willingness to pay, rising property prices may crowd out potential housing demand from a segment of the population.

3. In a more general setting, forced liquidation will also have repercussions on real production.
4. Consider Alan Greenspan's remark before the Joint Economic Committee of the United States Senate on 21 April 2004: 'Rates must rise at some point to prevent pressures on price inflation from eventually emerging'. This statement was accompanied by the hint that 'no increase is imminent', and similarly by a statement of the Federal Open Market Committee: 'The Committee believes that policy accommodation can be removed at a pace that is likely to be measured'.

REFERENCES

Allen, Franklin and Douglas Gale (2005), 'From cash-in-the-market pricing to financial fragility', *Journal of the European Economic Association*, **3** (2–3), pp. 535–46.

Cao, Jin and Gerhard Illing (2008), 'Liquidity shortages and monetary policy', CESifo Working Paper Series No. 2210, Munich.

Diamond, Douglas and Raghu Rajan (2005), 'Liquidity shortages and banking crises', *Journal of Finance*, **60** (2), pp. 615–47.

Eichberger, Jürgen and Martin Summer (2005), 'Bank capital, liquidity, and systemic risk', *Journal of the European Economic Association*, **3** (2–3), pp. 547–55.

Eisenberg, Larry and Thomas H. Noe (2001), 'Systemic risk in financial systems', *Management Science*, **47**, pp. 236–49.

Franke, Günter and Jan Pieter Krahnen (2005), 'Default risk sharing between banks and markets: the contribution of collateralized debt obligations', CFS Working Paper 2005/06, Ifk-CFS Frankfurt.

Goodhart, Charles and Gerhard Illing (eds) (2002), *Financial Crises, Contagion and the Lender of Last Resort: A Reader*, Oxford: Oxford University Press.

Holmström, Bengt and Jean Tirole (1998), 'Private and public supply of liquidity', *Journal of Political Economy*, **106**, pp. 1–40.

Illing, Gerhard (1992), 'Private information as transaction costs: the Coase theorem revisited', *Journal of Institutional and Theoretical Economics*, **148**, pp. 558–76.

Illing, Gerhard (2004), 'Financial fragility, bubbles, and monetary policy', in Hans-Werner Sinn, Mika Widgrén and Marko Köthenbürger (eds), *European Monetary Integration*, Cambridge, MA: MIT Press, pp. 141–69.

Illing, Gerhard (2005), 'How to escape contagion in the interest rate trap', in Reiner König and Hermann Remsperger (eds), *Financial Stability and Globalisation*, Frankfurt: Deutsche Bundesbank, pp. 49–62.

Milgrom, Paul and John Roberts (1994), 'Comparing equilibria', *American Economic Review*, **84**, pp. 441–59.

Sauer, Stephan (2007), 'Liquidity risk and monetary policy', Munich Economic Discussion Papers 2007-27, University of Munich.

Shin, Hyun Song (2005), 'Financial system liquidity, asset prices and monetary policy', in *The Changing Nature of the Business Cycle*, Sydney: Reserve Bank of Australia, pp. 312–35.

Shin, Hyun Song (2008), 'Risk and liquidity in a system context', *Journal of Financial Intermediation*, **17** (3), July, pp. 315–9.

Upper, Christian and Andreas Worms (2004), 'Estimating bilateral exposures in the German interbank market: is there a danger of contagion?', *European Economic Review*, **48** (4), pp. 827–49.

Woodford, Michael (2003), *Interest and Prices: Foundations of a Theory of Monetary Policy*, Princeton, NJ: Princeton University Press.

5. Coordinating expectations in monetary policy

Stephen Morris and Hyun Song Shin

INTRODUCTION

The last 15 years have seen a remarkable revolution in both the conduct of and the common understanding of monetary policy around the world. This revolution has encompassed instruments, with an increased emphasis on transparency about short- and medium-run central bank policy planning and a decreased emphasis on intermediate targets such as monetary aggregates. This revolution has also encompassed objectives, with an increased emphasis on medium-run inflation targets. However, the objective question cannot be separated from the instrument question. In particular, inflation targeting is seen as a key component of transparent monetary policy.

At the heart of this revolution is a change in perspective about what monetary policy is all about. The traditional perspective viewed monetary policy as an engineering problem. Central bankers had a set of instruments under their control, faced uncertainty outside their control and sought to manipulate their instruments to achieve targets. The modern perspective views monetary policy as a strategic problem. Most of the action comes neither from instruments under the direct control of central bankers, nor from exogenous uncertainty outside their control, but rather from the actions of market participants who are mostly concerned about variables outside the direct control of the central bank – for example, long-term interest rates – but are acutely aware that everyone else is looking at the central bank for clues about where those variables are headed. As Michael Woodford (2005, p. 2) put it, 'central banking is not like steering an oil tanker, or even guiding a spacecraft, which follows a trajectory that depends on constantly changing factors, but that does not depend on the vehicle's own expectations about where it is heading'. Charles Goodhart (in a personal communication) has coined the term 'expectationalists' to denote this school of thought that includes not only Michael Woodford, but other leading monetary economists such as Alan Blinder, Lars Svensson and Ben Bernanke.

In this view, monetary policy is – at its heart – the problem of managing and coordinating expectations in the economy. The instruments under the direct control of the central bank – such as overnight interest rates – are less important than the messages the central bank sends out. But how easy is it to use communication to manage and coordinate expectations, and what are the costs and benefits of doing so? Most readings of the evidence of the last 15 years suggest that it is possible to manage expectations and that the benefits outweigh any costs. None the less, a recent theoretical literature has identified some potential costs and difficulties in trying to coordinate expectations. Sometimes these costs seem related to the concerns expressed by the old-fangled secretive central bankers about talking too much. Sometimes these costs offer some insights into the 'limits of transparency', in other words, the question of how much should be made public. The next section will review some of these arguments from our earlier work. The subsequent section will discuss how these arguments may relate to some current debates on central bank communication policy. The final section concludes.

The type of theoretical models of social value of information and optimal communication in strategic settings that we shall describe assume away too much institutional detail and microfoundation to offer concrete lessons for the design of central bank policy. On the other hand, we believe it is fair to say that the theoretical models that monetary economists use to debate inflation targeting and transparency assume away too much about strategic interaction and expectations formation to adequately address the real questions. We would say – especially to our academic colleagues – that research has not caught up with the revolution in monetary policy practice, and there is much work to be done.

COORDINATING EXPECTATIONS

An economy consists of a large number of economic actors making individual decisions. Since Adam Smith, we have been aware of the remarkable role that prices and free markets can play in coordinating those decisions into a balanced and perhaps efficient outcome. Each actor cares greatly about what others will do. In our models of perfect competition, however, market prices – and the ability to transact freely at those prices – allow each actor to understand and analyse the market without worrying about what other actors will do, and therefore without worrying about what they think.

The price level, however, creates special difficulties. There is a fundamental indeterminacy in the level of prices. When businesses set prices, they must form beliefs about how others are setting prices now and in the future.

How others set prices will depend on what they think about inflation, and so on. When traders take positions in the financial markets, they must form beliefs about the evolution of short-run rates, knowing that short-run interest rates in turn are influenced by market expectations. Beliefs may be self-fulfilling and – in the absence of good monetary policy – there may be excessive levels and inflation volatility. Thus it is no coincidence that monetary policy in particular is subject to much commentary on how people are interpreting it, how they think others are interpreting it, and so on. There is a large coordination dimension with – in the absence of good monetary policy – much indeterminacy in outcomes.

Economists employ the suggestive metaphor of the 'sunspot' to understand outcomes in such settings. Suppose that sunspot activity were observed by everyone in the economy. When sunspot activity was high, economic actors expected inflation to be high and – we are still living in a world of bad monetary policy – this led them to set high prices, which translated into high inflation. When sunspot activity was low, economic actors kept price rises small, and there was low inflation. In this world, sunspot activity has no intrinsic relevance for inflation. From the viewpoint of each individual actor, sunspot activity happens to be a good predictor of others' pricing behaviour, and thus becomes an important determinant of their pricing decision.

Let us pause to ask what features of these metaphorical sunspots would allow them to coordinate expectations in this economy. We noted that they must be observed by everybody. But more is required: it must be common knowledge among actors in the economy that everyone is observing the sunspot, and everyone is acting on the sunspot in the same way. To stretch the metaphor further, there must also be a common understanding of what is meant by 'high sunspot activity' or 'low sunspot activity'. If some actors classified an intermediate level of sunspot activity as 'high' while others classified it as 'low', then sunspots would no longer be able to play their expectation coordination role. In short, there must be transparency about sunspots in order for them to coordinate expectations.

Now enter the central bank. One way of summarizing the modern expectationalist view of central banking is to say that central banks have successfully taken over the role of sunspots. If economic actors can be persuaded that it is a central bank announcement, rather than the level of sunspot activity, that will coordinate expectations about interest rates and prices, and thus determine interest rates and inflation, then here is a free instrument for the central bank that offers a more predictable and smoother way of influencing outcomes than actually intervening in markets. The 'efficacy of central banking as sunspots' requires that central bank pronouncements acquire the same features as the sunspots outlined above:

they must be observed by all; it must be common knowledge that they are observed by all; and, there must be common knowledge of the exact meaning of the pronouncements. In short, central bank communication must be transparent.

It is, of course, a little more complicated than that. The economists who use the metaphor of sunspots do not believe that it is actual sunspots that serve as equilibrium selection devices. Rather, they think that economic actors could focus on a piece of news that is only a little bit payoff relevant, and via its role in coordinating expectations, that piece of news could play the role of a sunspot.

Likewise, central bank announcements convey real information that is directly relevant to economic actors. In particular, they can or might convey information about current actions of the central bank, future actions of the central bank and the state of the economy. This information is relevant to economic actors, not just in assessing the variables that are the subject of the announcements, in other words, the bank's current and future actions and the state of the economy, but also about other variables, for example, long-run interest rates and asset prices. Nevertheless – in an environment that is subject to self-fulfilling expectations – this information could play a role in coordinating expectations about long-run interest rates and stock prices that is far greater than could be justified by the information content of the announcement. Indeed, this is simply to repeat the main claim of the modern expectation coordination view of central banking: central banks might be able to coordinate expectations well even when their actions have only small, lagged and unpredictable effects on outcomes.

This analogy between sunspots and central bank communication policy then begs the question: transparent central bank communication may be successful in coordinating expectations, but under what circumstances will expectations be coordinated on something desirable – as in recent experience – and under what circumstances might they be coordinated on something undesirable? We now turn to this question.

Can More Transparency Reduce Informational Efficiency by Crowding Out Private Information?

Morris and Shin (2002) considered this question in a stylized model of public communication that we shall use to illustrate a number of points in this chapter. Consider a large group of economic actors. Suppose that each actor wants to set his or her action equal to his or her expectation of an average of (i) the state of the world and (ii) the average actions of others. Each actor has some private information about the state of the world in addition to hearing a public announcement about the state of the world from the central bank. How accurately should we expect average actions to reflect the information that actors obtain from public and private signals?

Because of people's desire to have their actions close to others' actions, they will have an incentive to put more weight on public rather than private signals, even if those signals are equally informative about the true state of the world. If it is socially desirable for actions to reflect the best information available, the strategic motive will lead private information to be inefficiently ignored. Now, if the precision of public announcements is increased – think of this reflecting increased transparency of the central bank – there will be two countervailing effects. On the one hand, given any rule by which actors aggregate private and public signals, the increased accuracy of the public signal will improve outcomes. On the other hand, if private information is already being inefficiently ignored, increasing the precision of public announcements will just lead to more inefficient discounting of private information. Which effect prevails? If public announcements are accurate relative to the accuracy of private information, then increased transparency (increased precision of public announcements) is unambiguously good. If, however, public announcements are relatively inaccurate, then their effect in crowding out private information predominates, and increased transparency could be bad.

What lessons might this benchmark observation have for central bank transparency? Note first that the excess reaction of the market to public announcements seems to capture the traditional concern of central bankers that the market may overreact to apparently innocuous statements and that extreme caution in speaking to the public might be a safe response to such overreaction. Moreover, in the extreme case where people's beliefs about others' actions are especially important, public announcements will have a large impact on outcomes even when they convey very little payoff-relevant information. In this sense, they act like sunspots.

Two reasons have been suggested for why these observations might have limited relevance for central bank communication in practice.

First, the negative welfare impact relies on the assumption that while economic actors' desire to coordinate with others yields private benefits, it does not yield social benefits. In many microfounded models, this may not be the case. For example, Christian Hellwig (2005) has shown that when the coordination motive represents strategic complementarities in a monopolistic price-setting model, the social benefit of coordinated action is sufficiently high to prevent the negative welfare impact.

Second, the negative impact of a marginal increase in the accuracy of public announcements arises only when public signals are inaccurate relative to private signals. If the central bank is not significantly less informed than the private sector about the subjects on which it communicates, then the welfare impact is unambiguously positive. Lars Svensson (2006) has argued forcefully that this is the empirically relevant case. Surely, the central bank is more informed about the central bank's conduct of monetary policy now and in the future. Even in forecasting the economy, there is evidence that, for example, the Federal Reserve performs well relative to the private sector.

These are both important points, but let us argue why we none the less think that there might be lessons here for central bank communication policy.

First, it matters whether the welfare objective is merely to coordinate expectations on *some* thing or to coordinate expectations on the *right* thing. Much analysis of monetary policy focuses on reduced-form modelling where heterogeneous expectations are not explicitly modelled and where the loss function is a weighted sum of the output gap and deviation of inflation from its target. Here, coordination of expectations is assumed, but the level of expectations matters, that is, it matters that the expectations (coordinated by assumption) are coordinated at the right level. It is clearly unsatisfactory to have a theory motivated by expectation coordination where coordination is assumed. But the reduced-form loss function presumably reflects some intuition that it does matter what you coordinate on. Remember, it is exactly when levels rather than coordination *per se* matter that the potentially negative effect of increased precision of public announcements arises. It is important to study further the nature of the relevant coordination for monetary policy. There is some recent work on this topic: Angeletos and Pavan (2007) give an overview of when welfare losses associated with public information might be expected to arise or not arise. In the monopolistic competition pricing model of Hellwig (2005), public information is always valuable, intuitively, because getting relative prices right matters more than the absolute level of prices. Angeletos et al. (2007) describe a scenario in which public information can introduce volatility in asset prices that leads to socially inefficient investment choices.

To understand the welfare impact of using central bank communication to coordinate private-sector expectations, we must take a position on why coordination is required, and what the trade-off is between coordination *per se* and coordination at the right level.

Second, if central bank communication is to play such an important and beneficial role in coordinating private-sector expectations, it must be because – in the absence of such communication – expectations would not be coordinated, or, in other words, there would be heterogeneous interpretations about what is going on in monetary policy and the economy. Where do these heterogeneous interpretations come from? If you are confident that these heterogeneous viewpoints have no informational value, then no socially valuable information is lost when these viewpoints are no longer reflected in economics actors' choices. But how confident should we be that no socially valuable information is lost? It certainly sounds safe to argue that if the central bank's information is better than all the information among private-sector actors, the social loss from transparency cannot arise. Proponents of transparency would argue that this is the case at the relevant margins of the debate on transparency. Even if this rule is accepted, there may not be agreement on whether the central bank has more relevant information. Since future central bank actions are crucial to forming coordinated expectations in the market, many central banks have been saying more and more about future policy plans. Mervyn King (2006), on the other hand, insists that he and the Bank of England's Monetary Policy Committee (MPC) have no more information about future policy actions than the private sector: 'We don't say where interest rates will go next for the simple reason that we don't know. And it would be quite misleading to pretend otherwise'.

A closely related issue is the revealed preferences of the central bank as embodied in the forecasts it issues on the path of its policy interest rate. Charles Goodhart (2007) notes that when a central bank issues forecasts of inflation and the output gap, together with its forecast of the policy rate, there is an implied weighting over inflation and the output gap that is revealed in the combined forecasts. Such preferences may not be explicitly held or agreed among MPC members, nor will such preferences necessarily pass the time-consistency test.

Finally, note the important implicit assumption that a central bank has control over the inferences the private sector draws from its communication. Mervyn King may not wish to communicate about the Bank of England's future policy actions, because he believes that he does not have relevant insights over and above his explanation of objectives and current policy. The market, however, will make inferences about future policy, and the MPC minutes might play a role in coordinating expectations about future policy decisions. In doing so, the MPC minutes might crowd out private-sector information that otherwise would have been reflected in market expectations.

Now let us consider more transparent central banks, such as those of Norway and New Zealand (and recently Sweden), which seek to communicate what future policy decisions will be conditional on the future state of the economy. Such announcements may coordinate expectations about future policy, but may also be relevant to private-sector assessments of future stock prices, and might play a role in coordinating expectations about stock prices. Nevertheless, it is surely true that the private sector has valuable information about stock prices that we would not like to see crowded out by either sunspots or misunderstood central bank communication.

Is There a Conflict between Managing Expectations and Learning from Markets?

Ben Bernanke (2004a) has argued:

> [W]hen the monetary policy committee regularly provides information about its objectives, economic outlook, and policy plans, two benefits result. First, with more complete information available, markets will price financial assets more efficiently. Second, the policy makers will usually find that they have achieved a closer alignment between market participants' expectations about the course of future short-term rates and their own views.

In other words, Bernanke argues that when the central bank conveys its own views more clearly, (i) market prices are more informationally efficient, and (ii) market expectations may be closer to the central bank's own expectations.

Prima facie, there seems to be a conflict between these two claims. If the central bank is able to successfully coordinate market expectations, it is because market participants put a significant weight on central bank announcements. This means that they must put less weight on their own private information. This would seem to lessen the informational efficiency of market prices. To the extent that the central bank collects information about the economy from the private sector, this suggests that more transparent communication by the central bank might reduce the informativeness of information from the private sector and reduce the central bank's ability to conduct monetary policy in the future. Morris and Shin (2005) formally modelled this tension between managing expectations and learning from them, as well as noting anecdotal evidence consistent with this view.

Advocates of transparent central bank communication downplay a conflict here. Bernanke would surely argue that the economic data that serve as inputs into US monetary policy are distinct from the asset prices that reflect the coordinated expectations generated by transparent central bank communication, and that there is no feedback between the two. This question surely merits further theoretical and empirical investigation.

The Precision–Commonality Trade-off

In our discussion so far, we have assumed that if the central bank has some information, it is feasible for it to make that information public. We have noted that the 'publicity' or common knowledge of the information enables the central bank to have a large role in coordinating expectations, hopefully in the social interest (but conceivably not).

As any central banker knows, however, it is not so easy to communicate information in such a way that it becomes common knowledge within the private sector. If different listeners interpret an announcement differently, then the content of the announcement does not become common knowledge. The same result is obtained if some listeners pay attention to the announcement, while others do not. Intuitively, the more one attempts to communicate, the more likely it is that some listeners will not pay attention to all the information, resulting in less common knowledge. In this sense, there is a trade-off between the commonality of information communicated and the accuracy of that information.

Morris and Shin (2007) used the following example in illustrating this trade-off. Consider again the coordination problem that we described earlier: each actor is trying to match his or her action to some average of his or her expectation of the state and his or her expectation of the average action of others. Suppose I know the true state and have two alternative communication scenarios available. Under scenario one, I could collect everyone together into one lecture hall and announce the state. This lecture hall, however, would have to be very large, and there would be a large amount of noise added to my announcement of the state. In other words, while I announced the true state of the world, everyone would hear the same noisy signal of what I said. In this case, there would be common knowledge of an inaccurate signal of the state. Under scenario two, however, I could divide everyone into two equal groups and put them in smaller lecture halls with better acoustics. In each lecture, my announcement of the true state would be heard with less noise. Nevertheless, each audience would have a different noise term. In this case, everyone's information about the state would be more accurate than under scenario one, but there would not be common knowledge of their beliefs. If these were the only communication scenarios available, then there would be an important, non-trivial trade-off between precision and accuracy of communication even if increased accuracy of public signals were always desirable.

There is a trivial sense in which this trade-off is reflected in the design of central bank communication. The MPC goes to some lengths to ensure that there is a single, definitive statement of their policy decisions and reasoning. This enhances the commonality of understanding of what they have said. Repeating their position to multiple audiences, offering further clarifications when confusion arises, might unambiguously increase the accuracy of the public's understanding of their position. It would not, however, enhance the commonality of the understanding, since some people might miss the clarification.

This trade-off must surely arise in understanding the limits to transparency. Many central bankers comment that markets may absorb unconditional forecasts of future policy; conditional forecasts are too much for the market to bear. One way of understanding this claim is that there is a greater hurdle in attaining common knowledge than merely conveying information to a single individual. An inflation target or unconditional forecast may be sufficiently simple for there to be confidence that 'everyone' is observing it, but more complex communication strategies may erode common knowledge and – in this sense – lessen transparency.

CURRENT DEBATES

How can we relate the theoretical ideas outlined above to the current debates surrounding the conduct of monetary policy? We shall focus in greater detail on one issue that we have touched on already – namely, on whether a central bank should publish its own forecast of its policy rate. This question recently came to the fore of the debate following the decision of Sweden's central bank, the Riksbank, in 2006 to join the central banks of Norway and New Zealand in publishing the forecast of its policy rate. Even among those central banks that have explicit inflation-targeting policy regimes, the practice of publishing the forecast of the policy rate puts these three countries (New Zealand, Norway and Sweden) at the vanguard of the trend towards greater central bank disclosure. The Bank of England (another inflation-targeting central bank) has been less willing to go down this route, as already noted earlier in our discussion.

The Bank of England's position is at odds with a body of work both in academia and policy circles that has advocated forward-looking guidance by the central bank on its future actions as a way to enhance the effectiveness of monetary policy. We have already noted the key planks in this argument. The argument starts with the observation that the central bank generally controls directly only the overnight interest rate. The links from the overnight rate – the direct lever of monetary policy – to the prices that matter, such as long-term interest rates, depend almost entirely on market expectations, and monetary policy is effective only to the extent that the central bank can shape the beliefs of the market participants.

A second plank in the argument for the central bank providing guidance on its future actions is some version of the expectations theory of the yield curve – in other words that long-term interest rates are determined (or at least influenced in large part) by market participants' expectation of the future course of short-term rates set by the central bank. By charting a path for future short rates and communicating this path clearly to the market, the central bank can, it is argued, influence market expectations, thereby affecting mortgage rates, corporate lending rates and other prices that have a direct impact on the economy. Having thus gained a lever of control over long-term rates, monetary policy works through the IS (investment–savings) curve – through quantities such as consumption and investment.

Indeed, as we have commented already, the management of expectations is seen by many leading monetary economists of the expectationalist school as *the* task of monetary policy. For Svensson (2004, p. 1), 'monetary policy is to a large extent the management of expectations', or as Woodford (2005, p. 3) has put it, 'not only do expectations about policy matter, but, at least under current conditions, very little else matters'. The arguments are laid out particularly clearly in a policy speech given by (then Federal Reserve Governor) Ben Bernanke (2004b) entitled, 'The logic of monetary policy'. Here, Bernanke explores the analogy between driving a car and steering the economy through monetary policy. The economy is a car and the Federal Open Markets Committee (FOMC) is the driver, and monetary policy actions are akin to taps on the accelerator or the brake in order to stimulate or cool the economy as appropriate, based on its current state. Bernanke notes that while this analogy is superficially attractive, the analogy breaks down due to the importance of the expectations of future actions by the central bank. If the economy is like a car, then it is a car whose speed at a particular moment depends not on the pressure on the accelerator at that moment, but rather on the expected average pressure on the accelerator over the rest of the trip.

In addition to the argument that monetary policy is more effective when central banks disclose the path of their future policy rates, there is also an argument that appeals to consistency. Rudebusch and Williams (2006) examine the current practice of some inflation-targeting central banks of arriving at forecasts of inflation and output that are based either on the assumption that the policy rate will remain constant, going forward, or on the path of the policy rate as revealed in market prices of short-term interest rate futures contracts. If the central bank knows that its own forecast diverges from either or both of these paths, then the central bank's own forecast of inflation and output will build in an inconsistency. Thus, in addition to the reasons arising from policy effectiveness, even from the viewpoint of consistency, the disclosure of future expected policy actions is seen as being desirable.

The Market as a Single Agent

There are, however, a number of issues that may give us cause to pause and reconsider the arguments. Let us begin, first, with the practice of treating the market as a single, coherent agent with beliefs that satisfy the consistency requirements that apply to a rational individual. In referring to movements in market prices, we often employ the shorthand to refer to the 'market's expectations'. In simple formal models with a representative agent, there is indeed a representative individual whose beliefs correspond to the 'market's expectations'. In practice, however, there is no such thing as the 'market's expectations'. The market is not an individual, and market prices do not correspond to the beliefs of a particular individual. Instead, market prices are determined as the result of the interactions of a large number of individuals who may have their own respective windows on the world, and who do their best to infer the information of other individuals in the market.

When traders have differential information and short trading horizons, Allen et al. (2006) show that the prices that emerge from the forward-looking rational expectations equilibrium of an otherwise standard asset-pricing model exhibit the tell-tale features of the excessive influence of public information over private information. One symptom of the over-reliance on public information is the fact that the (arithmetic) average of the traders' expectations concerning the fundamental value of an asset two periods from now need not be equal to the average expectation today of the average expectation tomorrow of the fundamental value. In other words, the 'law of iterated expectations' fails for the average expectations of the market as a whole. Such a failure would never occur if the market were a single, coherent agent capable of holding beliefs as a single individual.

Once we break free from the straitjacket of construing the market as a single, coherent individual, some of the anomalies that have been raised as potential obstacles to publishing guidance on future policy actions of the central bank appear to be on stronger ground. As mentioned by Rudebusch and Williams (2006, p. 2), one of the strongest central bank taboos is the prohibition against talking publicly about future interest rates. This taboo is attributed to the belief that financial markets would tend to interpret any central bank statements about the likely future path of policy as commitment to future action, as opposed to conditional projections based on existing information and subject to considerable change. Mervyn King's argument alluded to above rests on similar misgivings. To the extent that the 'market' is not one, single individual with coherent beliefs, such misgivings do not attribute irrationality or bounded rationality to the 'market'. There is no such attribution of irrationality, since there is no one individual called the 'market' that can be the subject of such attribution. To think otherwise would be to commit what philosophers call a 'category mistake'.[1]

Expectations Theory of the Yield Curve

We have already seen that an important (perhaps the most important) plank in the argument for the desirability of publishing guidance on the future path of central bank policy rates is some version of the expectations theory of the yield curve. According to this theory, long-term interest rates are determined by the expectations of the future path of short-term rates. It is through this channel that the central bank gains a lever over prices that matter – in particular long-term rates that determine the key interest rates that determine mortgage rates, corporate lending rates and so on. While there is some empirical support for the expectations theory of the yield curve, the evidence is mixed. Gerlach and Smets (1995) find supporting evidence for the expectations theory for a number of European countries, but there is little evidence for it for countries that host the major financial markets.

Indeed, in a paper published 25 years ago, Shiller et al. (1983, pp. 174–5) summarize the state of discussion on the expectations theory in the following unflattering terms.

> The simple expectations theory, in combination with the hypothesis of rational expectations, has been rejected many times in careful econometric studies. But the theory seems to reappear perennially in policy discussions as if nothing had happened to it. It is uncanny how resistant superficially appealing theories in economics are to contrary evidence. We are reminded of Tom and Jerry cartoons that precede feature films at movie theatres. The villain, Tom the cat, may be buried under a ton of boulders, blasted through a brick wall (leaving a cat-shaped hole), or flattened by a steamroller. Yet seconds later he is up again plotting his evil deeds.

Their paper was published in the Brookings Papers of 1983, but the force of their argument remains as strong as ever. The bond market crash of 1994, and the fluctuations in the yield curve in the summer of 2003 are two of the more glaring instances of apparent 'overreaction' by the market to central bank communication.

When considering the workings of financial markets and the motivation of traders, the failure of the expectations theory of the yield curve is perhaps not a surprise. Although it is very plausible that central bank guidance is the pivotal factor in pricing out one or two years in the yield curve, it seems more of a stretch to believe that longer-term rates are determined by traders' expectations of central bank actions in the distant future. When hedge funds and fixed-income traders trade ten-year swaps, could we plausibly believe that they are influenced primarily by their beliefs of central bank policy seven, eight or nine years from today? Evidence from the markets tend to undermine such a hypothesis.

Even among those central banks that have begun to publish the forecast of their future policy rates, the markets have not always taken the cue from the central bank's forecast in setting prices. Goodhart (2007) notes that when the Norges Bank (Norway's central bank) published its interest rate projections in autumn 2006, very short-term rates fell into line, but the longer ones did not.[2] The expectations theory of the yield curve seems even less secure in the face of such evidence.

Monetary Policy and Informational Efficiency

To the extent that market prices guide real economic decisions, the informational value of market prices ought to be of interest to central banks. Following the recent cooling of the residential housing market in the USA, the excesses of the lending practices of some financial institutions to the 'sub-prime' mortgage market has become a subject of topical debate and a cause for concern.[3] Many of the sub-prime loans were extended in the period of unusually low short-term interest rates earlier in the decade, illustrating the long-lasting nature of some investment and financing decisions. As such, informational efficiency should be of concern to central bankers. In contrast to monetary models based on the IS curve that emphasizes *flows* (such as consumption flows), many important decisions affected by monetary policy are concerned with *stocks* (such as debt). Stock decisions can sometimes be difficult to reverse.

Irving Fisher in his *Theory of Interest* (1930) gives the example of three possible uses for a plot of land: forestry, farming or mining. The interest rate used to discount future cash flows largely determines the ranking of the three projects. Long-duration projects such as forestry, where the bulk of the payoffs arrive in the distant future, do best in an environment of low interest rates. When interest rates are high, short-duration projects like strip mining dominate. Since investment decisions are often difficult to reverse, distortions to investment can have a lingering effect long after the initial misallocations.

Central bankers have a large impact on financial markets. Indeed, it could be argued that the central bank's impact can sometimes be *too* large. By the nature of the problem, it is difficult to gauge whether the reactions in the financial market are excessive or justified by the fundamentals. Behaviour of financial intermediaries as illustrated above show, however, that it cannot be taken for granted that informational efficiency will be guaranteed. Apparent 'overreactions' will be the rule rather than the exception.

CONCLUSION

In the middle of the twentieth century, there was an earlier attempt to use transparent communication to coordinate private-sector expectations to socially efficient outcomes. It was called 'indicative planning'. The idea was that missing markets might lead to market failures: in five years' time, if the manufacturing sector made the right investments, there would be an increased demand for steel; if the new steel plants had been built, there would have been supply to meet the demand. The lack of a future steel market meant, however, that the invisible hand would not equate them in an efficient way. If, on the other hand, the planning agency could collect information from the managers of the manufacturing sector and the steel sector and publicly and transparently announce this information, then they might be able to coordinate market expectations to a socially efficient level. A recent book by Barry Eichengreen (2006) gives an overview of the process and the outcomes.

In the event, the plans did not always work as intended. Coordination was evidently more difficult to achieve than this. Some of the problems of indicative planning are orthogonal to the new view of monetary policy (for example, the relevant private-sector entities would be large actors who would have an incentive to misreport their private information). Others might be more relevant (would an 'independent' planning agency insulated from short-term political considerations have performed better?). One of the lessons from the global games literature is that when the costs of mis-coordination are large, the inherent strategic uncertainty about others' actions entails some degree of inefficiency in the outcome.

The public policy instrument of 'coordinating expectations' through transparent communication has not always been a success. Nevertheless, the last few years show that it seems to be working well for monetary policy in a number of countries. This raises an interesting question. What is so special about monetary policy that allows coordination failure to be fixed with such apparent ease? One important factor is surely that, while successful communication can reduce the importance of the central bank's direct instruments (such as controlling overnight interest rates), those instruments are still there and 'off the equilibrium path'. In other words, if the communication policy failed to coordinate expectations, these instruments would be used and could have a large, if less predictable, impact than the first-best option of using communication alone.

If coordinating expectations is possible, then it is a powerful force for good, as illustrated by the successes of increased transparency of central bank communication over the last 15 years. This power could – in some circumstances – be damaging, however. In this chapter, we have tried to describe how taking expectations coordination seriously suggests when it could be damaging. In doing so, it offers some insights into what the limits to transparency should be.

NOTES

1. The Wikipedia entry on 'category mistake' gives the following definition: 'Category mistake, or category error is a semantic or ontological error by which a property is ascribed to a thing that could not possibly have that property'.
2. Goodhart (2007, p. 19) quotes the following passage from the speech by Deputy Governor Jarle Bergo: 'It is now almost three months since the previous Inflation Report was published. Since that time forward rates have increased and approached Norges Bank's interest rate path. Forward rates somewhat further out are still lower than our forecast. The reason may be that market participants have a different perception of the interest rate path that is necessary to stabilize inflation at target and to achieve stable developments in output and employment. Alternatively, the market may have the same short-term interest rate expectations as Norges Bank, but because of extraordinary conditions long-term bond prices are being pushed up and, consequently, long-term bond yields are being pushed down'.
3. This lecture was delivered in November 2006.

REFERENCES

Allen, Franklin, Stephen Morris and Hyun Song Shin (2006), 'Beauty contests and iterated expectations in asset markets', *Review of Financial Studies*, **19**, pp. 719–52.

Angeletos, Marios, Guido Lorenzoni and Alessandro Pavan (2007), 'Why the prospect of Wall Street can be bad for efficiency in Silicon Valley', working paper, Massachusetts Institute of Technology, Cambridge, MA.

Angeletos, Marios and Alessandro Pavan (2007), 'Efficient use of information and social value of information', *Econometrica*, **75** (4), pp. 1103–42.

Bernanke, Ben (2004a), 'Central bank talk and monetary policy', Remarks at the Japan Society Corporate Luncheon, New York, 7 October, www.federal reserve.gov/boarddocs/speeches/2004/200410072/default.htm, accessed 16 May 2008.

Bernanke, Ben (2004b), 'The logic of monetary policy', Remarks before the National Economists Club, 2 December, www.federalreserve.gov/boarddocs/speeches/2004/20041202/default.htm, accessed 16 May 2008.

Eichengreen, Barry (2006), *The European Economy since 1945: Coordinated Capitalism and Beyond*, Princeton, NJ: Princeton University Press.

Fisher, Irving (1930), *The Theory of Interest*, London and New York: Macmillan.

Gerlach, Stefan and Frank Smets (1995), 'The monetary transmission mechanism: evidence from the G7 countries', CEPR Discussion Paper 1219, London.

Goodhart, Charles (2007), 'The interest rate conditioning assumption', working paper, London School of Economics, Financial Markets Group.

Hellwig, Christian (2005), 'Heterogeneous information and the welfare effects of public information disclosures', working paper, University of California, Los Angeles, CA.

King, Mervyn (2006), 'Mansion House speech', City of London, 21 June.

Morris, Stephen and Hyun Song Shin (2002), 'Social value of public information', *American Economic Review*, **92**, pp. 1521–4.

Morris, Stephen and Hyun Song Shin (2005), 'Central bank transparency and the signal value of prices', *Brookings Papers on Economic Activity*, **2**, 1–66.

Morris, Stephen and Hyun Song Shin (2007), 'Optimal communication', *Journal of the European Economics Association Papers and Proceedings*, **5**, pp. 594–602.

Rudebusch, Glenn and John Williams (2006), 'Revealing the secrets of the temple: the value of publishing central bank interest rate projections', Working Paper 2006–31, Federal Reserve Bank of San Francisco, CA.

Shiller, Robert, John Campbell and Kermit Schoenholtz (1983), 'Forward rates and future policy: interpreting the term structure of interest rates', *Brookings Papers on Economic Activity*, **1**, pp. 173–223.

Svensson, Lars (2004), 'Challenges for monetary policy', paper presented at the Bellagio Group Meeting at the National Bank of Belgium, January, www.princeton.edu/svensson/papers/401bru.pdf, accessed 16 May 2008.

Svensson, Lars (2006), 'Social value of public information: Morris and Shin (2002) is actually pro-transparency, not con', *American Economic Review*, **96**, pp. 448–51.

Woodford, Michael (2005), 'Central bank communication and policy effectiveness', paper presented at the Federal Reserve Bank of Kansas City Economic Symposium at Jackson Hole, WY, August.

6. Central bank transparency: where, why and with what effects?

Nazire Nergiz Dincer and Barry Eichengreen[1]

INTRODUCTION

Transparency represents the most dramatic difference between central banking today and central banking in earlier periods.[2] In recent years, a number of central banks have moved in the direction of greater transparency about their objectives, procedures, rationales, models and data. The question is whether the trend is widespread and whether it is likely to be transitory or enduring. Below we show that this movement in the direction of greater policy transparency is remarkably general. The answer to the question of whether it is likely to prove durable or to be a passing phase is likely to depend on the consequences; our analysis suggests that so far, there have been broadly favourable impacts on inflation and output variability. If institutional arrangements that produce favourable results retain public support, then this suggests that the trend towards greater monetary policy transparency is here to stay.

While there have been a few studies along these lines, relatively little is known about actual trends in transparency or their correlates and implications. Theory has provided useful insights, as we shall see below, but it has not produced general conclusions. Our goal in this study is therefore to contribute new evidence.

We shall construct an index of central bank transparency, distinguishing its components and dimensions, for a larger range of countries and years than in previous studies. Both the time dimension and the international dimension shed light on recent trends in transparency. They allow us to ask questions such as: in what countries have central banks been growing more transparent, and why? Next, we analyse the impact of transparency on inflation persistence, inflation variability and output variability. An advantage of considering both the determinants and the effects of transparency is that we can use our analysis of the determinants to identify instrumental variables that address the concern that an observed correlation between outcomes and transparency reflects the impact of outcomes on transparency, rather than the other way around.

REFLECTIONS ON THE DEVELOPMENT OF CENTRAL BANK TRANSPARENCY

Central banks originated as closely held, privately owned suppliers of credit to the government. Because they competed with other financial institutions, they tended to be less than forthcoming about their pricing and portfolio decisions. Given their privileged relationship with the state – often with the head of state himself – information was treated as confidential, as properly known only to the bank and its client. That they were less than transparent about their decision making is understandable given these circumstances.

As part of this bargain, central banks gradually acquired their modern competency of regulating supplies of money and credit. Typically they acquired it in the era of commodity money. The obligation of converting their liabilities into specie at a fixed rate of exchange ensured an important element of transparency in their operations. Observers thus knew something about the institution's objective function: the central bank assigned a high weight to the maintenance of convertibility. They also knew something about the model that the central bank used – typically some variant of the price–specie flow model – and were knowledgeable of the instruments the central bank used to pursue its objectives, typically the rate at which it discounted other obligations to regulate currency fluctuations, together with ancillary measures to render that discount rate effective.[3] They observed the success with which the central bank regulated the price of specie. Reflecting the public or semi-public nature of this commitment, central banks published information on changes in gold reserves that were used by market participants to forecast future policies.[4] In modern studies, one aspect of transparency is whether a central bank provides an explicit policy rule or strategy that describes its monetary policy framework; an exchange rate target is one such rule. So it was in this earlier period. The existence of this modicum of transparency was what made it socially acceptable to assign consequential public-policy functions to entities that often had private shareholders, mixed motives and a good deal of bureaucratic autonomy.

The persistence of currency pegs through much of the twentieth century and the tendency to regard as aberrant and exceptional periods when those pegs were in abeyance is one way of understanding why there was not more intense pressure for central banks to reveal more information about their operations. It was easy enough to judge, on the basis of events in foreign exchange markets, whether the central bank was true to its mandate. This perspective suggests that it is no coincidence that the tendency in the last ten years for central banks to become more transparent in other aspects of their operations has coincided with a shift towards more flexible exchange rates.[5] In a growing number of countries, the one element that had done the most to lend transparency to monetary policy disappeared. The result was pressure to increase other aspects of transparency, if for no other reason than to enhance society's ability to hold central banks accountable to their ultimate stakeholders.

To be sure, this shift towards greater exchange rate flexibility was not exogenous. It did not occur in isolation from other events in the economy or society. As Eichengreen (1996) has argued elsewhere, it is best understood in terms of two other late-twentieth-century trends: financial liberalization and political liberalization. The deregulation of financial markets and the removal of controls on international financial flows made it impossible for central banks and governments to use one instrument to hit two targets, pegging the exchange rate while at the same time using monetary policy to pursue other goals. Meanwhile, democratization made it more difficult to privilege the exchange rate – to credibly commit to pegging the exchange rate without regard to the implications for other socially relevant economic variables. When unemployment rose to high levels, for example, political pressure for the central bank to do something about it became irresistible. In an environment of deregulated financial markets and capital flows, the exchange rate peg was increasingly a casualty. This was a first channel through which came the impetus to develop further other aspects of central bank transparency.

There were also other channels linking democratization and financial liberalization to central bank transparency. Democratization directly increased demands for public accountability. Compared to other forms of government, democratic governments are intrinsically more open about their affairs as a way of achieving accountability to their constituents; in this sense central bank transparency (the central bank being an agency of the government) is only a specific instance of the general point. Transparency is one way in which such public accountability can be brought about. It is surely not coincidental that the rise in central bank transparency in Latin America, in Eastern Europe and in Asian countries from Korea to the Philippines coincided with the third wave of democratization.

Democratization also strengthened the argument for central bank independence, a trend that is closely allied to increased transparency. In democratic societies, political pressures are intense (in a sense, this is the very definition of democracy), and there are a variety of arguments for why central banks, when deciding on their tactics, should be sheltered from those pressures via independence.[6] With independence, however, comes demands for adequate accountability; central banks are asked to provide more information about their operations to enable citizens and their representatives to evaluate the central bank's actions, praise it for its achievements, and take it to task for its failures. In addition, independence may render the central bank more willing to volunteer information about its operations; when a central bank is dependent on the government, keeping information private is one way that it can advance its own goals relative to those of its political masters.[7]

Finally, financial liberalization made it important that central bank actions have a stable and predictable impact on market variables. Deregulation eliminated the authorities' ability to control market outcomes directly. The growth of financial markets and transactions made the market response to policies all the more essential for achieving the central bank's ultimate objectives. Volatility, when it occurred, was even more disruptive than before. This made it more important that the central bank communicate with market participants in a way that inspired confidence and avoided causing excessive volatility. In so far as communication means the regularized transmission of information, the implication was an increase in transparency.[8]

It is against this backdrop that we ask the following questions: what exactly is the state of central bank transparency and what has been the impact on economic outcomes?

THEORY

Economists are instinctively of the view that more information is better. In the present context, they argue that greater communication from central banks about their objectives, their assessment of the effects of policy actions and information about general economic conditions will enhance social welfare. Policy thus being more predictable, agents will be better able to align their decisions with those of the central bank. The economy will adjust more smoothly in so far as agents can more accurately forecast the time paths of relevant variables.

By the same token, the theory of the second best suggests that removing one distortion may not always lead to a more efficient allocation when other distortions are present. Adding distortions, theorists have thus provided counterexamples where greater transparency may not lead to a welfare improvement.

Transparency has typically been modelled in a Barro–Gordon (1983) set-up where there is uncertainty about the central bank's preferences and the central bank may wish to stimulate output to levels above the natural rate. As in Backus and Driffill (1995), the public will use outcomes or actions to infer the central bank's preferences. Because private-sector decisions are made before disturbances are known, there may be a role for stabilizing policy. If the central bank prefers a level of output above the natural rate, however, stabilizing policy may have an inflationary bias. Thus, such models include a number of distortions that make it possible to obtain different results about whether transparency is welfare improving and whether it is preferred by the central bank.

Faust and Svensson (2001) consider a model in which the public attempts to infer the central bank's type from information on policy outcomes. Inference is imperfect because of unanticipated monetary control errors that the public observes incompletely. Greater transparency about control errors enables agents to infer the central bank's preferences more accurately. This in turn acts as an incentive for the monetary authority to build a reputation for valuing price stability. The private sector becomes more sensitive to unanticipated policy responses and actions, attenuating the incentive for the central bank to engage in them. The result is thus greater sensitivity of inflation expectations to policy actions, less benefit to the central bank of inflating, and less inflationary bias. In this way, increased transparency about control errors improves social welfare.

Greater transparency about the central bank's objectives has similar effects – the central bank is led to moderate its inflationary bias – but in certain cases extreme transparency about objectives may be welfare reducing. Greater transparency about objectives not only eliminates uncertainty about inflation and output, but also removes the central bank's incentive to curtail inflation in order to signal its type. Hence neither the central bank nor society may prefer goal transparency.

Making minor modifications to the Faust–Svensson framework, Jensen (2002) shows that increases in transparency about outcomes can be welfare reducing as well. In Faust and Svensson, inflation expectations are formed at the start of the period, and current policy decisions affect output only in the future; this means that there are no costs in terms of forgoing stabilization policy. In Jensen's model, in contrast, not every firm is permitted to change its prices at the beginning of every period, so there are implications for output in the current period. Inflation expectations, and hence current inflation, become more sensitive to policy when the public is able to infer the central bank's preferences, and hence to predict its future behaviour. The central bank is led to pay more attention to inflation.

Transparency may be welfare increasing if the central bank lacks credibility, because market expectations and reactions provide discipline that prevents excessive inflation. It may, however, be welfare reducing if shocks to output are large and stabilization policy is hamstrung. In general there will be an optimal degree of transparency that trades off these two considerations.

Geraats (2002a) models the private-sector response to policy actions themselves, not to the outcomes from which policy actions are inferred. The public is imperfectly informed about shocks to the economy and uses the interest rate to infer the central bank's target. Contrary to Jensen, greater transparency may not hamstring stabilization policy. An opaque central bank, on the other hand, may have to limit the variability of its interest rate in order to signal its type. It is forced to smooth the interest rate in order to avoid exciting inflation expectations. Hence it may be less able to counter output shocks.

In addition, when the degree of transparency is endogenous, signalling and self-selection can arise. The public will expect opaque central banks to be more inflationary, and it will form higher inflation expectations. Geraats shows that this may be sufficiently costly that even weak central banks will prefer transparency, contrary to the implications of other models.

Assuming that inflation expectations are set by the private sector acting strategically instead of by agents passively forming rational expectations further weakens the presumption that more transparency about objectives enhances welfare. Sørensen (1991) considers the case where wages are set by a risk-averse labour union whose demands depend on inflation expectations. Again, uncertainty about the central bank's objective raises the variance of inflation and output. Since the union is risk averse, however, it may demand wages lower than those corresponding to its unbiased forecast of inflation in order to limit volatility. This second effect will work to reduce the level of inflation and increase the level of output.[9] This effect disappears, however, if the central bank makes its objectives public information, so that the risk aversion of the wage-setting union no longer matters.

Morris and Shin (2002) address a related coordination problem, where individual welfare depends not only on the state of the world, but also on the actions of other individuals. Starting from a position where both private and public information are imperfect, they show that greater precision of public information can lead individuals to attach inadequate weight to private information. In the absence of coordination motives, the precision attached to the public and private signals will be commensurate with their relative precision. When coordination motives are present, however, agents attach greater weight to the public signal, since they know this to be common information. But since the public signal is noisy, this weight on the public signal may be suboptimal from a social-welfare point of view; agents may be led to coordinate on an inefficient equilibrium. This adverse outcome is more likely, the more precise the private information. Svensson (2006) argues that this result obtains only under extreme parameter values: when the public signal is very noisy relative to its private counterpart.

This brief survey suffices to make the point.[10] General conclusions based on theory remain elusive. Results are sensitive to what one assumes about the structure of the economy (the determinants of supply and demand, the channels through which monetary policy affects output and inflation), the stochastic structure (what relationships are subject to disturbances), the information environment (what the central bank knows that the private sector does not, and the relative and absolute precision of their signals), the timing of actions and decisions, and the institutional setting (whether the central bank has the political independence to make decisions on the basis of an objective function that differs from that of the private sector or the government).

PREVIOUS EMPIRICAL STUDIES

Empirical studies of central bank transparency are still in their infancy. Most take the form of detailed studies of individual central banks, describe disclosure practices in detail, and/or attempt to identify an effect of changes in disclosure practices on specific financial and economic variables using time-series data.[11] They are valuable for demonstrating the feasibility of bringing the concept of transparency to the data. Their limitations are the difficulty of knowing how far to generalize the findings of individual cases and the difficulty of identifying the impact of increased transparency on the basis of a time series, especially when there may be only one significant change in disclosure practices in the sample period and other things were going on at the same time.

More recently, a number of studies have attempted to compare the transparency of different central banks. Typically they measure transparency for either a very limited number of central banks or a single point in time. Examples include Eijffinger and Geraats (2006), who distinguish political transparency (that is, openness about policy objectives), economic transparency (openness about data, models and forecasts), procedural transparency (openness about the way decisions are made, achieved mainly through the release of minutes and votes), policy transparency (openness about the policy implications, achieved through prompt announcement and explanation of decisions) and operational transparency (openness about the implementation of those decisions, in other words about control errors and macroeconomic disturbances affecting their magnitude), as well as three subcategories within each of these five dimensions. Their overall index is the sum (equally weighted average) of the subindices for these five dimensions. The strength of this approach is its comprehensive, multi-dimensional definition of transparency; its limitation is that it is constructed for just nine central banks (the Reserve Bank of Australia, the Bank of Canada, the European Central Bank (ECB), the Bank of Japan, the Reserve Bank of New Zealand, the Swedish Riksbank, the Swiss National Bank, the Bank of England and the US Federal Reserve System).[12] The results indicate sharp differences between more and less transparent central banks (with the Reserve Bank of New Zealand, the Bank of England and the Swedish Riksbank being the most transparent, and the Reserve Bank of Australia, the Bank of Japan and the Swiss National Bank being the least).

A related study is Bini-Smaghi and Gros (2001), who like Eijffinger and Geraats consider 15 aspects of central bank transparency.[13] They implement their index for four central banks: the Federal Reserve, the Bank of England, the Bank of Japan and the ECB. De Haan et al. (2004) develop a similar index for six central banks.[14] Siklos (2002) expands coverage to 20 central banks, all from advanced industrial countries. There is again considerable overlap with the contemporaneous work of Eiffjinger and Geraats and Bini-Smaghi and Gros.[15] Siklos ranks the Bank of England, the Federal Reserve and the Riksbank one, two and three. The Austrian National Bank, the Bank of France and the National Bank of Belgium bring up the rear.

The most comprehensive such study is Fry et al. (2000). The strength of their analysis is its wide country coverage, based on a survey of 94 central banks. Its limitation is a more restrictive definition of transparency. Their measure is an equally-weighted average of three elements: whether the central bank provides prompt public explanations of its policy decisions, the frequency and form of forward-looking analysis provided to the public, and the frequency of bulletins, speeches and research papers. The index, however, may not be unbiased: it is based on a survey of central banks administered by an official institution with a known interest in transparency. That their data are for 1998 is also less than ideal, given the changes that have taken place in transparency practices since then.

A number of authors have examined the relationship of these measures to economic and financial variables. Demertzis and Hughes Hallett (2003) employ the Eijffinger–Geraats index for 2001 to examine the relationship between central bank transparency and the level and variability of inflation and the output gap in the 1990–2001 period. The results suggest a negative relationship between inflation variability and central bank transparency, but not between the level of inflation and transparency. The former relationship appears to be driven by the subindices for economic and operational transparency (whether the central bank discloses information about data, its models, its forecasts, and the disturbances to which monetary policy is subject). There is no evident relationship between transparency and average output deviations, but a strong positive relationship between transparency and the variability of output. The latter seems to be driven by the subindex for operational transparency. The positive association of transparency with output variability is consistent with theoretical studies suggesting that more transparency may make for more volatile inflation expectations, to which a central bank may respond by using its monetary instruments less actively, limiting its effectiveness as an instrument of stabilization policy.[16] The fact, however, that the transparency data are for the end of the period over which economic performance is analysed suggests that what these correlations may be picking up are the economic determinants of transparency rather than its consequences.[17]

Chortareas et al. (2001) and Cecchetti and Krause (2001) utilize the Fry et al. index. Chortareas et al. focus on whether the central bank publishes a forward-looking analysis of economic prospects: they find that this aspect of disclosure reduces average inflation, even in the presence of controls.[18] Cecchetti and Krause examine the impact of transparency on inflation and output variability and find a weak negative association with a weighted average of the two variability measures.

In sum, existing empirical studies do not all reach consistent conclusions. Many are based on very limited country samples or utilize evidence for a single point in time. Cross-sections, unlike panels, do not permit the inclusion of country-fixed effects; the worry is that an observed correlation between transparency and economic outcomes may be picking up the effects of other country characteristics that are difficult to capture. Moreover, central banks that are transparent about their policies are not likely to be selected randomly from the larger population. The theoretical literature suggests that there are systematic reasons – having to do with a country's history, its economic structure, and even the behaviour of the economic and financial variables of interest – why a central bank may prefer more or less transparency. A convincing empirical analysis will have to take these considerations into account.

DATA

Our indices of central bank transparency build directly on the work of Eijffinger and Geraats. Their approach has the advantage of acknowledging that the phenomenon has multiple dimensions.[19] The result is 15 subindices, described in detail in the appendix, designed to capture five broad aspects of transparency: political, economic, procedural, policy and operational. The overall index thus runs from 0 to 15. Adopting the same criteria used by these previous investigators facilitates comparison across studies and frees us of suspicions that we have constructed our measures so as to maximize or minimize the impact of transparency.

We draw our data from information on central banks' websites and in their statutes, annual reports, and other published documents, rather than sending a survey instrument to the central banks themselves and relying on the subjectivity of responding staff. We follow Fry et al., however, by gathering this information for as large a number of central banks as possible. In addition we gather the same information for every year from 1998 through 2005. Where there was a change in some aspect of transparency over the course of a calendar year, we took the value that prevailed for the largest share of the year.[20]

We were able to assemble this information for 100 central banks. This is the majority of central banks in the world.[21] Most of the omissions are central banks of micro-states: our sample includes the central banks of all large, systemically significant countries.[22]

Table 6A.1 (pp. 134–9) shows the results by country and region. The most transparent central banks in 2005, according to our coding, were, in descending order, the Reserve Bank of New Zealand, the Swedish Riksbank, the Bank of England, the Czech National Bank, the Bank of Canada, the ECB, and the Central Bank of the Philippines. We see here a number of countries that have received high marks for transparency in previous studies (New Zealand, Sweden, the United Kingdom, Canada), but also others (the Czech Republic, the Philippines), which is a reminder of the advantages of broad country coverage and of the fact that a number of countries with relatively opaque central banking practices have been moving in the direction of greater transparency. The seven least transparent central banks were those of Aruba, Bermuda, Ethiopia, Kuwait, Libya, Saudi Arabia and Yemen. Table 6A.2 (p. 140) shows our coding of the 15 individual components for these 14 countries as of 2005.

More generally, we can compare different dimensions of central bank transparency. In 2005, 63 central banks received scores of 2 or more for political transparency (including, *inter alia*, providing a quantitative definition of their objectives to the public).[23] Only five central banks, however, received the highest possible rating for economic transparency (disclosing data, the policy model and forecasts). The picture is similar for procedural transparency (the release of minutes and votes), where only three central banks received the highest possible score,[24] and again for

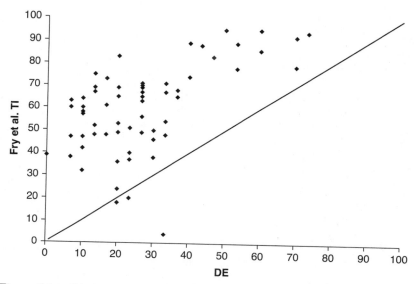

Figure 6.1   Comparison of DE and Fry et al. indices for 1998

policy transparency (prompt announcement and comprehensive explanation of policy decisions), where only the Reserve Bank of New Zealand, the
Swedish Riksbank and the Federal Reserve received a score of 2.5. No
central bank received a perfect score of 3 for operational transparency
(release of information about disturbances, control errors, and so on).

Taking unweighted averages of the countries making up a region (as in
Table 6A.1), we see the highest level of transparency in Australia–New
Zealand, followed by Western Europe, Northern Europe, South East Asia,
Southern Africa and North America. That South East Asia and Southern
Africa are scored as more transparent than North America is a figment of
the unweighted averages. When we instead take GDP-weighted averages, as
in Table 6A.3 (p. 141), the most transparent regions as of 2005, in descending order, are Europe (led by Northern Europe), Oceania, Southern Africa
(dominated by South Africa) and North America; lower weights on its relatively transparent small economies cause South East Asia to drop down.
Either way, the lowest levels of transparency, starting from the bottom, are
those of Northern Africa, Eastern Africa, Western Africa and Melanesia –
no surprises there.

We can compare our index (Dincer–Eichengreen, denoted DE) for 1998
with that of Fry et al. for the same year for the 67 countries that are
common to the two samples. The two measures have a correlation
coefficient of 0.57. For ease of comparison, in Figure 6.1 both indices are

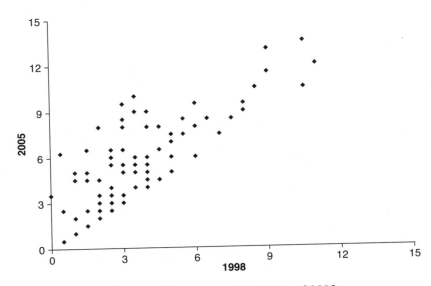

Figure 6.2   Comparison of transparency in 1998 and 2005

scaled to run from 0 to 100.[25] The case where our estimate of transparency exceeds that of Fry et al. by the most is Uruguay, while the opposite is true for Indonesia.[26] We do not have a ready explanation for the coding differences for these particular observations.

Turning to trends over time, the average transparency score in our sample rises from 3.4 in 1998 to 5.2 in 2005. Strikingly, none of our 100 countries moved in the direction of less transparency over this period. Figure 6.2 compares our measure of transparency in 1998 and 2005 (with 2005 on the vertical axis). There are only 11 countries on the diagonal, indicating no increase in transparency, while the remaining 89 cases are all above and to its left.

Figure 6.3 shows transparency by level of economic development (again, using weighted averages). Consistent with the preceding discussion, central banks in the advanced countries are more transparent than central banks in emerging markets (defined as middle-income countries with significant links to international financial markets), which in turn are more transparent than central banks in developing countries. Consistent with Figure 6.2, there have been increases in central bank transparency in all three country groups. Perhaps most strikingly, the increase among emerging markets is, on average, as large in absolute value as the increase among advanced countries; the corresponding increase among developing countries is smaller. Much of the increase in emerging markets is centred in the period following the Asian crisis and again in the early parts of the current decade.

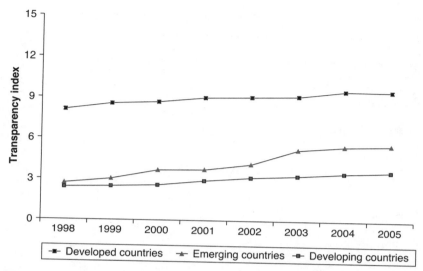

Figure 6.3   *Trends in transparency by level of economic development: weighted averages*

DETERMINANTS

We now use regression analysis to further characterize differences in central bank transparency. Our goals here are to work towards an explanation for these variations and also to identify instruments for our analysis of the consequences of transparency.

We start with the 1998–2004 cross-section, with all variables averaged over the period.[27] We regress transparency on a vector of economic determinants: per capita income, inflation history (defined as the lagged log first difference of the consumer price index), the de facto exchange rate regime (the Reinhart–Rogoff 2004 version as updated by Eichengreen and Razo-Garcia, 2006) and financial depth (defined as the ratio of M2 to GDP). In addition, we include a range of potential political determinants: rule of law, political stability, voice and accountability and government efficiency (all taken from Kaufmann et al., 2005). Since the political variables are highly correlated, we include them one at a time.

The results (Table 6.1) suggest, not surprisingly, that per capita GDP, which proxies for the general level of economic and institutional development, is the most robust correlate of overall transparency. This could have been predicted from Figure 6.3. In addition, countries with more flexible exchange rates (where a larger value of the index denotes greater flexibility)

Central banks as economic institutions

Table 6.1   Determinants of transparency, 1998–2004 averages[†]

	I	II	III	IV
Constant	−8.69*	−9.49*	−7.29*	−7.01*
	(−3.31)	(−3.85)	(−3.12)	(−2.46)
Past inflation	−1.17	−1.90	−0.50	0.02
	(−0.53)	(−0.88)	(−0.24)	(0.01)
Exchange rate regime	−0.29*	0.30*	0.24*	0.28*
	(4.66)	(4.77)	(4.09)	(4.52)
Financial depth	−0.00	−0.00	0.00	−0.01
	(−0.63)	(−0.37)	(0.30)	(−0.85)
GDP per capita	1.10*	1.25*	0.86*	0.80
	(3.07)	(3.88)	(2.81)	(1.90)
Rule of law	0.03			
	(1.66)			
Political stability		0.02		
		(1.43)		
Voice and accountability			0.04*	
			(3.41)	
Government efficiency				0.04*
				(2.18)
R-squared	0.55	0.54	0.60	0.56

Note: [†] *t*-statistics in parentheses; * denotes significance at 5%.

tend to be more transparent in the conduct of monetary policy, as anticipated in the section above on the development of central bank transparency: the absence of an exchange rate peg eliminates one traditional device for monitoring central bank actions.[28] A number of the political variables are significant, although at levels that vary with the proxy used.[29] Greater transparency characterizes central bank operations in countries that rank higher in terms of rule of law, that have more stable political systems, that have higher ratings in terms of voice and accountability, and that are more favourably regarded in terms of government efficiency.[30] The correlation of these political variables with central bank transparency will be useful when we consider the impact of transparency on economic and financial variables below.[31] As a form of sensitivity analysis, Table 6.2 adds openness and interacts it with the exchange rate regime; the results suggest that greater openness is associated with greater transparency if a country has a relatively flexible exchange rate, but with less transparency if the country has a relatively rigid currency. Again, this accords with intuition and casual observation.

Table 6.2   Further determinants of transparency, 1998–2004 averages†

	I	II	III	IV
Constant	−7.02*	−8.04*	−5.51*	−4.87
	(2.46)	(2.83)	(−2.13)	(−1.60)
Past inflation	−0.65	−1.27	0.35	0.83
	(−0.27)	(−0.52)	(0.15)	(0.33)
Openness	−0.01*	−0.01*	−0.01*	−0.01*
	(−2.17)	(−2.28)	(−2.12)	(−2.13)
Openness* ER regime	0.01*	0.01*	0.01*	0.01*
	(3.18)	(3.06)	(2.30)	(3.14)
Financial depth	−0.01	0.01	0.01	−0.01
	(−0.38)	(0.01)	(0.57)	(−0.62)
GDP per capita	1.14*	1.35*	0.87*	0.73
	(2.93)	(3.74)	(2.53)	(1.62)
Rule of law	0.03			
	(1.70)			
Political stability		0.02		
		(1.13)		
Voice and accountability			0.04*	
			(3.28)	
Government efficiency				0.05*
				(2.46)
R-squared	0.49	0.48	0.55	0.52

Note: † *t*-statistics in parentheses; * denotes significance at 5%.

We can also use this specification to consider factors influencing trends in transparency. In Tables 6.3 and 6.4 we pool the annual observations and estimate fixed-effects models (including separate intercepts for each country).[32] The estimates are now driven by the time-series variation in the data; they thus tell us something about why central bank practice is evolving in the direction of greater transparency. The exchange rate regime and per capita income continue to enter as before. Greater political and social stability now appears, however, to have a negative impact on monetary-policy transparency.[33] The result is not intuitive because, as Figure 6.4 shows, there is a positive cross-section correlation between the two variables. Recall, however, that fixed-effects regressions eliminate the cross-section variation. We suspect that what we are seeing is that advanced countries with highly transparent central banks and stable political systems cannot move much further in those directions (they contribute relatively little to the variation in the data), while countries that are not as admirable in terms of political stability and rule of law (Brazil, Colombia, Thailand,

Table 6.3   Determinants of transparency, fixed-effects models[†]

	I	II	III	IV
Constant	−34.52 (−0.09)	−40.65 (−0.11)	−41.50 (−0.11)	−40.87 (−0.11)
Past inflation	−0.03 (−0.09)	0.10 (0.25)	0.10 (0.27)	−0.04 (−0.11)
ER regime dummy	0.09* (2.52)	0.12* (3.41)	0.12* (3.39)	0.11* (3.19)
Financial depth	−0.00 (−0.16)	−0.00 (−0.10)	−0.00 (−0.13)	−0.00 (−0.19)
GDP per capita	4.61* (9.35)	5.05* (10.41)	5.11* (10.70)	5.15* (10.79)
Rule of law	−0.04* (−3.22)			
Political stability		−0.00 (−0.47)		
Voice and accountability			0.00 (0.33)	
Government efficiency				−0.01 (−1.27)
Haussman test	15.96*	22.61*	25.58*	23.70*
R-squared	0.97	0.97	0.97	0.97

*Note: † t-statistics in parentheses; * denotes significance at 5%.*

the Philippines) have been moving in the direction of greater central bank transparency precisely in order to insulate monetary policy from political problems.[34]

Overall, the analysis confirms that transparency is greater in countries with more stable and developed political systems and deeper and more developed financial markets. The one surprise is the negative association between some components of transparency and economic openness, although the robustness of this association may be questioned.

EFFECTS

We now explore the effects of monetary policy transparency. Some previous studies (see Mishkin, 2004) suggest that greater transparency should be associated with a reduction in uncertainty about future policy actions, and thus with a reduction in inflation volatility. Others (see Ball and Sheridan,

Table 6.4   Further determinants of transparency, fixed-effects models†

	I	II	III	IV
Constant	−31.95	−38.33	−39.40	−38.37
	(−0.08)	(−0.10)	(−0.10)	(−0.10)
Past inflation	−0.09	0.07	0.09	−0.12
	(−0.24)	(0.19)	(0.22)	(−0.29)
Openness	−0.01	−0.01	−0.01	−0.01
	(−0.70)	(−0.43)	(−0.40)	(−0.37)
Openness* ER dummy	0.01	0.01*	0.01*	0.01*
	(1.97)	(2.33)	(2.26)	(2.29)
Financial depth	−0.01	−0.01	−0.01	−0.01
	(−0.55)	(−0.54)	(−0.61)	(−0.69)
GDP per capita	4.46*	4.89*	4.94*	4.99*
	(8.71)	(9.54)	(9.76)	(9.87)
Rule of law	−0.04*			
	(−3.68)			
Political stability		−0.00		
		(−0.31)		
Voice and accountability			0.01	
			(0.83)	
Government efficiency				−0.02*
				(−1.72)
Haussman test	13.36*	19.10*	21.92*	19.47*
R-squared	0.97	0.97	0.97	0.97

Note: † *t*-statistics in parentheses; * denotes significance at 5%.

2005) have found evidence of a reduction in the average rate of inflation, but not in the level or volatility of growth. Here we consider the impact on output variability, inflation variability, and inflation persistence. In contrast to previous studies, we acknowledge the endogeneity of monetary policy transparency, using the same political variables utilized to explain the degree of transparency as instruments for transparency in this section's (second-stage) regressions. Specifically, in the results reported below we use the rule of law as an instrument for central bank transparency.[35]

Table 6.5 reports the estimates for inflation variability. Note that in each column we report the sum of squared residuals comparing the change in the point estimates with the loss of efficiency when instrumental variables are used; the change in the point estimates being relatively large, this supports our use of instrumental variables. The regressions suggest that past inflation is positively related to inflation variability, while financial depth is negatively related to inflation variability. Of particular interest is the

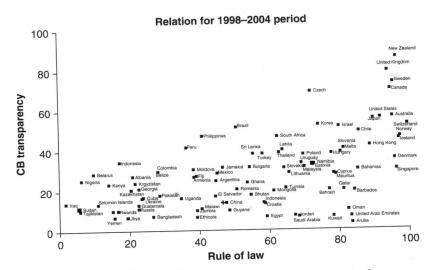

Figure 6.4   *Rule of law and central bank transparency, average for*
              1998–2004

coefficient on transparency, which is negative and, in most cases, statistically significant. This is consistent with theories suggesting that greater monetary-policy transparency allows the public to react more quickly to policy adjustments, in turn discouraging the authorities from attempting to manipulate inflation in the pursuit of other objectives.

Table 6.6 considers inflation persistence. Transparency enters negatively, consistent with the notion that greater policy transparency allows the public to adjust more quickly, in turn limiting the incentive for the central bank to run persistently inflationary policies in an effort to achieve objectives other than price stability. The coefficient in question is statistically significant at the 90 per cent level in only two of six specifications, however. Table 6.7 considers an alternative formulation where the dependent variable is current inflation and the explanatory variables include lagged inflation (the coefficient on which picks up inflation persistence) and also the interaction of lagged inflation with the fitted value of transparency (from the first-stage regression). The coefficient on the interaction term, which tells us whether inflation persistence is greater, lesser or no different in countries where monetary policy is more transparent, is negative, consistent with earlier results, and it is also significantly different from 0 at the 90 per cent level in all three columns.

Finally, in Table 6.8 we consider the determinants of output variability. Here analytical work offers competing predictions: as noted above, some

Table 6.5 Effect of transparency on inflation variability (instrumental variables pooled regressions)†

	I	II	III	IV	V	VI
Constant	7.59*	7.41*	7.43*	1.45	6.94*	1.66
	(7.44)	(7.93)	(7.21)	(1.36)	(7.73)	(1.64)
Transparency index	−1.23*	−1.27*	−1.00*	−0.30	−1.04*	−0.49*
	(−5.79)	(−5.54)	(−4.69)	(−1.66)	(−4.67)	(−2.69)
Openness		0.01			0.01*	0.00
		(1.51)			(2.24)	(0.21)
Financial depth			−0.01*		−0.02*	0.01*
			(−2.60)		(−3.18)	(2.12)
Past inflation				29.36*		29.67*
				(6.17)		(6.18)
Number of observations	579	546	562	578	524	531
Sum of sq. res.	19,561	19,452	19,452	8,216	19,242	8,131

Notes:
1. Dependent variable is inflation variability, which is the standard deviation of the inflation rate for 12 months.
2. Transparency is the fitted value of transparency from the first-stage regression on constant and rule of law.
† *t*-statistics in parentheses; * denotes significance at 5%.

models suggest that greater policy transparency should be associated with more stability, because it allows the public to adjust more quickly to policy actions; others, on the other hand, suggest that a more transparent monetary policy may be associated with more output volatility, because it prevents the authorities from using policy as actively to offset output fluctuations (policy actions instead feeding through more quickly into inflation, and hence deterring policy activism), or because coordination externalities cause individuals to attach excessive weight to the public signal. A limitation of these results is that we have only annual data on output for our broad sample of countries, forcing us to measure the output variable as the standard deviation of the growth rate over the most recent three-year period.[36] Be that as it may, the results are consistent with a negative impact of monetary policy transparency on output variability.[37]

CONCLUSION

Greater transparency in central bank operations is the most dramatic recent change in the conduct of monetary policy. We understand it as a response to other changes in the monetary policy environment. It is a way of ensuring the accountability of policy makers when the traditional

Table 6.6   *Effect of transparency on inflation persistence (instrumental variables pooled regressions)*[†]

	I	II	III	IV	V	VI
Constant	0.79*	0.82*	0.79*	0.77*	0.80*	0.79*
	(18.90)	(18.80)	(18.27)	(14.91)	(17.72)	(15.74)
Transparency index	−0.02*	−0.02	−0.01	−0.02	−0.01	−0.01
	(−2.05)	(−1.90)	(−0.45)	(−1.57)	(−0.91)	(−0.81)
Openness		−0.01			0.01	0.01
		(−0.79)			(0.28)	(0.18)
Financial depth			−0.01*		−0.01	−0.01
			(−2.26)		(−1.93)	(−1.73)
Past inflation				0.10		0.06
				(0.65)		(0.40)
Number of observations	568	538	552	567	524	523
Sum of sq. res.	49	44	46	49	42	42

Notes:
1. Dependent variable is inflation persistence, which is the estimated coefficient of the regression where monthly inflation data is used and inflation is regressed on the inflation in the previous month.
2. Transparency is the fitted value of transparency from the first-stage regression on a constant and rule of law.
†   *t*-statistics in parentheses; * denotes significance at 5%.

mechanisms for doing so – public monitoring of compliance with an exchange rate commitment and direct supervision by a government with formal control – are in decline, reflecting the shift to flexible exchange rates and central bank independence.

In this chapter we have presented new information on the extent of the trend and its effects. The trend is general: a large number of central banks have moved in the direction of greater transparency in recent years. The question is whether it will prove durable or be a passing phase. In part, the answer depends on the consequences. Our preliminary analysis suggests broadly favourable, but relatively weak impacts on inflation and output variability. If institutional arrangements that produce favourable results retain public support, then this suggests that the trend towards greater monetary policy transparency is here to stay.

The other way of approaching this question is to ask whether the changes in the larger policy environment that precipitated the move towards greater transparency in monetary policy might themselves be rolled back. We see the abandonment of pegged exchange rates as a response to financial liberalization, and greater central bank independence as a way of insulating the

Table 6.7 *Alternative specification for inflation persistence (instrumental variables pooled regressions)*[†]

	I	II	III
Constant	0.01*	0.02*	0.02*
	(3.77)	(3.19)	(3.71)
Lagged inflation	1.00*	1.00*	0.92*
	(4.28)	(4.26)	(4.05)
Lagged inflation* transparency	−0.16	−0.16	−0.15
	(−1.92)	(−1.93)	(−1.85)
Openness		−0.00	0.00*
		(−0.45)	(2.45)
Financial depth			−0.00*
			(−4.96)
DW test	1.42	1.42	1.40
R-squared	0.48	0.47	0.49

Notes:
1. Dependent variable is inflation.
2. Transparency is the fitted value of transparency from the first-stage regression on a constant and rule of law.
[†] t-statistics in parentheses; * denotes significance at 5%.
Transparency is instrumented as described in the text.

Table 6.8 *Effects of transparency on output variability (instrumental variables pooled regressions)*[†]

	I	II	III	IV	V	VI
Constant	3.81*	3.63*	3.76*	3.38*	3.52*	3.18*
	(10.81)	(9.00)	(10.48)	(9.00)	(8.38)	(7.35)
Transparency index	−0.33*	−0.41*	−0.38*	−0.27*	−0.39*	−0.36*
	(−4.51)	(−5.66)	(−4.46)	(−3.50)	(−4.49)	(−4.06)
Openness		0.01*			0.01*	0.00*
		(2.98)			(2.52)	(2.21)
Financial depth			0.01*		0.01	0.01
			(1.87)		(0.51)	(1.11)
Past inflation				2.24*		2.36*
				(3.48)		(3.29)
Number of obs.	648	606	626	618	586	566
Sum of sq. res.	3181	2987	3064	2946	2906	2748

Notes:
1. Dependent variable is output variability.
2. Output variability is computed as the standard deviation of the annual GDP growth rate over the period $t-2$ to t (where t denotes the current year).
3. Transparency is the fitted value of transparency from the first-stage regression on a constant and rule of law.
[†] t-statistics in parentheses; * denotes significance at 5%.

conduct of monetary policy from short-term political pressures in democracies. If financial globalization and political democratization are here to stay, then so too is greater transparency in the conduct of monetary policy.

NOTES

1. We thank Petra Geraats, Pierre Siklos and the participants of the Cournot Centre conference, 'Central Banks as Economic Institutions' held 30 November and 1 December 2006 in Paris, for helpful comments.
2. Here we use transparency to mean information disclosure. This minimal definition leaves unspecified whether or not the information set has more than one dimension and, if so, which dimension is relevant. For more on this, see below.
3. Meaning that changes had an immediate impact on market conditions.
4. And, increasingly, on other portfolio aggregates that were deemed relevant to the prospective future maintenance of convertibility.
5. Eichengreen and Razo-Garcia (2006) show that the share of soft pegs in all exchange rate regimes fell from about 70 per cent in 1990 to 45 per cent in 2004. Soft peggers move to hard pegs (including the monetary union in the case of European countries) and floats in a ratio of 3 to 4. Note that, since the euro floats against other currencies, one would want to group the members of the Eurozone together with the floating-rate countries for purposes of this argument.
6. The standard approach to this problem focuses on time inconsistency and inflationary bias when the central bank adopts the objective function of the median voter. Independence is then a way of permitting the appointment of central bankers who are more conservative than the median voter as a way of offsetting the inflationary bias that results from inability to precommit. There are other models, however, that also suggest a link from democratization to central bank independence, such as models of the political business cycle suggesting that a politically dependent central bank may feel pressure to inefficiently loosen monetary policy in the run-up to elections.
7. On these arguments, see Geraats (2005) and below.
8. To what extent this desire to avoid excessive volatility and avoid destabilizing financial markets, while advancing the central bank's other goals, implies the desirability of greater transparency is a disputed issue, as we shall see below.
9. In a similar set-up, Grüner (2002) demonstrates that if the union is sufficiently risk averse, not only the level, but also the variance of inflation may turn out to be lower as a consequence of greater uncertainty about the central bank's objectives.
10. More comprehensive surveys of the theoretical literature include Geraats (2002b) and Carpenter (2004).
11. Examples of studies that attempt to estimate the impact of greater disclosure include Muller and Zelmer (1999) for Canada, Chadha and Noland (2001) for the United Kingdom, Haldane and Read (2000) for the United Kingdom and the United States, and Kuttner and Posen (2000) for the United States, Germany and Japan. There is a related literature that examines the association of having an inflation-targeting regime with various measures of economic performance. This is a good point at which to observe that transparency is generally regarded as integral to the effective implementation of inflation targeting, although countries conventionally characterized as inflation targeters tend to differ in exactly how transparent they are, and inflation targeting as conventionally defined entails more than simply the disclosure of information. Thus, while the concepts overlap, they are distinct. It follows that empirical indices of whether or not a central bank targets inflation and how transparent it is, while correlated, measure different things.
12. The index covers the 1998–2002 period.

13. Although they group these into three broad categories rather than five.
14. In an unpublished companion paper (De Haan and Amtembrink, 2002), two of the authors apply a similar methodology to 15 countries.
15. Siklos takes an unweighted average of 11 subindices, whereas Eiffjinger and Geraats take an unweighted average of five. Eiffjinger and Geraats distinguish three equally-weighted aspects of each of their five dimensions, making for a total of 15 questions. Siklos distinguishes subtopics in the case of three of his 11 questions.
16. That said, it is clear that one should not put too much weight on empirical results when there are only nine observations and nothing is done to control for other country characteristics and the possibility of reverse causality.
17. In Eijffinger and Geraats (2004) the authors show that there is no relationship between their index for nine central banks and subsequent economic performance.
18. Not surprisingly, it does not hold for countries with pegged exchange rates, for which inflation is largely determined by foreign conditions.
19. Rather than focusing on a small handful of dimensions, as in Fry et al.
20. Starting in 1998 facilitates comparisons of our measure with that of Fry et al. Adding this time dimension was particularly challenging, since many central bank websites describe current practice, but not that of prior years. For this we had to rely mainly on published documents. We were able to access a relatively complete run of these on the basis of holdings in the University of California and Joint IMF–World Bank libraries. We are grateful to the staff of the Joint Bank–Fund library for granting us access to their collection.
21. Recall that there are more countries than there are central banks, given the existence of monetary unions.
22. There are a few additional omissions, reflecting cases where we were not able to glean information from a central bank's website or its publications, as well as in cases where the central bank provides this information only in the language of its own country, and we could not translate it. Among the omissions from our sample are Bolivia, Ecuador, Chad, Iran and Afghanistan. We are aware that this creates a form of sampling bias: we tend to oversample more transparent central banks. There exist econometric corrections for this bias (involving strong assumptions), although we have not implemented these yet. Our defence is that the number of consequential omissions is relatively slight.
23. Up from 47 in 1998.
24. Up from 2 in 1998, the addition being Sweden.
25. It is not surprising that central bank staff, when asked their subjective opinion of the transparency of their own institution, rank it higher than we rate it on the basis of published information.
26. The other two cases where our measure of transparency is most dramatically above that of Fry et al. are Mauritius and Bahrain.
27. The most recent year for which all the ancillary variables are available is 2004. The results for individual years show the same patterns, but lower levels of significance. This makes sense, in so far as changes in central banking practices develop gradually and are unlikely to respond to changes in economic or political conditions in a single year; looking at longer-period averages thus increases the signal-to-noise ratio.
28. Readers may be concerned that the exchange rate regime is endogenous – that countries with experience with monetary policy transparency may be better able to operate regimes of greater flexibility. Fortunately, dropping the exchange rate regime variable left the other results unchanged.
29. The other variables do not approach statistical significance at conventional confidence levels. For what they are worth, the point estimates suggest that central banks of countries with a history of inflation tend to be more transparent, presumably as part of a credibility-building strategy. This is not something that would have been anticipated from the contrast between transparency in advanced and developing countries. Central banks in more open economies appear to be less transparent; again, this is not something that we would have anticipated from high-profile cases such as New Zealand or Sweden. We shall have more to say about these correlations below.

30. When we include multiple political variables (as we do in additional regressions available on request), significance levels vary, but it is voice and accountability and government efficiency that are most often significant at standard confidence levels.

31. That is, while it is not hard to come up with an argument for why the transparency of monetary policy should affect inflation, financial markets or the development of trade, it is harder to concoct a story for why it should have a first-order effect on, say, rule of law, which depends on the larger political and social setting and is the product of a country's history. It can thus be argued that such political variables satisfy the two criteria for a valid instrument: exogeneity and correlation with the explanatory variable of interest.

32. The standard Hausman and Breusch–Pagan tests reject random effects and simple pooling in favour of fixed effects (the Hausman test statistic is reported at the foot of the tables). See also the discussion below.

33. We find the same thing when we include different political variables, individually or in combination.

34. We can also analyse the determinants of the components of the transparency index to gain further insight into exactly how practice responds to these economic and political factors. Not surprisingly, political transparency is a positive function of political development and stability (whether this is measured by rule of law, political turnover, voice and accountability or government efficiency). The cross-section regressions for 2004 also suggest, more surprisingly, that political transparency appears to decline with financial depth. Regressions for other years and for the period averages indicate, however, that this result is not robust. Economic transparency (the public disclosure of data, the policy model and forecasts) is again positively related to political development and stability. It is positively related to financial development, as one would expect. More surprisingly, it appears to be less present in more open economies, other things being equal. Procedural transparency (the release of minutes and votes) is related, again positively, only to political development and stability. In contrast, policy transparency (prompt announcement and comprehensive explanation of policy decisions) is greater in countries with more stable and open political systems, but less in more open economies, or so the regressions on the period averages suggest. Finally, it would appear that operational transparency (release of information about disturbances, control errors, and so on) is again greater in countries with more stable political systems, but also in countries with more developed financial markets, while there is less in more open economies. These results are available from the authors on request.

35. Results using alternative instrument lists are discussed below and are available from the authors on request.

36. The current calendar year and its two immediate predecessors.

37. We also conducted a number of robustness checks. For example, we re-estimated the equations using fixed effects; doing so, and relying exclusively on the time-series variation in the data, produces weaker evidence of real effects of transparency. Rather than taking an unweighted average of our 15 dimensions of transparency, we constructed their first principal component and used its instrumented value as the transparency-related explanatory variable in Tables 6.5–8. Again the results are somewhat weaker than before. As noted above, we alternatively used different political variables, or combinations of political variables, as instruments for transparency in Tables 6.5–8. Doing so did not weaken the results for output variability in Table 6.8, although some alternative combinations of instruments produced lower levels of significance in Tables 6.5–7.

REFERENCES

Backus, David and John Driffill (1995), 'Inflation and reputation', *American Economic Review*, **75**, pp. 530–38.

Ball, Lawrence and Niamh Sheridan (2005), 'Does inflation targeting matter?', in Ben Bernanke and Michael Woodford (eds), *The Inflation-Targeting Debate*, Chicago, IL: University of Chicago Press, pp. 249–78.

Barro, Robert and Roger Gordon (1983), 'A positive theory of monetary policy in a natural rate model', *Journal of Political Economy*, **91**, pp. 589–610.

Bini-Smaghi, Lorenzo and Daniel Gros (2001), 'Is the ECB sufficiently accountable and transparent?', European Network of Economic Policy Research Institutes Working Paper no. 7 (September).

Carpenter, Seth (2004), 'Transparency and monetary policy: what does the academic literature tell policymakers?', Finance and Economics Discussion Series 2004-35, Washington, DC: Board of Governors of the Federal Reserve System.

Cecchetti, Steven and Stefan Krause (2001), 'Central bank structure, policy efficiency and macroeconomic performance: exploring the empirical relationships', NBER Working Paper 8354 (July), Cambridge, MA.

Chadha, Jagjit and Charles Nolan (2001), 'Inflation targeting, transparency and interest rate volatility: ditching "monetary mystique" in the UK', *Journal of Macroeconomics*, **23**, pp. 349–66.

Chortareas, Georgios, David Stasavage and Gabriel Sterne (2001), 'Does it pay to be transparent? International evidence from central bank forecasts', Bank of England Working Paper 143, London.

De Haan, Jakob and Fabian Amtenbrink (2002), 'A non-transparent European Central Bank: who is to blame?', paper presented at the conference on Monetary Policy Transparency, Bank of England, London (May).

De Haan, Jakob, Fabian Amtenbrink and Sandra Waller (2004), 'The transparency and credibility of the European Central Bank', *Journal of Common Market Studies*, **42**, pp. 775–94.

Demertzis, Maria and Andrew Hughes Hallett (2003), 'Central bank transparency in theory and practice', unpublished manuscript, Netherlands Bank and Vanderbilt University (January).

Eichengreen, Barry (1996), *Globalizing Capital: A History of the International Monetary System*, Princeton, NJ: Princeton University Press.

Eichengreen, Barry and Raul Razo-Garcia (2006), 'The International Monetary System in the last and next twenty years', *Economic Policy*, **47**, pp. 393–442.

Eijffinger, Sylvester and Petra Geraats (2004), 'How transparent are central banks?', Cambridge University Working Papers in Economics no. 0411 (January), UK.

Eijffinger, Sylvester and Petra Geraats (2006), 'How transparent are central banks?', *European Journal of Political Economy*, **22**, pp. 1–22.

Faust, Jon and Lars Svensson (2001), 'Transparency and credibility: monetary policy with unobservable goals', *International Economic Review*, **42**, pp. 369–97.

Fry, Maxwell, Deanne Julius, Lavan Mahadeva, Sandra Roger and Gabriel Sterne (2000), 'Key issues in the choice of monetary policy framework', in Lavan Mahadeva and Gabriel Sterne (eds), *Monetary Policy Frameworks in a Global Context*, London: Routledge, pp. 1–216.

Geraats, Petra M. (2002a), 'Why adopt transparency? The publication of central bank forecasts', unpublished manuscript, University of Cambridge (July).

Geraats, Petra M. (2002b), 'Central bank transparency', *Economic Journal*, **112**, pp. 532–65.

Geraats, Petra M. (2005), 'Political pressures and monetary mystique', Cambridge University Working Papers in Economics no. 0557 (December), UK.

Grüner, Hans-Peter (2002), 'How much should central banks talk? A new argument', *Economics Letters*, **77**, pp. 195–8.

Haldane, Andrew and Vicky Read (2000), 'Monetary policy surprises and the yield curve', Bank of England Working Paper 106, London.

Jensen, Henrik (2002), 'Optimal degrees of transparency in monetary policy-making', *Scandinavian Journal of Economics*, **104**, pp. 399–424.

Kaufmann, Daniel, Aart Kraay and Massimo Mastruzzi (2005), 'Governance matters IV: Governance indicators for 1996–2004', unpublished manuscript, World Bank, Washington, DC (May).

Kuttner, Kenneth and Adam Posen (2000), 'Inflation, monetary transparency, and G3 exchange rate volatility', Working Paper 00–6, Institute for International Economics, Washington, DC (July).

Mishkin, Frederic (2004), 'Why the Fed should adopt inflation targeting', *International Finance*, **7**, pp. 117–27.

Morris, Stephen and Hyun Song Shin (2002), 'The social value of public information', *American Economic Review*, **92**, pp. 1521–34.

Muller, Philippe and Murray Zelmer (1999), 'Greater transparency in monetary policy: impact on financial markets', Bank of Canada Technical Report 86, Ottawa: Bank of Canada (August).

Reinhart, Carmen and Kenneth Rogoff (2004), 'The modern history of exchange rate arrangements: a reinterpretation', *Quarterly Journal of Economics*, **119**, pp. 1–49.

Reinhart, Carmen, Kenneth Rogoff and Miguel Savastano (2003), 'Debt intolerance', *Brookings Papers on Economic Activity*, **1**, pp. 1–74.

Siklos, Pierre (2002), *The Changing Face of Central Banking: Evolutionary Trends Since World War II*, Cambridge and New York: Cambridge University Press.

Sørensen, Jan R. (1991), 'Political uncertainty and macroeconomic performance', *Economics Letters*, **37**, pp. 4377–81.

Svensson, Lars (2006), 'The social value of public information: Morris and Shin (2002) is actually pro-transparency, not con', *American Economic Review*, **96**, pp. 448–52.

DATA APPENDIX

Construction of the Transparency Index

The index is the sum of the scores for answers to the 15 questions below (min = 0, max = 15).

1. *Political transparency* Political transparency refers to openness about policy objectives. This comprises a formal statement of objectives, including an explicit prioritization in case of multiple goals, a quantification of the primary objective(s), and explicit institutional arrangements.

(a) Is there a formal statement of the objective(s) of monetary policy, with an explicit prioritization in case of multiple objectives?
No formal objective(s) = 0.
Multiple objectives without prioritization = 1/2.
One primary objective, or multiple objectives with explicit priority = 1.

(b) Is there a quantification of the primary objective(s)?
No = 0.
Yes = 1.

(c) Are there explicit contracts or other similar institutional arrangements between the monetary authorities and the government?
No central bank contracts or other institutional arrangements = 0.
Central bank without explicit instrument independence or contract = 1/2.
Central bank with explicit instrument independence or central bank contract although possibly subject to an explicit override procedure = 1.

2. *Economic transparency* Economic transparency focuses on the economic information that is used for monetary policy. This includes economic data, the model of the economy that the central bank employs to construct forecasts or evaluate the impact of its decisions, and the internal forecasts (model-based or judgemental) that the central bank relies on.

(a) Is the basic economic data relevant for the conduct of monetary policy publicly available? (The focus is on the following five variables: money supply, inflation, GDP, unemployment rate and capacity utilization.)
Quarterly time series for at most two out of the five variables = 0.
Quarterly time series for three or four out of the five variables = 1/2.
Quarterly time series for all five variables = 1.

(b) Does the central bank disclose the macroeconomic model(s) it uses for policy analysis?
No = 0.
Yes = 1.

(c) Does the central bank regularly publish its own macroeconomic forecasts?
No numerical central bank forecasts for inflation and output = 0.
Numerical central bank forecasts for inflation and/or output published at less than quarterly frequency = 1/2.
Quarterly numerical central bank forecasts for inflation and output for the medium term (one to two years ahead), specifying the assumptions about the policy instrument (conditional or unconditional forecasts) = 1.

3. *Procedural transparency* Procedural transparency is about the way monetary policy decisions are made.

(a) Does the central bank provide an explicit policy rule or strategy that describes its monetary policy framework?
No = 0.
Yes = 1.

(b) Does the central bank give a comprehensive account of policy deliberations (or explanations in case of a single central banker) within a reasonable amount of time?
No, or only after a substantial lag (more than eight weeks) = 0.
Yes, comprehensive minutes (although not necessarily verbatim or attributed) or explanations (in case of a single central banker), including a discussion of backward-and-forward-looking arguments = 1.

(c) Does the central bank disclose how each decision on the level of its main operating instrument or target was reached?
No voting records, or only after substantial lag (more than eight weeks) = 0.
Non-attributed voting records = 1/2.
Individual voting records, or decision by single central banker = 1.

4. *Policy transparency* Policy transparency means prompt disclosure of policy decisions, together with an explanation of the decision, and an explicit policy inclination or indication of likely future policy actions.

(a) Are decisions about adjustments to the main operating instrument or target announced promptly?

No, or only after the day of implementation = 0.
Yes, on the day of implementation = 1.

(b) Does the central bank provide an explanation when it announces policy decisions?
No = 0.
Yes, when policy decisions change, or only superficially = 1/2.
Yes, always and including forwarding-looking assessments = 1.

(c) Does the central bank disclose an explicit policy inclination after every policy meeting or an explicit indication of likely future policy actions (at least quarterly)?
No = 0.
Yes = 1.

5. *Operational transparency* Operational transparency concerns the implementation of the central bank's policy actions. It involves a discussion of control errors in achieving operating targets and (unanticipated) macroeconomic disturbances that affect the transmission of monetary policy. Furthermore, the evaluation of the macroeconomic outcomes of monetary policy in light of its objectives is included here as well.

(a) Does the central bank regularly evaluate to what extent its main policy operating targets (if any) have been achieved?
No, or not very often (at less than annual frequency) = 0.
Yes, but without providing explanations for significant deviations = 1/2.
Yes, accounting for significant deviations from target (if any); or, (nearly) perfect control over main operating instrument/target = 1.

(b) Does the central bank regularly provide information on (unanticipated) macroeconomic disturbances that affect the policy transmission process?
No, or not very often = 0.
Yes, but only through short-term forecasts or analysis of current macroeconomic developments (at least quarterly) = 1/2.
Yes, including a discussion of past forecast errors (at least annually) = 1.

(c) Does the central bank regularly provide an evaluation of the policy outcome in light of its macroeconomic objectives?
No, or not very often (at less than annual frequency) = 0.
Yes, but superficially = 1/2.
Yes, with an explicit account of the contribution of monetary policy in meeting the objectives = 1.

Table 6A.1   Central bank transparency, by region

	1998	1999	2000	2001	2002	2003	2004	2005
AFRICA	2.2	2.2	2.5	3.0	3.2	3.5	3.5	3.9
Eastern Africa	*1.7*	*1.8*	*1.9*	*2.4*	*2.6*	*2.6*	*2.6*	*2.8*
Ethiopia	1	1	1	1	1	1	1	1
Kenya	2	2	2.5	4.5	4.5	4.5	4.5	4.5
Malawi	0.5	0.5	0.5	2.5	2.5	2.5	2.5	2.5
Mauritius	3.5	3.5	3.5	3.5	5	5	5	5
Rwanda	1.5	1.5	1.5	1.5	1.5	1.5	1.5	2.5
Uganda	2	2.5	2.5	2.5	2.5	2.5	2.5	2.5
Zambia	1.5	1.5	1.5	1.5	1.5	1.5	1.5	1.5
Northern Africa	*1.4*	*1.4*	*1.6*	*1.6*	*2.0*	*2.0*	*2.0*	*2.3*
Egypt	1	1	1	1	1	1	1	2
Libyan Arab Jamahiriya	1	1	1	1	1	1	1	1
Sudan	1	1	2	2	2	2	2	2
Tunisia	2.5	2.5	2.5	2.5	4	4	4	4
Southern Africa	*3.0*	*3.0*	*3.7*	*5.0*	*5.3*	*5.7*	*6.0*	*7.2*
Lesotho	1	1	1.5	1.5	1.5	2.5	2.5	4.5
Namibia	4	4	4.5	4.5	5.5	5.5	6.5	8
South Africa	4	4	5	9	9	9	9	9
Western Africa	*2.7*	*2.7*	*2.7*	*2.8*	*2.8*	*3.5*	*3.5*	*3.5*
Ghana	3	3	3	3	3	5	5	5
Nigeria	3.5	3.5	3.5	4	4	4	4	4
Sierra Leone	1.5	1.5	1.5	1.5	1.5	1.5	1.5	1.5

AMERICAS	3.8	4.0	4.2	4.5	4.5	4.9	5.2	5.2
Latin America and Caribbean	2.7	2.8	2.9	3.4	3.7	3.8	4.0	4.0
East Caribbean	2.5	2.5	3	5.5	5.5	5.5	5.5	5.5
Aruba	0.5	0.5	0.5	0.5	0.5	0.5	0.5	0.5
Bahamas	4.5	4.5	4.5	4.5	4.5	4.5	4.5	4.5
Barbados	2.5	3	3	3	3	3	3	3
Cuba	2.5	2.5	2.5	2.5	2.5	2.5	2.5	2.5
Jamaica	3	3	3	4.5	6.5	6.5	6.5	6.5
Trinidad and Tobago	3.5	3.5	3.5	3.5	3.5	4	5.5	5.5
Central America	2.4	2.4	2.4	3.0	3.0	3.1	4.1	4.1
Belize	2	2	2	3.5	3.5	3.5	3.5	3.5
El Salvador	2	2	2	3	3	3	3	3
Guatemala	1.5	1.5	1.5	1.5	1.5	1.5	4.5	4.5
Mexico	4	4	4	4	4	4.5	5.5	5.5
South America	3.9	4.3	4.9	5.1	5.7	6.1	6.1	6.1
Argentina	3	3	3	3	3	5.5	5.5	5.5
Brazil	3.5	5.5	9	9	9	9	9	9
Chile	7	7	7.5	7.5	7.5	7.5	7.5	7.5
Colombia	2.5	3.5	3.5	3.5	6	6	6	6
Guyana	1.5	1.5	1.5	1.5	1.5	1.5	1.5	1.5
Peru	4.5	4.5	4.5	6	8	8	8	8
Uruguay	5	5	5	5	5	5	5	5
North America	6.3	6.7	6.7	6.7	6.7	6.7	6.7	6.7
Bermuda	1	1	1	1	1	1	1	1
Canada	10.5	10.5	10.5	10.5	10.5	10.5	10.5	10.5
USA	7.5	8.5	8.5	8.5	8.5	8.5	8.5	8.5

Table 6A.1 (continued)

	1998	1999	2000	2001	2002	2003	2004	2005
OCEANIA	5.4	6.4	6.4	6.8	7.3	7.3	7.4	7.4
Australia and New Zealand	*9.3*	*10.5*	*10.5*	*10.5*	*11.3*	*11.3*	*11.3*	*11.3*
Australia	8	8	8	8	9	9	9	9
New Zealand	10.5	13	13	13	13.5	13.5	13.5	13.5
Melanesia	*1.5*	*2.3*	*2.3*	*3.1*	*3.3*	*3.3*	*3.5*	*3.5*
Fiji	1.5	4.5	4.5	4.5	4.5	4.5	4.5	4.5
Papua New Guinea	1	1	1	3.5	4	4	5	5
Solomon Islands	2	2	2	2	2	2	2	2
Vanuatu	1.5	1.5	1.5	2.5	2.5	2.5	2.5	2.5
ASIA	3.0	3.2	3.5	3.8	4.3	4.6	4.9	5.1
Central Asia	*2.7*	*2.7*	*2.7*	*3.0*	*3.0*	*2.7*	*3.3*	*4.0*
Kazakhstan	3.5	3.5	3.5	3.5	3.5	3.5	3.5	5.5
Kyrgyzstan	3	3	3	4	4	3	5	5
Tajikistan	1.5	1.5	1.5	1.5	1.5	1.5	1.5	1.5
Eastern Asia	*4.6*	*4.8*	*5.2*	*5.2*	*5.7*	*6.3*	*6.6*	*6.6*
China	1	1	1	1	1.5	4.5	4.5	4.5
Hong Kong	5	6	6	6	7	7	7	7
Korea	6.5	6.5	8	8.5	8.5	8.5	8.5	8.5
Japan	8	8	8.5	8	8	8	9.5	9.5
Mongolia	2.5	2.5	2.5	2.5	3.5	3.5	3.5	3.5

Southern Asia	2.3	2.3	2.3	2.4	3.0	3.5	3.9	3.9
Bangladesh	0	0	0	0.5	0.5	3	3.5	3.5
Bhutan	2	2	2	2	3.5	3.5	3.5	3.5
India	2	2	2	2	2	2	2	2
Pakistan	2.5	2.5	2.5	2.5	2.5	2.5	3.5	3.5
Sri Lanka	5	5	5	5	6.5	6.5	7	7
South East Asia	3.0	3.9	4.9	5.5	6.4	7.1	7.3	7.5
Indonesia	3	4.5	4.5	4.5	4.5	7	8	8
Malaysia	4	4	5	5	5	5	5	5
Philippines	3.5	5	5	6	10	10	10	10
Singapore	2.5	4	4	5.5	4.5	5.5	5.5	6.5
Thailand	2	2	6	6.5	8	8	8	8
Western Asia	2.3	2.4	2.5	2.8	3.2	3.2	3.3	3.4
Armenia	4	4	4	4	4	4	4	4
Bahrain	3	3	3	3	3	3	3	3
Cyprus	2.5	2.5	2.5	3.5	6	6	6.5	6.5
Georgia	3	3	3	3	3	3.5	3.5	3.5
Iraq	2	2	2	2	2	2	2.5	2.5
Israel	5.5	7	7.5	8.5	8.5	8.5	8.5	8.5
Jordan	1	1	1	1	1	1	1.5	2
Kuwait	1	1		1	1	1	1	1
Oman	1.5	1.5	1.5	1.5	1.5	1.5	1.5	1.5
Qatar	3	3	3	3	3	3	3	3
Saudi Arabia	1	1	1	1	1	1	1	1
Turkey	3	2	4	5.5	8.5	8.5	8.5	8.5
United Arab Emirates	1	1	1	1	1	1	1	1
Yemen	1	1	1	1	1	1	1	1

Table 6A.1 (continued)

	1998	1999	2000	2001	2002	2003	2004	2005
EUROPE	5.2	5.5	5.8	6.2	6.7	7.1	7.4	7.5
Eastern Europe	*3.4*	*3.9*	*4.3*	*4.5*	*5.4*	*5.5*	*6.0*	*6.4*
Belarus	1.5	3.5	5	5	5	5	5	5
Bulgaria	4.5	4.5	4.5	4.5	4.5	4.5	6	6.5
Czech Republic	9	10	10	10	10.5	11.5	11.5	11.5
Hungary	3	3	4.5	5.5	8	8	8	9.5
Poland	3	5	5	6.5	6.5	6.5	7	8
Republic of Moldova	4	4	4	5	5	5	5	5
Romania	1.5	1.5	1.5	1.5	4.5	4.5	6.5	6.5
Russian Federation	1.5	1.5	1.5	1.5	1.5	1.5	2.5	2.5
Slovakia	4	4	4.5	3.5	5.5	5.5	5.5	6
Ukraine	2	2	2	2	3	3	3	3
Northern Europe	*6.4*	*6.6*	*6.9*	*7.2*	*7.6*	*7.8*	*7.8*	*7.9*
Denmark	5	5	5	5	5	6	6	6
Estonia	5	5	5.5	5.5	5.5	5.5	5	6
Iceland	5.5	5.5	7	7	7.5	7.5	7.5	7.5
Latvia	6	6	6	6	6	6	6	6
Lithuania	4	4	4	4.5	4.5	4.5	4.5	4.5
Norway	6	6	6	7.5	7.5	7.5	8	8
Sweden	9	9	10	10	13	13	13	13
United Kingdom	11	12	12	12	12	12	12	12

Southern Europe	*3.8*	*3.8*	*3.9*	*4.1*	*4.8*	*5.5*	*5.8*	*5.8*
Albania	3.5	3.5	3.5	3.5	3.5	5	6	6
Croatia	1.5	1.5	1.5	2.5	2.5	2.5	2.5	2.5
Malta	5	5	5.5	5.5	5.5	7	7	7
Slovenia	5	5	5	5	7.5	7.5	7.5	7.5
Western Europe	*7.3*	*7.8*	*8.0*	*9.0*	*9.0*	*9.5*	*10.0*	*10.0*
Switzerland	6	7	7.5	8	8	9	9.5	9.5
European Union	8.5	8.5	8.5	10	10	10	10.5	10.5

Table 6A.2 Components of the index for the 14 countries with extreme values

	TI	1a	1b	1c	2a	2b	2c	3a	3b	3c	4a	4b	4c	5a	5b	5c
New Zealand	13.5	1	1	1	1	1	1	1	1	1	1	0.5	1	1	0.5	0.5
Sweden	13	0.5	1	0.5	1	1	1	1	1	1	1	0.5	1	1	1	0.5
UK	12	1	1	1	0.5	1	1	1	1	1	1	0.5	0	1	0.5	0.5
Czech Republic	11.5	1	1	1	1	1	1	1	1	0.5	1	0.5	0	0	0.5	1
Canada	10.5	1	1	1	1	1	0.5	1	0	0	1	1	0	1	0.5	0.5
Euro Area	10.5	1	1	1	1	1	1	1	0	0	1	0.5	0	1	0.5	0.5
Philippines	10	1	1	1	1	0	1	1	1	0.5	1	0.5	0	0	0.5	0.5
Bermuda	1	0.5	0	0.5	0	0	0	0	0	0	0	0	0	0	0	0
Ethiopia	1	0.5	0	0.5	0	0	0	0	0	0	0	0	0	0	0	0
Kuwait	1	0.5	0	0.5	0	0	0	0	0	0	0	0	0	0	0	0
Libya	1	0.5	0	0.5	0	0	0	0	0	0	0	0	0	0	0	0
Yemen	1	0.5	0	0.5	0	0	0	0	0	0	0	0	0	0	0	0
Aruba	0.5	0	0	0	0	0	0	0	0	0	0	0	0	0	0	0
Saudi Arabia	0	0	0	0	0	0	0	0	0	0	0	0	0	0	0	0

Table 6A.3 Regional transparency index (weighted)

	1998	1999	2000	2001	2002	2003	2004	2005
Africa								
Eastern Africa	2.58	2.56	2.90	4.27	4.46	5.05	5.32	5.38
Northern Africa	1.83	1.91	2.08	2.85	3.06	3.10	3.03	3.00
Northern Africa	1.21	1.20	1.25	1.27	1.55	1.62	1.67	2.10
Southern Africa	3.98	3.98	4.97	8.84	8.86	8.87	8.90	8.95
Western Africa	3.37	3.38	3.42	3.86	3.84	4.08	4.08	4.07
Americas								
Latin America and Caribbean	7.02	8.04	8.20	8.20	8.30	8.37	8.43	8.43
Central America	2.84	2.88	3.14	4.62	4.94	5.13	5.54	5.54
South America	3.84	3.86	3.88	3.90	3.89	4.36	5.41	5.41
North America	3.59	4.71	6.67	6.60	7.63	7.94	7.94	7.98
North America	7.70	8.63	8.64	8.63	8.63	8.65	8.65	8.66
Oceania								
Australia and New Zealand	8.22	8.54	8.51	8.56	9.51	9.54	9.55	9.56
Australia and New Zealand	8.32	8.62	8.59	8.62	9.57	9.59	9.60	9.61
Melanesia	1.21	2.19	2.10	3.69	4.02	4.04	4.61	4.62
Asia								
Central Asia	5.60	5.75	6.20	5.81	5.90	6.48	7.16	7.08
Eastern Asia	3.36	3.35	3.37	3.44	3.44	3.38	3.48	5.33
Southern Asia	6.51	6.60	7.04	6.47	6.48	7.16	8.05	7.89
South East Asia	1.98	1.98	1.99	2.02	2.06	2.23	2.38	2.38
Western Asia	2.89	3.80	4.91	5.40	6.05	7.06	7.39	7.54
Western Asia	2.59	2.46	3.04	3.52	4.34	4.47	4.56	5.03
Europe								
Eastern Europe	8.27	8.57	8.58	9.60	9.70	9.74	10.10	10.02
Northern Europe	2.82	3.71	3.62	3.98	4.50	4.53	5.05	5.22
Northern Europe	9.78	10.49	10.62	10.74	11.07	11.12	11.18	11.13
Southern Europe	3.37	3.46	3.50	3.87	4.89	5.12	5.17	5.13
Western Europe	8.40	8.44	8.46	9.92	9.92	9.96	10.46	10.46

7. Global imbalances: origins, consequences and possible resolutions

Takatoshi Ito[1]

INTRODUCTION

The international financial system shared by industrialized countries has evolved through many phases in the last two centuries: the silver standard, the gold standard, competitive devaluation, the Bretton Woods system, the managed float regime, and the free-floating exchange rate. Exchange rate behaviour under the free-floating system from 1973 on was not what its advocates had predicted, nor was it truly free from intervention. The US dollar crisis of 1978 was reversed only through large-scale intervention by the United States and the issuance of foreign currency-denominated bonds (the so-called Carter bonds). The Plaza Agreement and other concerted interventions by the Group of Five in September 1985 helped depreciate the overvalued dollar. The Plaza Agreement was followed by the Louvre Accord of February 1987, which aimed at stabilizing exchange rates among the Group of Seven. The Group of Seven has since continued its efforts to manage exchange rates through policy coordination and communication with the markets whenever the monetary authorities of each country have judged the major exchange rates to be misbehaving.

In each international monetary regime, currency crises occurred in one form or another. During the gold standard system, parity with gold was so important that any adjustment tended to result in a political crisis. When the exchange rate is misaligned, overvalued, for example, the economy tends to fall into recession and deflation. Under the Bretton Woods system, the adjustment of the fixed exchange rate (to the US dollar) was permitted, but it was as difficult to do as under the gold standard. Several countries were forced to devalue their currencies under the Bretton Woods system, with or without loans from the International Monetary Fund (IMF).

Just before the collapse of the Bretton Woods system, advocates of the floating exchange rate system argued that the stigma of adjusting the exchange rate would disappear and that the exchange rate would automatically, most likely gradually, adjust to changes in macro fundamentals. The currency of a country with trade deficits would depreciate, and the trade account balance would be restored. Soon after the major currencies moved to the floating system in the spring of 1973, however, it became clear that the nominal exchange rate was much more volatile than any macro-based model could have predicted.

Although over the short term, movements (level and volatility) could not be explained with macro models, over the medium term, the exchange rate tended to move back to fundamental levels. Indeed, the process of medium-term trend and cyclical movements worked in line with macro models most of the time for most of the currencies, except on rare occasions when the exchange rate stayed way out of the range of what many considered normal. When the exchange rate remained too depreciated or too appreciated to restore the internal and external balances for a period of time, say a few years, the situation was called a 'misalignment'. Famous cases of exchange rate misalignment include the US dollar crisis of 1978, the US dollar appreciation of 1984–85, and the yen appreciation of 1994–95.

As capital accounts became liberalized, the ability of the exchange rate to equalize the current account became weaker. It became possible to finance current account deficits by capital inflows if investors, for various reasons, were willing to put money into the country by acquiring financial or real assets. In the case of emerging market countries, sustained deficits have usually ended up provoking a currency crisis.

In the 1990s, currency crises of a new type affected some emerging market economies such as Mexico, Thailand and other Asian countries, Russia, Brazil and Argentina; these were called capital account crises. These countries, which had fixed exchange rates and liberalized capital accounts, developed large current account deficits, and then experienced sudden, massive capital outflows. Once an exodus had started, it was difficult to stop.

The section that follows describes the problem of global imbalances while the third section explores their origins. The fourth section examines the view that global imbalances may continue for some time, and the fifth section proposes a possible way of resolving global imbalances without a global recession. The final section concludes.

GLOBAL BALANCE OR IMBALANCE?

The 'global imbalances' that have emerged since 2003 comprise the following four components:[2]

1. large US current account deficits;
2. large current account surpluses in China, other East Asian countries and oil-producing nations;
3. accumulation of foreign reserves among those surplus countries due to resistance to currency appreciation; and
4. large capital inflows to the United States and low interest rates worldwide.

Increasing US current account deficits have been financed by increasing capital inflows from current account surplus countries. The magnitude is large, reaching more than 6 per cent of GDP. The phenomenon is similar to the situation of emerging market economies that have suffered currency crises. The difference here is that the US dollar is a key currency, and the rest of the world seems to have an insatiable demand for US assets, especially US bonds.

Many of the current account surplus countries – mainly China, other East Asian countries and oil-producing nations – are intervening heavily in the exchange market to support the US dollar (preventing the exchange rate from appreciating too fast and too much), and their foreign reserves have increased accordingly. The motivation and intention of these countries in building up reserves is not clear. Do they want to keep the exchange rate more competitive in order to promote exports (and foreign reserve build-up as a byproduct)? Or, do they want to increase foreign reserves while the exchange rate is not too depreciated? The difference between the two may be subtle, but when one attempts to predict future behaviour, motivation and intentions become important. If export promotion is being seriously pursued, the behaviour may continue indefinitely. If the build-up of foreign reserves, up to a certain target level, is a main goal – possibly due to self-insurance against a currency crisis – then the build-up will stop when the target is reached.

As most foreign reserves are kept in US Treasuries, US dollars earned by current account surpluses and interventions by emerging market and oil-producing nations are recycled into US capital markets. Consequently, the US domestic interest rate has been kept relatively low. An economic boom in the United States has increased imports, and current account deficits have become even larger. Hence, current account surpluses in emerging market economies will be maintained, completing the cycle.

The value of the US dollar, when measured in real effective terms, has remained more or less stable, even with growing trade imbalances. Although the euro has greatly appreciated over the last few years, other currencies, most notably those in East Asia, have tended to be stable in relation to the US dollar.

This steady state of global imbalances is interesting. Many believe that the United States cannot maintain large current account deficits – 6–7 per cent of GDP – forever, and foreign reserves in East Asia may become saturated with US dollar assets. Sooner or later, fundamental imbalances will tip the scales. Some predict that this steady state will collapse either because the rest of the world may diversify its assets away from the US dollar, or because the US boom – especially the strong consumption boom fuelled by the housing boom – may end. So far, however, this has not happened.

Others argue differently. Dooley et al. (2003, 2004a,b,c, 2005a,b) assert that the steady state of imbalances can be called the 'Revived Bretton-Woods system' (BWII). Some Asian emerging market countries, most notably China, have experienced both capital inflows and current account surpluses. They limit currency appreciation, however, by intervening in the foreign exchange market so that their currency value in relation to the US dollar remains stable. Their policy is motivated by a mercantilist view towards keeping their export industries competitive in the global export market. Central banks, as well as private-sector investors outside the United States, have shown extreme resilience to holding increasing amounts of US dollar assets. No one has an incentive to deviate from this steady state, and the situation may persist indefinitely.

In this chapter, I take the view that the current state – large US current account deficits and large Chinese current account surpluses – is not sustainable, and that something will have to happen to correct global imbalances. What will it take to do this? This chapter considers ways of restoring balance in the world trading system and financial flows.

THE ORIGINS OF GLOBAL IMBALANCES

US Deficits

Between 2001 and 2005, US bilateral deficits of merchandise trade continued to grow. The major increases came from bilateral balances against China (by 119 billion dollars, a 143 per cent increase), the Organization for Petroleum Exporting Countries (OPEC) (by 53 billion dollars, a 134 per cent increase) and the European Union (EU) (by 38 billion dollars, a 71 per cent increase). Among EU countries, Germany stood out with a 22 billion dollar increase (74 per cent increase) during the same period. Modestly large changes occurred against Canada (24 billion dollars, or a 45 per cent increase), Mexico (20 billion dollars, or 67 per cent), Japan (14 billion dollars, or 20 per cent) and Malaysia (10 billion dollars, or 79 per cent).

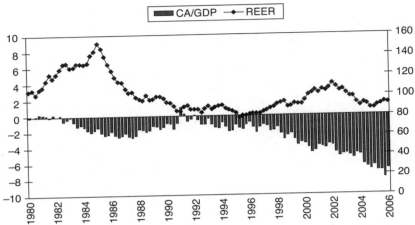

Figure 7.1   Current account/GDP real effective exchange rate, United States, 1980:I–2006:I

Bilateral deficits against Asian countries, other than China, Japan and Malaysia, were modest both in US dollars and percentage.

Figure 7.1 shows the current account deficits as a percentage of GDP and the real effective exchange rate of the United States over a somewhat longer period. In the 1980s, when the real effective exchange rate appreciated (1981–85), the current account deficits increased. The real effective exchange rate depreciated after it peaked during the first quarter of 1985. The decline of the US dollar from 1985 to 1990 resulted in the decline in the magnitude of current account deficits from 1987 to 1990, with some lag. The lag in the turnaround in the two variables was normal considering the delayed responses in prices and quantities.

The real effective exchange rate appreciated by more than 20 per cent from 1995 to 2001. This was accompanied by an increase in the current account deficits as a ratio of GDP. By 1999, the current account–GDP ratio exceeded the highest recorded in the 1980s, reaching 3 per cent. The real effective exchange rate peaked in 2002, then started to decline. The relationship between real effective exchange rates and current account deficits seems to have broken down since 2002.

In retrospect, the current account–GDP ratio worsened continuously, even with a moderate depreciation of the dollar from 1995 to 2005. Figure 7.2 shows the current account deficits (in billions of dollars) and net portfolio inflows (in billions of dollars). An increase in current account deficits does not seem to have been preceded by real effective exchange rate appreciation, nor was it followed by dollar depreciation. Why did the current account movement become independent from the exchange rate

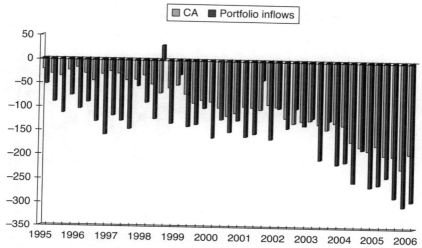

Figure 7.2 *US current accounts and portfolio inflows*

movement? One clue to this puzzle is that strong capital inflows to the United States after 1995, and more prominently after 2002,[3] increased regularly with a monotone trend.

The relationship between the real effective exchange rate and the current account deficits–GDP ratio seems to have broken down in the 1990s. The appreciation between 1990 and 2002 was gradual and small, but the current account deficits increased steadily. The dollar depreciated from 2002 to 2004, but the current account deficits did not shrink at all. The current account deficits rose to a record level, even as a ratio of GDP, by the end of 2005. The current account deficits did not seem to affect the exchange rate movement, nor did depreciation seem to have an impact on current account deficits.

Figure 7.3 shows which countries the United States is experiencing trade deficits with. The deficit with China doubled from 2001 to 2005, becoming the trading partner with the largest single bilateral trade deficit with the United States. OPEC countries also doubled their trade surpluses.

In addition, *bilateral* surpluses and deficits may not be used as a guide for obtaining the desirable exchange rate changes, although sharp increases or decreases of the bilateral exchange rates are indicative of changes in comparative advantages or in the competitive environment of the two countries. The most comprehensive exchange rate for measuring competitiveness is the real effective exchange rate, that is, multilateral exchange rates adjusted for inflation differentials. Thus measured, the dollar has not moved much since 2000.

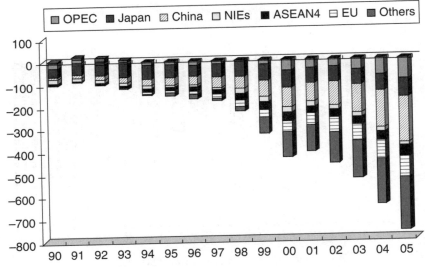

Figure 7.3 US trade deficits, by trading partner

Whether the United States is able to continue running such a large current account deficit depends on two factors: continuous inflows of foreign capital into US capital markets and buoyant domestic and import demands. If foreign investors, government and private, decide to shift away from US dollar assets and diversify into non-dollar assets, the US dollar would depreciate precipitously, and revenue switching from imports to domestic goods could occur, which would adversely affect East Asian exporters. If US domestic demands, such as consumption or fixed and housing investment fall, then a recession could also occur, reducing import demands. A recession would make the central bank lower the interest rate, which would in turn make foreign investors hesitant to hold US assets. Import demands would decrease, and so would capital inflows, resolving at least one part of the global imbalances.

Foreign Reserve Accumulation among Asian Countries

As explained earlier, the counterpart of US current account deficits is current account surpluses in China, other East Asian countries and oil-producing nations. The amounts of foreign reserves in East Asian countries are shown in Figure 7.4, while the foreign reserves as a ratio of their respective GDP (converted to US dollars at the market exchange rate) are shown in Figure 7.5.

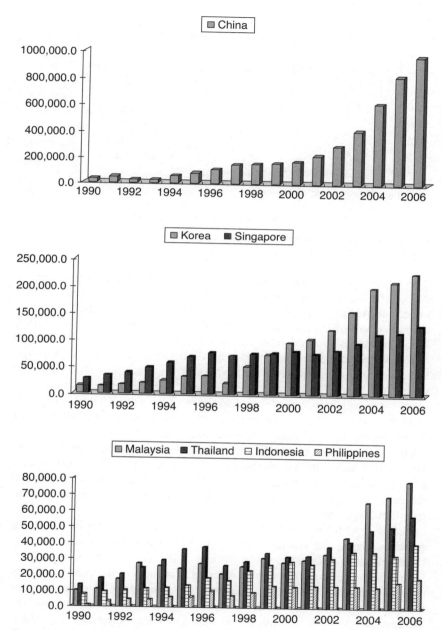

Figure 7.4   Foreign reserves of East Asian countries, December (except August 2006) (US$m)

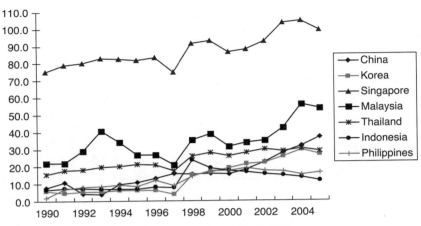

Figure 7.5   Foreign reserves as a ratio of GDP (%)

In China, foreign reserves increased to almost 1 trillion dollars by mid-2006. The accumulation accelerated sharply after 2002; the amount increased fivefold from 2001 to 2006. As a ratio of GDP, Chinese foreign reserves doubled from 15 per cent in 2000 to 37 per cent in 2005. Other Asian countries suffered from the Asian currency crisis of 1997–98 and reduced their foreign reserves in 1997. All of them have now made up the loss and accumulated reserves far beyond the pre-crisis peak. Although the timing and pace of economic recovery varied from one country to another, all of them greatly increased their foreign reserves after 2002. This is prima facie evidence of intervention, selling one's own currencies in exchange for foreign assets, most of them US dollar denominated.

Of the foreign reserve–GDP ratios, Singapore's is the highest, at almost 100 per cent, and Malaysia is the second highest, at more than 50 per cent. They are followed by China, at just less than 40 per cent, and Thailand and Korea, both at just under 30 per cent. Indonesia and the Philippines are at less than 20 per cent.

Before the Mexican crisis of 1994, which was a precursor of the Asian currency crises, the safety buffer against a currency crisis was casually talked about as a three-month equivalent of the imports of goods and services. Figure 7.6 shows the foreign reserves in months of imports. China has now accumulated foreign reserves that are equivalent to 14 months of imports. Other countries range from just below four months – the Philippines – to eight months. All countries increased their monthly equivalent of imports from 1997 to 2005. All countries have thus reached a safety level, at least in terms of the old measurement.

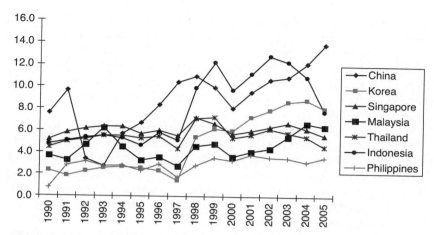

Figure 7.6   Foreign reserves in months of imports (goods and services)

The increase in foreign reserves plays a key role in maintaining global imbalances. If one thinks that Asian countries have accumulated enough of a buffer against another currency crisis, then the saturation point has almost been reached. If, on the other hand, they are willing to accumulate more, then global imbalances will persist.

There are three possible ways that decisions in East Asia may trigger a resolution to global imbalances. First, suppose that the central bank in an East Asian country has been intervening in order to maintain export competitiveness in order to help a weak domestic economy. Then imagine that the economy gains strength and that the interventions become unnecessary, and thus stop. Second, suppose that following the Asian crisis, the central bank in an East Asian country wants to build up foreign reserves in order to restore pre-crisis levels, then continues to build up reserves to avoid future crises. When the central bank has built up foreign reserves to the level it feels to be sufficient, then the building up of foreign reserves – that is, intervention – may stop, although it is difficult to calculate the optimal level of foreign reserves in the real world. Third, suppose that the central bank continues to build up foreign reserves, but diversifies its portfolio away from the US dollar to non-dollar assets, affecting flows of capital into the United States. In such a case, the cycle of capital flows that supports global imbalances may be broken.

There are several reasons why a central bank may want to limit the amount of foreign reserves it holds. If the domestic interest rate is higher than the US interest rate, holding the reserves would cost the central bank and the government the interest differential times the amount of foreign reserves. Moreover, the portfolio of foreign reserves would suffer capital losses if the domestic currency depreciates against the currency of the foreign reserve assets. Thus, extremely large holdings of foreign reserves are detrimental to the economy. Obviously, zero foreign reserves is not desirable for emerging market economies either. Therefore, an optimal level of foreign reserves should be some finite number (ratio to GDP, or ratio to gross external liability).

The BWII view states that East Asian countries are afraid of sharp currency appreciation, because their economic development strategy depends on exports. As East Asian economic development relies on export-oriented industrialization, the countries maintain stable exchange rates *vis-à-vis* the US dollar. According to this view, East Asian countries do not mind building up foreign reserves to extremely high levels, much higher than traditionally considered optimal.

In contrast, several scholars have attempted to explain this accumulation of foreign reserves as a consequence of the recovery from the currency crisis, one motive being precautionary in order to avoid another crisis (see, for example, Aizenman and Marion, 2003; Genberg et al., 2005). According to these views, there is a rationale behind the East Asian accumulation of foreign reserves; it is only a matter of time before East Asian countries find either the amount of their holdings or the proportion of the US dollar in their portfolios to be less than optimal.

BRETTON WOODS II: VIEW AND CRITIQUE

Dooley et al. argue in favour of the BWII view in a series of papers. They state that the current situation of global imbalances will continue to be sustained, because none of the players has any incentive to change his or her behaviour. Almost all US deficits are recycled into the US markets by capital inflows, mostly into US government bonds. US households are happy to spend the wealth generated from home refinancing via cashing out on home equities. The US government does not feel the pinch from increasing fiscal deficits, because interest rates have remained relatively low. As long as robust growth continues, the United States does not mind current account deficits.

One of the components of the BWII view is that East Asian countries have incentives to keep intervening in foreign exchange markets to avoid appreciation, because their development strategy depends on continued growth in exports. They accumulate foreign reserves as a natural result of these exchange market interventions, aimed at keeping the dollar peg. They have incentives to keep their foreign reserves in US dollar securities so that the dollar is supported. Diversification into the euro or the yen could trigger dollar depreciation, so East Asian countries would not dare attempt it. Thus, neither the United States nor East Asia has incentives to change their behaviour.

The BWII view appears to justify the status quo. Indeed, the degree of 'imbalances' has increased, yet the dollar has not depreciated significantly since 2005, while the issue of how to resolve imbalances has been debated. Is the BWII logic right?

There are several possible holes in the BWII argument. First, a changing configuration of global interest rates will cause consumption and investment in major economies to change. It is likely that higher interest rates and higher energy prices in the United States will have a significant dampening effect on household consumption. Although the US economy has been robust despite an increase in interest rates from 2003 to 2005, a consumption boom seems to be finally ending. Adverse effects on consumption in the United States had been slow to emerge, but housing investment finally began a sharp decline in 2006 as the sub-prime housing loans market started to see high delinquency rates. If the US economy slows down significantly, it would represent the first piece of the solution to the global imbalances puzzle.

Second, exchange rate regimes in East Asia are diverse, so stating that all East Asian countries fix to the dollar is inaccurate.[4] In several countries in East Asia, interventions have been stopped (as in Japan since March 2004), or reduced (as in Korea since 2005), so that purchases of US government securities by various public sectors have been, and will continue to be, gradually reduced. Instead, oil-producing nations have increased trade surpluses, thanks to oil price increases, and their holdings of foreign reserves, due to their de facto dollar peg policy. It is sheer coincidence that a decline in the purchase of US Treasuries by East Asian countries has been offset by an increase by oil-producing nations (possibly through European funds or financial institutions).

Third, in some East Asian countries, foreign reserve accumulation may reach a level that becomes harmful to their economies. If interventions are not perfectly sterilized, the economy may be overheated. Consumer price inflation and/or an asset price bubble could result. Many have predicted that China might experience such overheating. The Consumer Price Index (CPI) inflation rate has been none the less well within a tolerable range (below 5 per cent) for developing countries. For those countries where the domestic interest rate is higher than the US interest rate, maintaining large foreign reserves generates high fiscal costs. Accumulating foreign reserves may have political costs too, as it is viewed as evidence of intervention (which is true) by the United States and criticized. China and Korea started to operate the Sovereign Investment Fund in 2007 – similar to the Government of Singapore Investment Corporation (GIC). If they do diversify on a large scale, the preference for dollars may end (in which case the dollar may depreciate) or the purchase of Treasury bonds may be reduced (in which case the interest rate could rise).

Fourth, even if the size of foreign reserves is maintained, portfolios may be reshuffled to provide for better returns and for diversification. Singapore created a government-run investment fund, the GIC, to manage part of its foreign reserves. The GIC invests in equities, fixed income securities, real estate and other foreign assets in various countries. A similar investment-fund-type agency was established in Korea in 2006 and another one in China in 2007. The new Chinese agency decided to purchase a 3 billion dollar stake in the Blackstone Group. These developments are indications that some East Asian countries have become more aware of better return opportunities and of exchange rate risk. The size of those wealth funds, independent of traditional foreign reserves, has been limited so far, and as yet has had no visible effect on the value of the dollar.

It is likely that some East Asian countries have accumulated foreign reserves deliberately, partly in order to replenish them after the currency crisis of 1997–98, and partly in order to accumulate more so that future crises may be avoided. Fear of the IMF is so strong in these countries that they are willing to pay quasi-fiscal costs, if any, to maintain a high level of foreign reserves. In some countries, however, the level of foreign reserves has become so high that the costs and risks of future dollar depreciation now outweigh the benefits.

REBALANCING DEMAND

Resolving Global Imbalances without a Recession

As explained in previous sections, there are several triggers that may start unravelling global imbalances. Here, I present possible combinations of events necessary to avoid worldwide recession while global imbalances are being unwound. As explained earlier, one possible trigger is a US recession, most likely caused by a housing market slump, which would result in housing investment and consumption declines. If this occurs as an isolated incident, exporters to the United States would suffer declines in exports, foreign reserve accumulations and capital outflows to the United States. Thus, global imbalances would be resolved, but at the expense of recessions in every country. Hence, US domestic consumption declines would have to be matched by a corresponding increase in domestic demand in East Asian and oil-producing countries, as well as an increase in their import demands from the United States.

Thus, the first obvious answer to resolving global imbalances is to make US households consume less, and to make households and corporations in the rest of the world, particularly in East Asia and oil-producing countries, spend more through consumption, investment and imports.

Why would not the obvious answer to this be market forces? Is there any role for the governments of major countries to coordinate policy so that private-sector spending can be restrained (in the United States) or stimulated (in the rest of the world)? These questions shall be examined below.

Another possible trigger is the behaviour of the East Asian and oil-producing nations' central banks. If they (i) stop intervention, or (ii) diversify their portfolios or stop purchasing additional US Treasuries, then East Asian currencies would appreciate and the US interest rate would rise. This would have a dampening effect on all economies involved. Thus, in order to avoid a worldwide recession, each economy has to have an autonomous increase in private spending in consumption, government stimulus (in the form of increased fiscal spending) or a lowering of the interest rate by central banks. In the next subsection, the magnitude of such rebalancing demands will be calculated.

A Simple Simulation

Suppose that the United States decreases imports by x per cent of GDP and increases exports by y per cent, so that the net exports improve by 3 per cent ($x + y = 3$). Then suppose that the decrease in exports to and the increase in imports from the United States affects its trading partners proportionately, so that each partner country's exports to and imports from the United States decrease or increase by the same percentage. Table 7.1 shows the impacts of changes in US exports and/or imports on trading partners.

When US trade deficits change, how will the correction be allocated to trading partners in the rest of the world? Here only a crude estimate is provided. Suppose that US imports and exports change (without asking what triggered these changes) and that the change is allocated to trading partners without modifying the countries' shares of imports and exports.

Note again that no serious econometrics is conducted to arrive at the numbers. These are all mechanical calculations, which do not explicitly take into account the necessary exchange rate changes.

1.   *Scenario 1: a 3 per cent decline in imports*   Assume a decline in US imports by 3 per cent of GDP. The dollar amounts of the change are allocated to the trading partners so that the shares of imports by country will not change. Namely, declines in US imports are allocated proportionately to exporters to the United States. The decline in

Table 7.1 *Impact of a decline in US imports and an increase in exports on US trading partners*

Scenario 1: US: decline in imports of 3% of GDP, 2004* – decline in exports to the United States (in GDP of respective countries)

Trading partner	Decline
Newly industrialized Asian economies	−2.01
Asean+3	−2.19
Eurozone	−0.54
China	−2.86
Japan	−0.66

Note: * Declines in US imports of 3% of GDP are calculated in terms of US$, coupled with no change in US exports. Then, declines in US imports are allocated to exporters to the United States proportionately. The actual shares of US imports (exports to US) are assumed not to change. The impact, declines in exports by trading partners to the United States, is expressed in the ratio of GDP (in US$) of trading partners (countries or regions) in 2004.

Scenario 2: US: export rise of 1% of GDP and import decline of 2% of GDP, 2004* – decline in trade surpluses vis-à-vis *the United States (in GDP of respective countries)*

Trading partner	Decline
Newly industrialized Asian economies	−2.29
Asean+3	−2.29
Eurozone	−0.55
China	−2.18
Japan	−0.62

Note: * Declines in US imports of 2% of GDP and an increase of US exports of 1% of GDP are calculated in terms of US$, coupled with no change in US exports. Then, declines in US imports (and exports) are allocated to exporters to the United States (and importers from the United States) proportionately (respectively). The trading partners' shares of US imports and exports are assumed not to change. The impact – declines in exports to the United States on the part of trading partners and increases in imports from the United States on the part of trading partners – is expressed in the ratio of GDP (in US$) of trading partners (countries or regions).

    exports of trading partners to the United States is expressed as a ratio of the GDP of the trading partners (countries or regions).[5]

2. *Scenario 2: a 2 per cent decline in imports and a 1 per cent increase in exports* Suppose that US imports decrease by 2 per cent of US GDP and US exports increase by 1 per cent of US GDP. Then allocate the changes to the trading partners, so that the country shares of US imports and exports do not change, and calculate the changes in the trade balance of the trading partners.

Since the reduction in exports to, and/or increase in imports from, the United States are divided by the GDP of the trading partner country, the smaller countries suffer more, in terms of the ratio to GDP, from the reduction of trade with the United States. The difference between the scenarios is whether a country is more of an exporter to the United States or more of an importer. China exports more to the United States than it imports, so the impact on China is greater in Scenario 1 than in Scenario 2.

The resulting adjustments to trading partners are shown in Table 7.1. The impacts on China and newly industrialized economies (NIEs) in Asia (Korea, Taiwan, Hong Kong and Singapore) are large, because their GDP depends largely on exports to the United States. The reduction in exports and the increase in imports amount to more than 2 per cent of GDP in China and in other East Asian countries. Although Japan and European countries also trade in large amounts with the United States, their domestic economies are large too, so that decreases or increases in US exports or imports do not represent more than 1 per cent of GDP in their respective economies. In order to avoid a recession resulting from the deterioration of their trading position with the United States, US trading partners must find ways of stimulating domestic demand.

The Role of US Policy

If foreign reserves in East Asia are soon to be saturated with US Treasuries, a shift in demand for consumption and investment may occur naturally from the United States to East Asia and oil-producing countries. The question is how soon the shift will occur. Will it happen before the United States starts running large deficits even on the investment income account (repatriation income minus payments)? If the adjustment is regarded as being too slow, what could the government do?

Housing prices in some cities and regions of the United States, the United Kingdom, Australia and some other countries have risen considerably in recent years. Higher home equity values have encouraged consumer spending. The central banks of these countries have avoided applying sudden 'brakes' on asset prices. It is difficult to tell whether the rise in asset prices is a bubble or not. A hard landing in Japan in the early 1990s is remembered as a situation to be avoided: the bubble was burst deliberately by hiking up the interest rate.

If US current account deficits are an overriding concern, creating the fear of a future currency crash, a case can be made for tightening monetary policy so as to reduce consumption and investment before it is too late.

An opposing view is that it is not wise to raise interest rates to contract demand simply because of concern over current account deficits, unless the boom is accompanied by expected inflation. Prudential policy – monitoring a loan-to-value ratio and the balance sheet of financial institutions – rather than monetary policy should be applied in order to manage risks caused by a possible bubble.

Since housing prices in most US cities have stopped rising, and since the home mortgage interest rate has risen only modestly, consumption spending will soon be moderated. This would contribute to correcting current account deficits and to 'rebalancing' aggregate demand in the United States and in other parts of the world. Nevertheless, there is no overwhelming case for applying monetary policy to this end.

A more direct way of influencing US current account deficits would be to reduce fiscal deficits. A gradual reduction of fiscal spending or an increase in taxes may contribute to solving both the fiscal deficit problem and the current account deficit problem. Reducing fiscal deficits is also useful in preparing against a future drop in capital inflows from the purchase of US government securities.

A decrease in household and government consumption should be accompanied by an increase in exports. Expenditure switching from imports to domestically produced goods is needed to avoid a serious recession. The change in trade position has to be accompanied by dollar depreciation and lower capital inflows.

Now let us consider the impact of policy on the exchange rate. If monetary policy is tightened to curb consumption, it could invite more capital inflows and result in dollar appreciation. This would be counter-productive with regard to the need for expenditure switching from imports to domestic products. Tightening fiscal policy and reducing bond issuance would contribute to lowering the bond rate, so that the dollar would depreciate. Again, tighter fiscal policy rather than tighter monetary policy is more consistent with an objective of reducing current account deficits.

Several empirical studies show that the dynamic effects of reducing fiscal deficits on current account balances are rather small. Rebalancing will eventually have to come from adjustments in private-sector spending (expenditure switching).

The Role of Policy in the Rest of the World

One concern of a slowdown of the US economy is that it may trigger a worldwide recession rather than rebalancing global demand. East Asian economies are dependent on the export of final products to the United States, and a slowdown of the US economy may affect these economies adversely. Moreover, a sharp depreciation of the US dollar in relation to East Asian currencies would put more dampening effects on the East Asian economies. Nevertheless, some combination of a slowdown of the US economy, a depreciation of the US dollar, and a decline in US imports – or an increase in US exports to East Asia, Europe and the oil-producing nations – is an essential part of rebalancing. A decrease in US imports would have a major impact on East Asia (see crude estimates above). There are two ways to mitigate these adverse effects.

First, the exchange rate policies of East Asian countries should be coordinated so that the exchange rates float jointly against the US dollar and other major currencies outside the region. The East Asian economies are sufficiently integrated that the intra-regional trade ratio is as high as among EU countries, about 50 per cent. Therefore, a sharp fall in the US dollar would cause large changes in the intra-regional exchange rates (such as yen–yuan, yen–won, baht–yen, and so on), unless the Chinese and Malaysian authorities allow much more flexibility for their currencies. One way to ensure that East Asian currencies move in a coordinated fashion is to adopt a common basket, band regime so that they mutually stabilize each other, but float jointly against outside currencies.[6]

Second, economic policies in East Asia could be relaxed in anticipation of pressure from dollar depreciation. Fiscal spending may not be a wise choice in some East Asian countries, however. Japan, with a very large government debt, has little room for fiscal stimulus. Instead, monetary policy in Japan has room to manoeuvre as inflation is a remote fear. Monetary policy has been rather 'behind the curve' in lifting the economy out of 15 years of stagnation and eight years of deflation. Similarly, deficit spending by the government may not be wise in Korea, Thailand, Indonesia and the Philippines, which are still emerging from the fiscal deficit problem posed by the management of the 1997 currency crisis. Only China and Malaysia have some room to stimulate the economy via fiscal policy.

As oil prices have risen sharply since 2004, many oil-producing nations have recorded large trade surpluses. So far, most of the revenues seem to have been 'recycled' in the asset markets of advanced countries. If and when these oil revenues start to be used for investment in the domestic markets and abroad, they will help to rebalance global demand. It will nevertheless be difficult to think of a short-term aggregate demand policy to this end. How to redirect oil-export surpluses to investment and long-run growth in domestic economies is a challenge to those nations. Obvious candidates for domestic demand are government investment to improve social infrastructure and private investment in oil-related businesses. In addition, structural policies to strengthen legal and economic infrastructures in oil-producing nations may help to encourage investment in these countries.

CONCLUSION

In order to make a smooth transition, US policies should be on the side of restraining household consumption and fiscal spending. In order to counteract the recessionary impact, exports should increase and imports should be curtailed. A US dollar depreciation and the correction of trade deficits are necessary. The impact on East Asia will be significant, although there will be impacts on oil-producing nations and the EU as well.

A good solution does exist. Domestic demand in China, the EU and OPEC countries has to be promoted so as to increase imports from the United States. To a lesser extent, more domestic demand in Japan, Malaysia, Canada and Mexico should also be promoted. For advanced countries, more emphasis should be placed on promoting consumption, while for emerging markets and OPEC countries investment should be promoted, given that they lack adequate social infrastructure and modernized plants and machinery.

In some East Asian countries, domestic demand should be stimulated in order to offset declines in exports to the United States. Coordination of exchange rate policies will mitigate the impact of dollar depreciation on their trade relationship, since intra-regional trade is already high. Internal stability and joint floating against the rest of the world is important for East Asian countries. Lastly, monetary policy should be relaxed in order to stimulate investment.

NOTES

1. Any opinions and views expressed in this chapter are the author's own and do not necessarily reflect those of the institutions that the author is or has been affiliated with. The author is grateful for comments from the participants of the Cournot Center conference.
2. For other papers dealing with global imbalances, see, for example, Eichengreen (2004), Obstfeld and Rogoff (2004) and Blanchard et al. (2005).
3. The correlation between current account deficits and net portfolio inflows increased from 0.33 for the period from 1980:I to 1994:IV to 0.76 for the period from 1995:I to 2006:I.
4. Japan is a free-floating country. Korea, Thailand and Singapore can be regarded as having adopted a basket currency regime. China and Malaysia have maintained a de facto dollar peg, although China declared on 21 July 2005 that it was abandoning the dollar peg.
5. The statistics used here are from 2004.
6. Proposals based on a basket, band, and crawl (BBC) regime and its variants for East Asia have been around for some time. For more details, see Ito et al. (1998), Williamson (2000), and Ogawa and Ito (2002).

REFERENCES

Aizenman, Joshua and Nancy Marion (2003), 'The high demand for international reserves in the Far East: what is going on?', *Journal of the Japanese and International Economies*, **17** (3), pp. 370–400.

Blanchard, Olivier, Francesco Giavazzi and Filipa Sa (2005), 'The US current account and the dollar', NBER Working Paper 11137, Cambridge, MA: NBER.

Dooley, Michael, David Folkerts-Landau and Peter Garber (2003), 'An essay on the revived Bretton Woods system', NBER Working Paper 9971, Cambridge, MA: NBER.

Dooley, Michael, David Folkerts-Landau and Peter Garber (2004a), 'The revived Bretton Woods system: the effects of periphery intervention and reserve management on interest rates and exchange rates in center countries', NBER Working Paper 10332, Cambridge, MA: NBER.

Dooley, Michael, David Folkerts-Landau and Peter Garber (2004b), 'Direct investment, rising real wages and the absorption of excess labor in the periphery', NBER Working Paper 10626, Cambridge, MA: NBER.

Dooley, Michael, David Folkerts-Landau and Peter Garber (2004c), 'The US current account deficit and economic development, collateral for a total return swap', NBER Working Paper 10727, Cambridge, MA: NBER.

Dooley, Michael, David Folkerts-Landau and Peter Garber (2005a), 'Savings gluts and interest rates: the missing link to Europe', NBER Working Paper 11520, Cambridge, MA: NBER.

Dooley, Michael, David Folkerts-Landau and Peter Garber (2005b), 'Interest rates, exchange rates and international adjustment', NBER Working Paper 11771, Cambridge, MA: NBER.

Eichengreen, Barry (2004), 'Global imbalances and the lessons of Bretton Woods', NBER Working Paper 10497, Cambridge, MA: NBER.

Genberg, Hans, Robert McCauley, Yung Chul Park and Avinash Persaud (2005), 'Official reserves and currency management in Asia: myth, reality and the future', Geneva Reports on the World Economy, International Center for Monetary and Banking Studies (ICMB), Centre for Economic Policy Research (CEPR).

Ito, Takatoshi, Eiji Ogawa and Yuri N. Sasaki (1998), 'How did the dollar peg fail in Asia?', *Journal of the Japanese and International Economies*, **12** (4), pp. 256–304.

Obstfeld, Maurice and Kenneth Rogoff (2004), 'The unsustainable US current account position revisited', prepared for the NBER conference 'G-7 Current Account Imbalances: Sustainability and Adjustment', 12–13 July.

Ogawa, Eiji and Takatoshi Ito (2002), 'On the desirability of a regional basket currency arrangement', *Journal of the Japanese and International Economies*, **16** (3), pp. 317–34.

Williamson, John (2000), *Exchange Rate Regimes for Emerging Markets: Reviving the Intermediate Option*, Washington, DC: Institute for International Economics.

8.   Global imbalances: a contemporary 'Rashomon' saga

Nouriel Roubini

INTRODUCTION

The current debate on global current account imbalances is reminiscent of Akira Kurosawa's film *Rashomon*. In it, a terrible crime has been committed in a forest. Each of four characters agrees that something serious has occurred, but each gives a different story or personal interpretation of what happened and why it happened and who is to blame. Similarly, the facts of the global imbalances 'crime' are not a matter of dispute: everyone agrees that global current account imbalances are large and growing as the United States saves less than it invests and spends more than it earns, while most of the rest of the world saves more than it invests and spends less than it earns. But the debate over the causes of this 'crime' and which countries are to blame is very acrimonious, especially since, rather than four characters, this contemporary saga counts at least ten (and possibly more), each with a different argument or explanation of the causes and who is responsible.

To set the scene, we must first present the ten principal 'suspects'. First interpretation: according to many, the United States is to blame for the global imbalances saga because of its twin fiscal and current account deficits. Second: Federal Reserve Chairman Ben Bernanke (2005) argues that it has little to do with US fiscal deficits (as according to him, the world is Ricardian) and is instead all about a 'global savings glut' triggered by emerging market economies saving too much. Third: it is more of a global investment drought than a global savings glut. Fourth: the three musketeers (Michael Dooley, David Folkerts-Landau and Peter Garber) of the Bretton Woods II (BWII) hypothesis (Dooley et al., 2003, 2004, 2005a, b) say that China and many emerging markets are keeping their currencies undervalued to promote export-led growth and are thus causing global imbalances. Fifth: it is not China's exchange rate policy that leads to excessive savings, but rather structural factors in its financial and economic systems. Sixth: Richard Cooper (2005, 2006, 2007) argues that it is all due to demographics (and low productivity growth); Japan, Europe and even China need to save as their populations are ageing very quickly, and as they have little productivity growth (Japan and Europe). Seventh: it is all the fault of oil exporters, who have not spent their huge oil-price windfall gains on investment and consumption, but are instead saving it all. Eighth: it is due to housing bubbles partly driven by easy money, as in the United States and a few other countries such housing bubbles have increased national investment (in housing) and led to a consumption boom and savings fall. Ninth: financial globalization, as portfolios are diversified and home bias disappears, is leading a large global demand for US assets. Tenth: Ricardo Hausmann and Federico Sturzenneger (2006) argue that there is not even a current account problem to begin with – no crime to debate – because the data are not being measured correctly, especially what is referred to as 'dark matter', some intangible value of US foreign assets.

The debate on these different interpretations is important for two reasons. First, depending on one's view of the causes, global imbalances may be sustainable for a long time and adjustable in a slow, orderly manner, or they may be unsustainable and risk leading to a disorderly, hard landing for the global economy; in other words, some view global imbalances as a serious crime while others think of them as a minor misdemeanour, and some even believe that they are an outright blessing in disguise (as in the Panglossian,[1] BWII view of the world). Second, depending on one's view of the causes and who is to be blamed, the policy actions required to re-balance the global economy in an orderly manner vary greatly. There is much difference of opinion concerning which punishment best fits the crime or is the most dissuasive of recidivism, or upon whom justice should most rightly be brought, whose behaviour has been the worst, and thus whose burden should be greatest in rectifying the imbalances.

DEBATE ON THE DIFFERENT INTERPRETATIONS

While there is some truth to each one of these stories, there is also a lot of nonsense and misguided interpretation in this rather contentious debate. Clearing the air of confusing arguments and misinterpretations is essential before we can answer the two policy questions above, namely: (i) are the imbalances sustainable and (ii) what policy action should be taken, and by whom, in order to reduce them in an orderly way? So let us try to distinguish the chaff of speculative debate from the wheat of reality, beginning with the first culprits, US twin deficits and a global savings glut.

The twin deficit story made much more sense than the savings glut hypothesis until 2004. In the 1990s, the US current account deficit was driven by an investment boom that outstripped the increase in national savings, which came with that decade's sharp fiscal improvement. But, after the 'tech bust' of 2000, national investment fell by 4 per cent of GDP between 2000 and 2004. Thus, for unchanged savings, the current account should have improved by 4 per cent of GDP; instead, it worsened by another 2 per cent. Why? The answer is clear: US fiscal policy took a U-turn. The fiscal surplus of 2.5 per cent of GDP in 2000 turned into a huge fiscal deficit of 3.5 per cent of GDP in 2004, a change of exactly 6 per cent of GDP, which explains the worsening of the current account in spite of the investment collapse. This is as clear a case of 'twin deficits' as one can get. In the 1990s, the United States was borrowing from abroad to invest in new real capital; in the 2000s, it was borrowing from abroad to finance its fiscal deficits, its foreign wars and its lack of private savings. The pattern of capital inflows matches this story: in the 1990s, large net foreign direct investment (FDI) and equity investments into the United States; in the 2000s, net negative FDI and equity investments (net outflows, not inflows, as US equities slumped) and a massive accumulation of debt, mostly US Treasuries increasingly held by foreign central banks.

Thus, until 2004, the global savings glut story clashes with the data: a global savings glut should lead to a fall in world real rates, inducing a widening US current account deficit via an increase in real investment and a fall in private savings. Neither of these two occurred between 2000 and 2004, and the worsening of the US current account deficit in that period was driven by the 6 per cent turnaround in fiscal accounts. Furthermore, in equilibrium, a global savings glut should be accompanied by an increase in global savings and the global investment rate: an exogenous increase in savings in some regions, say China and oil importers, leads, at initial real interest rates, to an increase in global savings; this increase induces a fall in real interest rates that leads, in equilibrium, to an increase in global investment rates and global savings rates (as a share of GDP). Conversely, in equilibrium, an exogenous fall in global investment rates, or a global investment drought, should logically lead to a decrease in global savings and the global investment rate: an exogenous fall in investment rates in some regions – say East Asia after its currency crisis and in the European Union and Japan because of low growth – leads, at initial real interest rates, to a decrease in global investment; this decrease induces a fall in real interest rates that, in equilibrium, leads to a decrease in global investment rates and global savings rates (as a share of GDP). The same fall in global real interest rates (bond market conundrum) could be due to a global savings glut or to a global investment drought. The test of one hypothesis or the other is the equilibrium value of global savings and investment rates as a share of GDP. International Monetary Fund (IMF) data show that between 2000 and 2004 both global investment rates and global savings rates were falling, thus disproving the global savings glut hypothesis and being more consistent with a global investment drought story. Between 2000 and 2004, world savings rates fell from 22.3 to 21.4 per cent of GDP, while world investment rates fell from 22.5 to 21.7 per cent of GDP (with the very small difference between savings and investment due to statistical errors). Thus, until 2004, the global savings glut hypothesis has no empirical basis.

From 2005 on, things changed slightly. The US current account deficit worsened while the fiscal imbalance improved modestly. Indeed, since 2005, there has been an excess of savings (relative to investment) in China, and oil exporters have kept long rates low (one explanation of the now infamous 'bond market conundrum', but not the only one as easy monetary policies also played a role). This has fed the housing investment bubble, and the associated consumption bubble, and has led to a further reduction in private savings (with household savings becoming negative). The excess savings hypothesis is only a partial explanation of global imbalances and applies to only a few countries. It certainly does not represent a 'global' savings glut.[2] In 2005, global savings rates increased to 22 per cent (from 21.4 per cent in 2004) and global investment rates increased to 22.2 per cent from 21.7 per cent; both global savings and investment increased modestly in 2006. Note that, by 2005 both global savings and investment were below their 2000 levels and close to (but not above) their average levels from 1992 to 1999. Thus, there is little or no evidence of a global savings glut. Bernanke overreached in his view. Indeed, rather than a global savings glut, we saw a global investment drought as East Asia's investment rates fell after the 1997–98 crisis and never recovered, while investment rates in slow-growing Europe and Japan have also been low for quite some time. Rather than a global savings glut, the world is facing a massive US twin private and public savings drought, actually, more of a famine, as US household savings are now negative, and as the United States is still running a large structural fiscal deficit, even after four years of recovery and above potential growth.

BWII is certainly a part of the explanation of global imbalances. It is a variant of the Bernanke savings glut argument where excess savings are due to the mercantilist exchange rate policies of China and other emerging markets. Certainly, the BWII hypothesis supporters have been quite right, until now, that many emerging market economies are following mercantilist, export-led growth policies, driven by the attempt to maintain undervalued currencies and aggressively accumulate foreign reserves in order to avoid a currency appreciation. But the Panglossian view that these imbalances are optimal and sustainable for decades to come is mostly wishful thinking. Continued US current account deficits of the scale of 7 per cent or more of GDP will eventually make US external liabilities excessively large and unsustainable, thus triggering a serious hard landing for the US dollar and the global economy. Furthermore, instabilities inherent in the BWII system will not allow it to survive for a decade; the seeds of its unravelling, the triggers that will begin the process, are already in place.

China's high savings rates (in spite of high investment rates) are due in part to a series of structural factors that hamper consumption. Chinese households need to save in a precautionary manner for education, health care and old age as there is little formal social security, as well as for periods of unemployment as there is very little in the way of a social safety-net. Also, weaknesses in the financial system (lack of a sound consumer credit system and constraints in the way housing is financed) necessitate high household savings. Thus, structural reforms – which China plans to implement in the next few years – are necessary in order for China to rely less on net exports and investment and more on consumption for long-term growth.

Demographic trends (in Europe, Japan and China) and low productivity growth (in Europe and Japan) imply that part of these global imbalances are structural rather than cyclical (and are thus more sustainable over time). But the view that it is all due to demographics is far-fetched. For one thing China may have an ageing problem, but its productivity growth is massive; thus, a country like China does not need to save as much as the ageing and slow-growing Europe and Japan. Also, Europe and Japan may need a structural current account surplus, but they are not the major sources of global imbalances: for example, globally, the Eurozone is currently running a current account balance, not a surplus.

Easy money and other financial sector factors that lead to housing booms are a more likely partial explanation of global imbalances. In addition to the United States, other countries with large current account imbalances include Turkey, Hungary, Australia, New Zealand, Iceland and Spain among others. What do these countries have in common? A housing boom that led to an increase in residential investment and a fall in private savings via the wealth effect on private consumption: lower savings and higher investment equal a current account deficit. These countries also share other common features: an overvalued currency, a credit boom and an accumulation of external liabilities that may become dangerous. Indeed, in 2006, as opportunities for yield carry trades unwound, each of these economies experienced pressure on its currency, in some cases quite severe. The danger is that these housing bubbles may burst as rates are raised to control inflation. The adjustment of these large and unsustainable current account imbalances may then occur in a disorderly, recessionary way with falling investment and rising savings.

Paradoxically, the recent flight of capital out of emerging market economies with large current account deficits (the countries listed above, as well as South Africa, India, and so on) has led to a temporary appreciation of the US dollar as investors fleeing risky assets are seeking the safety of US Treasuries. But fleeing to the assets of the country with the biggest current account deficit of all is a paradoxical, temporary and unsustainable solution. In due time, the US dollar (USD) will again experience the downward pressures deriving from both structural (large current account deficit) and cyclical forces (a shrinking interest rate and GDP growth differentials between the United States and Europe and Japan) that are bearish for the US dollar; currencies cannot defy the laws of gravity forever.

Much has been made of the idea that financial globalization, less home bias and large foreign demand for US assets can explain global imbalances. As an explanation of the causes of global imbalances – as opposed to being an explanation of the sustainability of the financing of these imbalances – this argument does not make much sense. Financial globalization cannot explain changes in global savings and investment (which lead to current account imbalances) that depend on other factors. Portfolio diversification and reduction of home bias can be achieved without any countries running current account deficits: cross-border purchases and sales of domestic and foreign assets can lead to any level of diversification desired and a reduction of home bias with zero change in net positions, that is with zero current account deficits. Therefore, foreign demand for US assets does not explain the imbalances in the first place, and in the second, imbalances are not necessary in order to have portfolio diversification.

Additionally, returns on US assets (such as equities) have been significantly lower in the last five years than in the rest of the world. Net FDI and portfolio investment in US equities that used to be to the tune of a positive 200 billion USD inflow in the later 1990s, turned into a negative outflow of 200 billion USD in 2003–04 (2005 was distorted by the Homeland Investment Act). Thus, non-residents are not rushing to buy US assets; net flows of equity are leaving the United States, not entering, poking a big hole in the theory that foreigners are begging to buy US assets. It may be partly true, however, that financial globalization makes the sustainability of the US current account deficit viable for longer than it otherwise would have been. Any emerging market economy with twin deficits the size of the United States' would have had a currency crisis and a hard economic landing far earlier. That the United States is an advanced economy, that it has never defaulted on its external debt and that its currency is still the major global reserve currency in the world help, and have made its deficit more sustainable for longer. But as was stated before, one cannot defy gravity forever. The unsustainable dynamics of the net external foreign liabilities of the United States will catch up with it in due course.

Moreover, the 'exceptional privilege' argument – that the United States is able to borrow in its own currency and thus able to reduce the real value of its external liabilities via a persistent dollar depreciation – has a basic conceptual fallacy. As the proverb goes, you can fool all of the people some of the time (via an unexpected depreciation), and some of the people all of the time (those few central banks that will never care about the return on their USD assets), but you cannot fool all of the people all of the time: if a necessary dollar depreciation – even a modest 4–5 per cent per year – were expected by investors, the return and yields on US assets should adjust upward accordingly in order to account for the fall in the USD, leaving the United States no opportunity to reduce the real value of its foreign liabilities through a persistent fall of the dollar.

The 'dark matter' argument turns out to be rather a 'black hole' once one considers the evidence. It goes as follows: if the United States were truly a net debtor (to the tune of over 2 trillion US dollars as official data claim), then net factor income payments should be negative (if the returns on US foreign assets are on average equal to the return on US foreign liabilities). But, US net factor income payments have remained positive, even after the United States formally became a net debtor in the late 1980s. Thus, there must be some dark matter, some intangible value of US foreign assets – superior US technology or skills or superior financial intermediation – that explains this paradox; the United States is therefore not a net debtor, nor does it run a current account deficit.

Dark matter, however, is a fairy tale. First, net factor income became negative in 2006. Second, the composition of US foreign assets and liabilities explains the temporary difference in relative returns (with US liabilities being more debt and US assets being more equity and FDI), and when interest rates on US Treasury bills were as low as 1 per cent, net factor payments were also low. Now, however, with short rates going above 5 per cent, net interest payments on US foreign debt are surging. Third, tax arbitrage to take advantage of lower corporate tax rates in parts of Europe and the rest of the world leads US firms to do transfer pricing, but this leaves more of the profits of US multinationals abroad while the reverse happens for foreign multinationals in the United States. Fourth, the way FDI is measured, at historical and market values, creates a downward bias on the value of FDI in the United States and an upward bias on the value of US FDI abroad. Fifth, even if this dark matter truly existed, and the United States was a net creditor rather than a net debtor, it would not mean that the United States was not running a current account deficit, nor that it could run a trade deficit of 7 per cent of GDP forever. It would only mean that the trade balance that eventually stabilized US net external liabilities was a small deficit (about 1 per cent of GDP at most) rather than a small surplus: thus, going from a current 7 per cent trade deficit to a 1 per cent deficit still implies a massive reduction of the US external deficit, which will be painful to achieve. In conclusion, the alleged dark matter is only a big black hole sucking greater amounts of foreign savings to finance ever increasing US deficits.

Oil exporters do account for part of the recent increase in global imbalances, but the view that this is a main factor and that the recycling of petrodollars will provide persistent, easy and cheap financing for the US current account deficits is flawed in many ways. So far, the United States has reacted to the oil shock as if it was a temporary one by smoothing consumption (given the real income shock of high oil prices), and thus saving less and accumulating a large current account deficit. Oil exporters have also been behaving as if the shock is temporary and have saved most of the oil windfall. The only rational response to this semi-permanent (as at this point it is very persistent) oil shock has been in Europe and Asia: consumption has adjusted partially to the shock and current account balances have not worsened as much as they would have had the shock been perceived as temporary. This also implies that, in net terms, the increase in oil exporters' savings has been partly matched by a drop in oil importers' savings; the oil shock has not led to a large global savings increase, or to a glut, and cannot account, as naïve interpretations do, for a large part of the fall in global long-term interest rates.

Specifically, suppose that there is an oil shock and both oil exporters and importers behave as if the shock is temporary. Oil exporters' savings go up dollar for dollar, increasing their income, while the reverse happens to oil importers. In equilibrium, there are large current account imbalances (a huge surplus for the oil exporters and a huge deficit for the oil importers), but there is no global savings glut: global savings and real interest rates are unchanged. The change in current account imbalances is not due to a savings glut (as nothing happened to real interest rates), but to the rational behaviour of oil exporters and importers reacting to what they perceive as a temporary oil shock.

Similarly, if the oil shock is permanent, nothing happens to the current account balances of either oil exporters or oil importers (as they match consumption dollar per dollar to the change in income), and there is again no savings glut. Even if the shock is only partly temporary or permanent, there is no savings glut as long as both importers and exporters have the same view of whether the shock is transitory or permanent: the partial increase in the savings of the exporters is matched by a corresponding decrease in the savings of the importers.

It is only in the case in which, on average, oil exporters' perception of the shock is different from that of oil importers that one can get a savings glut. If the shock is more temporary in the eyes of the exporters than in the eyes of the importers, you get a case where the shock leads to an increase in global savings (as exporters' marginal propensity to spend their oil windfall exceeds on average importers' marginal propensity to spend, or dissave) that reduces real interest rates and triggers additional effects on the current account that have to do with a 'savings glut'.

In the case of the recent oil shock, the evidence for such a savings glut is ambiguous: oil exporters have perceived the shock as temporary and have thus saved the oil windfall rather than spend it on consumption and investment. But most oil importers have also behaved as if the shock is temporary and have accordingly dissaved by similar amounts. For example, the US current account deficit worsened sharply following the oil shock, and US agents have behaved as if the shock is temporary.

Even in Europe and Asia (with the exception of China) the current account surpluses have significantly worsened (relative to the pre-shock level); thus, the shock has been partially perceived as temporary (but less so than in the United States). The only case in which the oil shock has not led to any current account deterioration but, rather, an improvement of the current account balance is China. Thus, once one considers the effects of the oil shock on the total level of global savings, at initial unchanged world real interest rates, there is no clear evidence that the oil shock has led to an increase in global savings (as the increased savings of oil exporters have been matched to a large extent by the dissavings of the oil importers), nor that the low level of global interest rates – the bond market conundrum – has to do with the oil shock and the recycling of saved petrodollars.

Huge current account deficits triggered by a transitory oil shock and the recycling – dollar per dollar – of hundreds of billions of new petrodollars can have nothing to do with a savings glut: if the savings of the exporters match the dissavings of the importers, this is no savings glut, but rather a flow of capital, financing optimal full consumption, smoothing at unchanged equilibrium real interest rates. To argue that the oil shock is a source of a global savings glut, one has to prove that this shock increased the total supply of global savings at initial real interest rates, then that this increase in global savings had a significant effect on global real interest rates, and finally that the ensuing change in global real interest rates led to changes in private savings and investment behaviour that are consistent with a savings glut effect. So far, no one has provided any evidence of this.

It is important to note that oil exporters will soon start to spend a larger fraction of their oil windfall, as they have done in the past. When this happens, the consequences will be painful for countries such as the United

States that, like the infamous cricket from Aesop's fables, have not put aside money for bad times, while the ants in Europe and Asia responded to the shock by wisely cutting spending, as they would in response to a permanent income shock. When oil exporters start to spend more, it will be painful in many ways for the United States: oil exporters' marginal propensity to spend on European and Japanese goods is higher than their propensity to spend on US goods, but their propensity to invest in USD assets has so far been greater than their propensity to accumulate euro or yen assets. When the spending adjustment does occur, however, it will push down the US dollar as demand for US assets becomes demand for European and Asian goods. Moreover, oil exporters are more flexible in their portfolio choices than central banks are; they may diversify out of USD assets faster than central banks when the fortunes of the US dollar reverse. Recent episodes of asset protectionism in the United States (such as the *Dubai Ports* case) may accelerate the desire of these oil exporters to get out of USD assets. Once oil exporters spend more and diversify their assets to a greater degree, the implications for the US dollar and interest rates will be significant.

The United States is at least lucky in that China and other members of the BWII periphery are foolish enough to subsidize US consumption and housing by selling their goods to the United States too cheaply and by lending it so much that US interest rates are much lower than they would otherwise be. Yet strangely, many in the United States make bellicose threats to China to move its currency or else face protectionism. Given how much China and other Asian countries are financing US deficits, this is like biting the hand that feeds it. If these countries were to stop intervening before the United States has done anything to tackle its twin private and public savings droughts, the renminbi and other Asian currencies would surge and US import prices and interest rates sharply increase; the United States would risk a hard landing.

The biggest net debtor and net borrower in the world can little afford to be choosy about the ways in which its creditors are willing to finance it. Such creditors are telling the United States that they are getting tired of piling up hundreds of billions of low-yielding US Treasuries. If they are to continue to finance the United States at a rate of 1 trillion US dollars a year (soon to be the size of the US current account deficit), they expect to be able to buy US gems, that is equity/FDI and US firms, rather than just bonds. But, as the *Unocal–CNOOC* and the *Dubai Ports* cases show, the United States is now telling its creditors that it is not willing to let equity investments by such creditors into the country. So it comes as no surprise that China is starting to use its US dollar reserves to buy real assets – mines, natural resources, and so on – in Africa, Latin America and Asia since it is thwarted in its desire to buy US real assets rather than IOUs (Treasury bonds).

This 'asset protectionism' is dangerous for the United States. It may also be unfortunate that, unlike the 1980s, when the largest lenders to the United States were its allies (Germany, Japan), today its largest lenders are unfriendly countries that may also be geostrategic competitors, or potentially unstable (China, Russia, Saudi Arabia, oil exporters). It is hard for the United States to complain about the geostrategic rise of China and its scramble for resources when it is heavily subsidizing US consumption, housing and investment, and is financing a good chunk of the US fiscal deficit and the various wars – against Iraq, Afghanistan, terrorism – that the United States is fighting abroad. There is indeed a 'balance of financial terror' – as Larry Summers (2004) aptly put it – in these global imbalances, but this is a case of dangerous and self-inflicted vulnerability on the part of the United States.

CONCLUSION

It is now time to pass judgement and pronounce the sentence. Given the above analysis of the nature and causes of global imbalances, we can now go back to the two essential policy questions posed earlier. On balance, one can only argue that global imbalances of the size that we are observing represent not just a misdemeanour, but a serious crime: they are not sustainable over time and their continuation increases the risk of a disorderly adjustment. Many different countries are responsible for this imbalance crime, and each will have to contribute to an orderly rebalancing.

There is indeed a growing, if tentative, international consensus, at least rhetorically, on what needs to be done and by whom. The United States needs to address its twin savings deficits: its large budget deficit and its low level of private savings. This implies reversing certain tax cuts that the United States cannot afford to make permanent. China – and the rest of the BWII periphery in Asia and other emerging markets – needs to let its currency appreciate and to adopt structural reforms that will lead to more domestic consumption and lower net exports. Europe and Japan need to accelerate structural reforms that will increase investment, productivity and growth, thus shrinking their external surpluses. Oil exporters need to let their pegged currencies appreciate and start spending more on consumption and investment. In each region, a combination of expenditure switching policies (via changes in relative prices triggered by currency movements) and expenditure-level-change policies (a reduction for the United States relative to its income, increases in the other regions relative to their respective incomes) is necessary to achieve an orderly global rebalancing. A significant fall in the US dollar and an increase in US private and public savings without a corresponding increase in foreign expenditure and reduction in foreign savings could lead to a global slowdown. Thus the burden of rebalancing the global economy must be fairly distributed.

There is a somewhat general consensus on an appropriate, orderly rebalancing; the problem is the gap that exists between the rhetoric and the reality. The United States is doing little or nothing to address its structural fiscal deficit (the current improvement is only cyclical); China (and Asia) is resisting a currency adjustment and moving too slowly towards policies that will reduce savings and increase consumption; structural reforms are occurring at a snail's pace in Europe and Japan; oil exporters are sticking to their currency pegs and not investing more in exploration for, and production of, more oil. Indeed, oil exporters include disparate, geostrategically unstable countries such as Iraq, Iran, Venezuela, Saudi Arabia, Nigeria and Russia, which are highly unlikely to massively and collectively increase their national investment rates or increase the needed global oil production.

The IMF has been given the role of an impartial 'arbitrator' or 'referee' (to call it the 'judge' in this chapter would be incorrect as the IMF has little power of enforcement or even true leverage power over sovereign countries that do not currently borrow from it) in the debate, or international blame game, on the causes of global imbalances and what to do about them. But unless the IMF starts to be more assertive in its views and shows the courage to name names both among the borrowers and the lenders in this saga, it risks becoming irrelevant to the debate. Sometimes managers need to stand up to their shareholders and show true independence in their views and actions. One can only urge the IMF to stand up and speak up frankly. Each country or region is blaming a different one, and none is taking responsibility for its own actions.

Meanwhile, the problem is becoming increasingly unsustainable. As the twin spectres of trade and asset protectionism are now rearing their ugly heads in the United States and all over the world, it is the duty of the organization in charge of global economic and financial stability and cooperation to take charge and defuse these threats to the global economy.

Thus, (rhetorical) talk is cheap, and global imbalances are increasing, becoming less and less sustainable. In 2007, the US current account deficit will be as high as 1 trillion US dollars and rising. Every year the world needs to lend another trillion dollars to the United States, on top of what has already been lent to finance the US external imbalance. At some point, this will become an unsustainable Ponzi game – an unsustainable permanent accumulation of US external liabilities and an ever expanding ratio of these liabilities relative to its GDP.

To understand the scale of the massive net external financing needs that the United States faces – and the risks to a stable flow of financing on such a large scale – consider the following. In 2005, the US current account deficit was 785 billion US dollars. The conditions for a private sector financing of US deficits in 2005 were as ideal as possible: US interest rates were going up as the Federal Reserve tightened policy while the European Central Bank (ECB) and the Bank of Japan were holding rates steady; US real GDP growth was much higher than in Europe and Japan; the Homeland Investment Act heavily subsidized the flow of foreign profits back into the United States; and the dollar was going up, providing capital gains to foreign holders of USD assets. Yet even in these most ideal circumstances, only half of the US current account deficit was financed on net by private investors, as foreign central banks accumulated about 400 billion in USD assets.

In 2007, the US current account deficit is set to reach 820 billion US dollars, while: (a) the Federal Reserve, at some point, stops tightening policy, while the ECB and the Bank of Japan are starting to tighten theirs; (b) US growth is slowing down, but EU and Japanese growth are rising; (c) the Homeland Investment Act has expired; and (d) US assets (equities and housing) are falling return-wise. Under these conditions, the willingness of private foreign investors to hold USD assets will be lower than in 2005, while US financing needs will be greater. Unless foreign central banks are willing to accelerate their accumulation of USD assets – even relative to the massive amounts of 2005 – the US dollar will fall and interest rates will increase; the supply of financing will fall, while the US demand for it, to cover its twin deficits, still remains large.

Added to this, if central banks decide to accumulate foreign reserves at a slower pace than in 2005 (just a slower pace of accumulation of new dollar assets, not a dumping of their existing stocks), the willingness of private investors to compensate for the reduced official financing of US deficits will be sharply reduced. Private demand for USD assets is complementary to, not a substitute for, public demand. As long as Asian and other BWII currencies were stable – not rising – relative to the US dollar, it made sense for private investors to finance the United States, because the benefits of carry trades – for example, borrowing at 0 per cent in Japan and investing at 5 per cent in US assets – were large and the currency risk close to nil. But if central banks intervene less and allow some appreciation of their currencies, private demand for USD assets will fall sharply as capital losses on the holdings of those assets would be significant. Like Alice in Wonderland who had to run faster to stay in the same place, financing US deficits without adversely affecting the value of the US dollar and US interest rates depends on an ever more precarious Ponzi game where foreign central banks accumulate dollar assets at increasing rates year after year in spite of the fact that, once the dollar starts to weaken, the capital losses for both official and private investors on their holdings of USD assets will be massive. This Ponzi game cannot and will not continue.

There are plenty of factors that may reveal to investors that the Emperor has no clothes, thus triggering the unravelling of the BWII system of 'vendor financing' of the United States: the Federal Reserve stopping its tightening cycle; a sharp US economic slowdown; foreign central banks starting to diversify reserves (as they are currently doing); asset protectionism, or goods protectionism, towards China triggering – as did threats of a trade war in 1987, which led to a stock market crash – a sharp fall of the dollar and greater portfolio diversification out of dollar assets; an episode of systemic risk having its source in the United States; a Chinese currency revaluation followed by the appreciation of a wide range of Asian currencies; rising geostrategic shocks challenging US power in the Middle East, Iraq, Iran or North Korea.

The dangers of a hard landing in an increasingly imbalanced global economy are rising. Tackling global imbalances is urgent. Yet little is being done to avoid a disorderly rebalancing. The multilateral consultation mechanism launched by the G7 to give the IMF a role in achieving a consensus on global imbalances has turned out to be a disappointment, resulting in few real commitments and little substance. At the Spring 2006 meetings of the IMF, little was achieved apart from oft-repeated commitments to seriously tackle the imbalances. But this is not a time to delay the necessary policy steps that will reduce the risks of a disorderly global rebalancing. This risk is now becoming more serious, because the danger of a US economic hard landing in 2007–08 is rising. This could trigger a disorderly fall of the US economy and an increase in trade tension between the United States and countries such as China, which still peg their currency to the US dollar at undervalued levels. The eventual outcome of these currency tensions could be serious trade protectionism.

The only way to avoid an ending less acrimonious and painful than that of *Rashomon* is if each region or country assumes responsibility for its behaviour and, rather than spewing ineffective rhetoric, takes concrete action to rebalance the global economy. Time is running out. The time for endless debate is over. The time for action is now.

NOTES

1. In Voltaire's *Candide*, the catchphrase of the philosopher Pangloss is 'All is for the best in the best of all possible worlds'.
2. Also, a savings glut argument implies that the changes in the behaviours of China and oil exporters lead, for initially unchanged world real interest rates, to an increase in global savings that triggers a reduction in real interest rates, which in turn induces changes in US

private savings and investment, worsening the current account. Whether all this is true depends on whether such increases in global savings did occur and what its impact was on the world real interest rates. These are not uncontroversial issues, as discussed below.

REFERENCES

Bernanke, Ben (2005), 'The global saving glut and the U.S. current account deficit', speech given before the Virginia Association of Economics at the Sandridge Lecture, Richmond, Virginia, 10 March.

Cooper, Richard (2005), 'Living with global imbalances: a contrarian view', *Policy Briefs in International Economics*, No. PB05-3, Washington DC, December.

Cooper, Richard (2006), 'Understanding global imbalances', unpublished paper.

Cooper, Richard (2007), 'Living with global imbalances', *Brookings Papers on Economic Activity*, **2**, pp. 91–107.

Dooley, Michael, David Folkerts-Landau and Peter Garber (2003), 'An essay on the revived Bretton Woods system', NBER Working Paper no. 9971, Cambridge, MA.

Dooley, Michael, David Folkerts-Landau and Peter Garber (2004), 'The revived Bretton Woods system: the effects of periphery intervention and reserve management on interest rates and exchange rates in center countries', NBER Working Paper no. 10332, Cambridge, MA.

Dooley, Michael, David Folkerts-Landau and Peter Garber (2005a), 'Savings gluts and interest rates: the missing link to Europe', NBER Working Paper no. 11520, Cambridge, MA.

Dooley, Michael, David Folkerts-Landau and Peter Garber (2005b), 'Interest rates, exchange rates and international adjustment', NBER Working Paper no. 11771, Cambridge, MA.

Hausmann, Ricardo and Federico Sturzenegger (2006), 'The Implications of Dark Matter for Assessing the U.S. External Imbalance', Centre for International Development (CID) Working Paper no. 137, November, Harvard University.

Summers, Lawrence (2004), 'The United States and the global adjustment process', speech at the Third Annual Stavros S. Niarchos Lecture, Institute for International Economics, Washington DC, 23 March.

9. Round table discussion: monetary policy in the new international environment

Patrick Artus, Alan S. Blinder, Willem Buiter, Otmar Issing and Robert M. Solow

INTRODUCTION

The round table discussion brought together four speakers, Patrick Artus, Alan Blinder, Willem Buiter and Otmar Issing, under the chairmanship of Robert Solow, and covered a variety of topics to do with central banking. Rather than present a direct transcription, we have grouped together the different speakers' contributions into four broad themes, starting with the objectives of central banks and the tools at their disposal, moving on to explore the implications and effects of globalization on monetary policy and the problem of communication and transparency, and ending with the question of independence and accountability.

CENTRAL BANK OBJECTIVES AND TOOLS

Willem Buiter (London School of Economics) Economic first principles do not get us very far: the New Keynesian school, for example, tried to derive price stability as an objective – or even the overriding objective – of the central bank from first principles, but failed. All that can be obtained from first principles is a complex combination of three pillars:

- the Bailey–Friedman optimal quantity of money (OQM) rule (which is actually not an OQM rule, but only an interest rate rule) – setting the opportunity cost of holding central bank money equal to zero;
- the accommodation of 'core inflation' – avoiding relative price distortions between constrained and unconstrained price setters;
- the minimization of the deviation of output from the efficient level (not necessarily from capacity level, that is to say, not the output gap).

This is what the first principles of conventional welfare economics give us –
but it can be seen that price stability is markedly absent, and very few
central banks try to implement a zero nominal interest rate rule as even one
of the minor pillars of economic policy.

The alternative is to look for the objectives of central banks in a legalistic way, at what their constitutional legal mandates are. Here, the variety is
great. At one end of the spectrum lies the USA, where the Fed has a triple
mandate: the Federal Reserve Act defines the three objectives of maximum
employment, price stability and moderate long-term interest rates. The Fed
is the only central bank in the world to have a real economy objective, a price
stability objective and an asset market objective – a very ambitious portfolio. Most other central banks have a lexicographic ordering of objectives.
Priority is given to price stability, and subject to that objective being met,
'all things bright and beautiful'. Hence, the Bank of England's mandate is
to deliver price stability, and without prejudice to this objective, to support
the government's economic policy, including objectives for growth and
employment. The European Central Bank (ECB), the Bank of Japan and
many others have similar mandates. So the Fed is an outlier here, because
there is no lexicographic, hierarchical ordering of its three objectives.

What do these objectives imply? The Fed objective function can be
written:

$$L_t = (\pi_t - \pi^*)^2 + \lambda_1 (y_t - y_t^*)^2 + \lambda_2 (i_t^L - i^{L*})^2,$$

where $\pi_t - \pi^*$ is the deviation of inflation from target, $y_t - y_t^*$ is the deviation of the output from capacity level and $i_t^L - i^{L*}$ is the deviation of the
long-term interest rate from its 'moderate' target level. This is the ultimate
form of flexible inflation targeting, not just trading off output gap variability against inflation relative to target variability, but also against some
measure of financial stability.

The Fed has no choice; its mandate requires this strong form of flexible
inflation targeting. Central banks with a hierarchical mandate are better
off, because they are asked to concentrate on something that they can
influence not only in the short run, but also over the medium and long
terms. Some form of inflation targeting has now become the standard operational expression of price stability: minimizing the deviation of inflation
from target with secondary attention to the output gap. In practice,
however, flexible inflation targeting

$$L_t = (\pi_t - \pi^*)^2 + \lambda_1 (y_t - y_t^*)^2 \tag{9.1}$$

often turns into

$$L_t = \text{Var}\pi_t + \lambda_1 \text{Var}y_t, \tag{9.2}$$

minimizing a loss function or a period loss function defined simply over the *variance* of inflation and the *variance* of output. To get from (9.1) to (9.2), one has to make a number of important and dangerous assumptions. To put it another way, if the central bank starts targeting (9.2), trading off the variance of inflation against the variance of output, rather than the deviation of inflation from target and the output gap, it is assuming that:

1. there is no inflation target bias, that on average the inflation target is met;
2. there is no output gap bias;
3. the variance of capacity output is zero; and
4. there is no covariation between output and capacity output, which means that neither the servomechanisms of the market nor stabilization policy do anything.

Of these four assumptions, the first and fourth are highly unlikely to be satisfied, and the second, though it may hold over the long term, certainly cannot be maintained over the short or medium term. If the first assumption, that on average the inflation target is met, really is automatically satisfied, then the main problem faced by central banks has been solved, and they can be closed down. But the second-moment inflation objective is indeed second order, and the real inflation targeting challenge is to hit the first moment. And herein lies the danger with flexible inflation targeting, especially in the form of a trade-off between the variance in inflation and the variance in output. If governments lose track of the first-order problem, it risks becoming 'soft' inflation targeting and leading to inflation drift, such as we have seen in the USA in recent years, in New Zealand, in Australia, and undoubtedly in the Scandinavian countries that have been benighted enough to adopt a strong version of flexible inflation targeting.

Alan Blinder (Princeton University) [picking up on the idea that the variance of inflation doesn't matter, only the mean]   This is not what I teach my elementary students in economics! Take two economies, one with year-to-year inflation of 3 per cent, varying by plus or minus 0.2 per cent decided by a flip of the coin, the other with 5 or 0 per cent inflation, also decided by the flip of a coin. The second has a lower mean, but a much higher variance. Which has the bigger inflation problem? The second. The phrase seen so often in central bank statutes – price stability – encompasses that. Central banks don't want the inflation rate jumping around from one year to the next, and neither do the people.

Buiter   Of course, all other things being equal, one would like the variance of inflation to be smaller, but dropping the mean altogether is dangerous. Of course, one can drown in a river that is on average only 25 inches deep, and inflation going from −100 per cent to +100 per cent from one year to the next is no one's idea of a barrel of fun, but still, anyone who does not recognize in the specification of an objective function that the level of the inflation target may not be easy to achieve on average is assuming away the hardest part of what the central bank does.

Otmar Issing (European Central Bank)   The question of objectives has always been on the agenda, explicitly or implicitly. The objectives or mandates of the central bank cannot be seen in isolation, they must be seen within the macroeconomic institutional arrangement of the country or region. This implies that we need a clear allocation of responsibilities and competences which must coincide. We must make it clear from the beginning that blurring responsibilities, making everybody responsible for everything means, in the end, that nobody is responsible for anything. This has a lot to do with the issue of accountability, which we shall come back to later.

Let us look at the institutional arrangement of the monetary union in Europe. The ECB has a clear mandate: the primary objective is maintaining price stability. Following Richard Musgrave, the allocation of responsibilities and competences in fiscal policy can be divided into three categories:

1.   the allocation of resources to the public and private sectors;
2.   distribution responsibilities; and
3.   a stabilization function, which, in the context of the monetary union, on a national level, is defined by the Stability and Growth Pact (SGP).

Unfortunately, the SGP's definition of a 3 per cent deficit limit has always been the focus of attention. This is a misunderstanding of the main message, which is: keep the budget balanced in normal times. If you have high public debt, have a surplus, so that if real activity weakens, there is a long way to go to let the automatic stabilizers work. A budget change of 3 per cent of GDP is a long way. And it is often forgotten that in case of a severe downturn, the SGP has an emergency clause, so the 3 per cent limit does not apply. Other (real) objectives can be left to the economy, to markets, especially including labour markets, but not in a way that we need central planning for wage increases – quite the opposite – we need a different framework than centralized wage bargaining; we need competitive labour markets. We need a framework where real wages react timely to changes in the labour market situation at all levels, regional levels, especially in the monetary union.

To return to monetary policy, the ECB has made clear from the beginning that a central bank can only control inflation over the medium to long term – it cannot control headline inflation over the short term. It is obliged by its statutes to comply with the task mandated to it, ultimately by the people of Europe. And as far as the time length of monetary policy is concerned, here again only the medium to long term is relevant. This has two implications. First, monetary policy automatically takes into account changes in real activity, and this is included in any medium- to long-term approach, so the real economy is not a target, but one of the most important variables in the reaction function, as is the exchange rate, for example.

Second, maintenance of price stability over the medium term anchors inflation expectations. This stabilizes long-term nominal interest rates, reduces risk premiums on inflation and has a very important anchoring effect on wage negotiations. In discussions with union leaders, who may feel ECB policy as a constraint on wage negotiations, I have always stressed that we should look from the opposite angle. It is an obligation of the ECB to deliver on its mandate, because if the wage negotiators trust that you will deliver and are disappointed, this will be a macroeconomic disaster, because in the next round there will be higher wage demands to compensate for the losses. So the ECB must respect its obligations, and of course exogenous shocks like the oil price rises put both unions and the ECB in a difficult situation. The ECB must explain why it cannot control inflation over the short term and union leaders must explain that there is no compensation for increases in the price index caused by things like oil price rises. Looking back, the Euro area has done better in this respect than we might have expected when it started.

Finally, in this context, I'm not here to defend the ECB's monetary policy, but to explain how this arrangement has worked over the last eight years. The ECB has kept nominal interest rates at 2 per cent for two and a half years, which means that it has conducted a very expansionary policy: the real short-term interest rate has been negative or zero all the time. The result has been slow growth and persistently high unemployment. What is the reason for that? Might an even more expansionary policy have brought better results without creating inflationary risks? This is a clear illustration that expansionary monetary policy is not a substitute for nominal and real rigidities in an economy. The ECB, for example, has published an article on monetary policy 'activism' (*Monthly Bulletin*, November 2006) where it explains convincingly that we cannot obtain a good measure of the monetary policy stance simply by looking at the nominal level of central bank interest rates, or just counting the number of changes in the interest rate;

we must look at the size and kind of shocks. The reaction of the central bank is different when dealing with demand shocks and with supply shocks.

Benjamin Friedman (Harvard University) [from the floor]   I'm surprised that you [Otmar Issing] appear to be so sanguine about the prospects for counter-cyclical fiscal policy. The high-water mark of the notion of automatic stabilizers was back when Bob Solow and colleagues were on the Council of Economic Advisers in the early 1960s. The beginning of the turn of that tide, at least in American opinion, was the failure of the 1968 US tax surcharge to have much effect, the idea being that if we have forward-looking behaviour, what matters is either permanent income (taking Milton Friedman's view) or life-cycle behaviour (in terms of Franco Modigliani's formulation), and therefore not much that happens on the tax side matters. Spending programmes are difficult to gear up and difficult to shut off once they're in place, and so the spending side isn't much help either. If we attach so much importance to monetary policy in the present era, part of the reason is precisely because of the loss of confidence in the potential use of fiscal policy as a stabilizing device – not that you couldn't use it if you had the Great Depression all over again. But for ordinary business cycle frequency fluctuations, the view is that there's just not a lot to be done with fiscal policy. Otmar seems to be taking a much more confident view of the prospects for fiscal policy. Is it really something that either a government in a country like the US could use effectively, or even more so countries in Europe, where the task is made even more arduous by having to coordinate all of the fiscal policies in all of the European Union countries?

Issing   I certainly do not favour counter-cyclical fiscal policies. Benjamin's examples were taken from discretionary fiscal policies, perhaps the worst thing. My aim was to explain the design of the framework, and one of the problems, though not as important as structural rigidities, confronted by the monetary union is that fiscal policy does not play its intended role. In most cases it has been pro-cyclical, so the design has not been implemented; but this does not mean we should give up hope that the automatic stabilizers – which are somewhat independent of policy decisions – can play a role, albeit in a modest way.

Friedman   But then who is minding the store – looking after the real objectives? If it isn't fiscal policy, and it isn't the central bank, then that leads to the 'classical' view that real objectives are not to be looked after. This, rather than fiscal policy, may be the crux of the disagreement.

Buiter There is a difference between saying one should not have real objectives and what one expects to achieve in terms of these objectives through instrument design, whether it be monetary, fiscal or whatever. What can be done, either by monetary policy rules or by fiscal policy rules is helpful but extremely limited. So we should use automatic stabilizers, designed so that they have the maximum effect, and of course be ready, if the Great Depression hits us again, to use fiscal policy aggressively, although we should not expect to have to do that more than once every 150 years. Likewise for monetary policy: we should pursue an inflation target, which would, most of the time, when demand shocks are the main source of instability, also have a dampening effect on output (a pleasant byproduct), and only subject to the inflation target being pursued should we consider tinkering with monetary policy to pursue an independent output target – independent of the secondary effects of pursuing the inflation target. Otherwise, we should leave it entirely to the market to look after real activity.

Robert Solow (MIT) There is something in the background that has not been stated forcefully enough. It appeared that both Otmar Issing and Willem Buiter were thinking about an economy in which well-designed automatic stabilizers are in effect, whereas in fact the recent history of our economies has been that relatively weak automatic stabilizers have been allowed to weaken still further, and so some reform of fiscal stabilization mechanisms would help the situation. Whether or not that would run afoul of the same political malfunctioning that besets discretionary fiscal policy, it would be difficult to say. One could not set automatic stabilizers once for a century! Once for a decade might do the trick. The question is whether everyone is talking about an economy with strong economic (fiscal) stabilizers.

Buiter If the mechanism is too weak, we should try to redesign it. The whole political economic problem of the EU has been that the ceilings of the Maastricht criteria have intervened in the operation of the automatic stabilizers, and the response of the designers has been 'Too bad! Just get far enough below the ceiling, on average, so that they can be used in the proper way', and the political response has been 'Yes, but how to get there from here?'. There is real tension. It is very hard for policy makers not to override the automatic stabilizers during the upswing, to act perceptively. My own country, the Netherlands, has had notoriously pro-cyclical fiscal policy, even under a so-called conservative minister of finance in the latter part of the twentieth century and the first six years of this one. It is very hard for policy makers not to tinker with the tightening during the upswing. They're very happy to let the easing follow its course during the downswing. How can that be addressed? This is frustrating, because fiscal stabilizers could have a powerful dampening effect on the business cycle.

Patrick Artus (École polytechnique)　There are more and more supply shocks, rather than demand shocks. Look, for example, at China and commodity prices. How should the central bank react if inflation comes increasingly from adverse supply shocks rather than demand shocks?

Buiter　In principle, there isn't any problem. I don't think there are more supply shocks than demand shocks. China is both, and one of the causes of the misfiring of monetary policy in the US is that the Fed, with its focus on core inflation as the predictor of future headline inflation, has ignored the fact that the same globalization process (China's entry) lowers the inflation rate of manufactured goods – core goods – on the supply side, while it raises the inflation rate of non-core goods – commodities – on the demand side. The Fed welcomed the negative contribution of globalization to core inflation and decided to ignore the contribution to headline inflation, now or future, of China's demand side. As a consequence, the Fed has been 'barking up the wrong price index tree' for the last few years. It does make things more complicated, but if there is a supply shock, the appropriate policy response is to restrict output (depending on how persistent it is). That is not the problem; the real problem is to identify whether it is a supply or demand shock – and that is hard! When the oil crisis hit, from 1973 to 1979, nobody had seen a supply shock since Napoleon, so it took people by surprise. Not only did they not know how persistent it was, they didn't even know *what* it was! So there is a problem of identification, but in principle, it is a technical problem, not one of principle.

Artus　Several issues should be addressed by the central banks of modern economies. One important issue is the link or relationship between structural policies and monetary policies. Of course, in Europe, we know that we have to do something about structural rigidities. Economists are still arguing about the level of potential growth, but if we look at productivity gains (see Figure 9.1) and demographic prospects, then potential growth probably lies somewhere around 1.5 per cent, which calls for the implementation of a lot of structural reforms. The question is whether monetary policy can help to implement these reforms.

　　Some Scandinavian countries have already tackled this problem. In the 1990s, Sweden pursued very tough policies to reduce the fiscal budget deficit, restructuring the state, creating the so-called 'agency system'

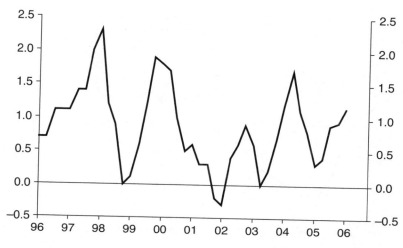

Sources: ECB; IXIS.

Figure 9.1 Eurozone: per capita productivity (Y/Y as %)

(Figure 9.2). Of course, this policy could have had an extremely restrictive effect on the economy: public spending was cut by 12 per cent of GDP in six years. The normal effect of that would have been dramatic recession, but this was avoided because monetary policy at the time switched to a very expansionary stance, with a considerable weakening of the currency and a very big decline in short-term rates. So instead of coordination between fiscal and monetary policies, coordination between monetary policies and structural policies is a much more important issue. This is something we should like to hear central banks talking about much more: how can they help governments to really start implementing structural reforms?

The second issue is more specific to Europe than the United States. How do you pursue monetary policy when there is a lot of uncertainty about the way it's working, about the transmission mechanisms of monetary policy? Europe is a very difficult case. The task of the ECB is much more complicated than that of the Fed, for example. Table 9.1 shows the share of variable rates in mortgage credits in Eurozone countries. Variable rates account for between 15 and 100 per cent of mortgages, so when the ECB moves interest rates this has a very different effect from one country to another. There is a lot of heterogeneity, which means that there is great uncertainty about the channels of transmission, about the effects of monetary policy. The literature is not very clear about what to do in the event of uncertainty about the

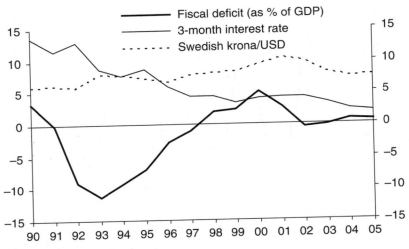

Source:　Datastream; IXISCIB.

Figure 9.2　Sweden: fiscal deficit, 3-month interest rate, exchange rate
　　　　　　against dollar

Table 9.1　Eurozone countries: percentage of variable rates in new
　　　　　　mortgage loans

Country	Variable rate (%)
Eurozone*	50.8
Eurozone excluding Germany	65.7
Germany	15
Austria	58
Belgium	52
Spain	95
Finland	97
France	35
Greece	88
Italy	85
Ireland	92
Luxembourg	81
Netherlands	44
Portugal	98

Note:　*By weighting of the 12.

Source: Bank of France.

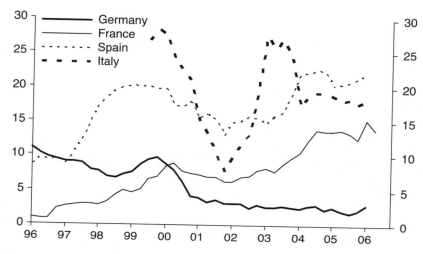

Sources: BUBA; BOE; Bank of Italy; Bank of France.

Figure 9.3 *Mortgage loans to households (Y/Y as %)*

effects of monetary policy. One school of thought argues that you should be less activist, more prudent, if you don't know what effect your moves will have on the economy, but modern theory says you should be more activist, so as to learn how the economy reacts. This is an important issue in Europe, and currently no one really knows what the increase in short-term rates will do to the European economy, at which stage it will really start to bite.

Figure 9.3 shows the consequences of heterogeneity: with low interest rates there are countries like Germany where mortgages increase by 2 per cent per year and Spain where they increase by 22 per cent per year. In the USA, a mortgage is a mortgage; in Europe a mortgage is not a mortgage, depending on whether you are in Germany or Spain, and this complicates matters a great deal for the ECB. The same is true for property prices (Figure 9.4).

Another important issue is the risk of deflation. It may seem strange to raise the subject now: the market mood is that it's over, even in Japan. Yet we are opening trade with countries where labour costs are seven times lower than they are here, and the idea that the disinflationary effect of emerging countries is over is completely erroneous. The market share of emerging countries is still growing a lot. China accounts for 7 per cent of world trade; this could rise to 15 or 20 per cent, with products with much lower prices, so we cannot exclude the risk that deflation might appear at some point. The case of Japan sparked a lot of debate about what should

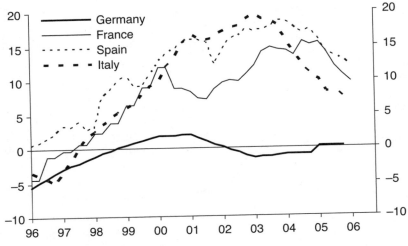

Source: FNAIM; National Statistics.

Figure 9.4   Real estate prices (Y/Y as %)

be done when deflation appears. There are different ways of operating monetary policy, for example, controlling base money, using exchange rate or price-level targets rather than inflation targets, but I'm not sure the ECB would be ready to face a renewal of deflation. It was a terrible thing in Japan and has only just finished.

The next point concerns asset prices. The consensus among central bankers appears to be that there cannot be a conflict between the objective of controlling inflation and the objective of controlling asset prices, because if you control inflation, there is no financial imbalance, and if there is no financial imbalance, then no such thing as an asset price bubble can appear. In reality, however, things are very different. Take the UK (Figure 9.5), where not just for the ten years shown in the graph, but for nearer 20 years, there was extremely low inflation (1 to 2 per cent) with an extremely strong increase in credit (between 10 and 15 per cent) and property prices rising between 15 and 25 per cent per year.

In reality, there can be a conflict between controlling asset prices and controlling inflation. So if the central bank has to choose between controlling a good or an asset – the supply of which is very inelastic – then probably asset prices are a better candidate than goods prices. That way, the central bank cannot hide behind the idea that controlling inflation is enough: we can have low or no inflation for a very long time and still have a very big problem with asset prices. And asset prices are very strongly correlated with household debt. It would appear to be important for the

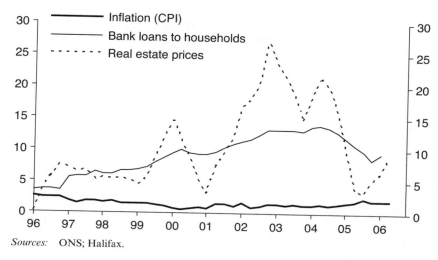

Sources: ONS; Halifax.

Figure 9.5 United Kingdom: inflation, house prices and loans to households (Y/Y as %)

central bank to prevent excessive growth in asset prices, in order to avoid banking crises, wealth loss and the obvious risk of deflation.

GLOBALIZATION

Artus Ten years ago we were in closed economies, and in that context, when unemployment goes down and capacity utilization goes up, then inflation lies ahead, and there is a very simple way of pursuing monetary policy: looking at straightforward leading indicators of inflation such as jobs and credit. But the world has changed radically since then. We have witnessed a big increase in the international mobility not only of goods, credit services and capital, but also labour. Research is still being conducted into the effects of migration on economies, but it is probably very much underestimated.

Monetarism is founded on the idea that an excessive increase in money supply or credit leads to an increase in the demand for goods, and at some stage the supply of goods, being rigid, cannot be extended any more, and we end up with inflation. But in a world where goods, labour and capital can flow very freely from one country to another, together with extreme excess capacity in emerging countries (China has an investment-to-GDP ratio of above 50 per cent), the supply of goods and services has become very flexible, at a national level. This calls for a change in the way we define

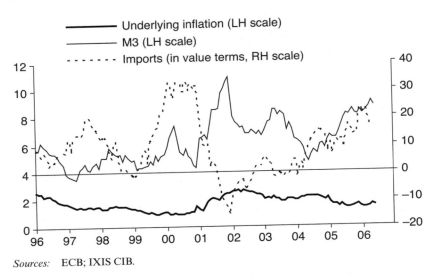

Sources: ECB; IXIS CIB.

Figure 9.6   Eurozone: M3, inflation and imports (Y/Y as %)

monetarism. An increase in credit still leads to an increase in the demand for goods and services, but if the supply of goods and services is very flexible, then this does not result in more inflation. All the leading indicators of future inflation give wrong signals: stronger domestic demand, more jobs, a quicker pace of credit distribution and a larger rate of M3 growth will not lead to greater inflation if they can be offset by more imports. This is a very important issue.

Let us look at a couple of illustrations, starting with the standard assumption that M3 growth is a leading indicator of future inflation (Figure 9.6). Here, for the Euro area, we can see that an increase in the money supply (for modern economies, this means increasing the credit supply) can result in more imports rather than higher inflation. Additional demand has been met by a rise in imports, not by increased demand for domestic products produced domestically. If you want to buy one more television, it's produced in China, so it does not add to European inflation. This is the starting-point for what globalization is doing to the economic environment.

In Figure 9.7, we can see that imports from developing countries have increased by about 300 per cent since the launch of the euro, so it is very difficult to keep thinking in terms of a closed economy. In an article in the *Financial Times* (9 November 2006), Jean-Claude Trichet defends the use of money supply growth and credit growth as leading indicators of future inflation. He is clearly still thinking in an environment of a closed economy.

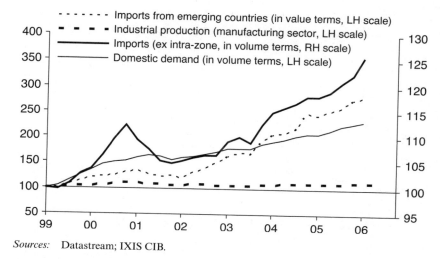

Sources: Datastream; IXIS CIB.

Figure 9.7   *Eurozone: domestic demand, imports, industrial production (1999 = 100)*

Twenty years ago, with our strong credit growth and a clear recovery in demand, we would have been facing inflation, but this is not the case today, because what we want to buy can be produced elsewhere, in countries with a huge potential for producing more. China has huge reserves of labour, in the form of 300 million disguised unemployed in the countryside. There is also surplus capacity, with investment rising by 30 per cent per year in China and other Asian countries. We must now start thinking in terms of this environment of very open economies for all factors.

If we consider that monetary policy looks at a variable factor that shows an increase in prices when there is excess demand for it, then goods and traded services no longer fit the bill, because their supply has become too flexible. Monetary policy needs something with a very rigid supply, and one natural candidate is assets, such as houses, equities, bonds, and so on.

Another question concerns what has to be done at a regional or national level and what at the global level. Inflation has become a purely global phenomenon; it will not reappear locally if it does not reappear globally. As long as there are countries like China, India, Brazil, and so on, producing more at low cost with a lot of unused capacity, then nothing like inflation will appear locally in Europe, the UK or the USA. So inflation, probably for a very long period of time, must be controlled at the global level – goods are extremely mobile, so inflation is the same everywhere. Targeting inflation locally is stupid: first because you cannot control it, as it is determined at the

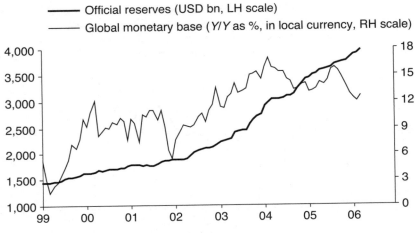

Sources: Central Bank; IXIS CIB calculations.

Note: * United States, Canada, EU15, Japan, China, India, other Asian emerging countries, Central and Eastern European Countries, Latin America (including Mexico), Russia, Norway and OPEC.

Figure 9.8   World*: monetary base and official reserves

global level, and second because there is no risk, as long as China is not operating at full capacity, which might be the case in about 50 years. So inflation probably has to be looked at and controlled globally by a coordination of monetary policies. We don't have that kind of coordination.

In Figure 9.8, we can see that base money growth at the world level is running at 12 to 15 per cent per year, so globally monetary policy is very expansionary. But nobody looks at that: monetary policy is still pursued at a local level. And at a local level, if inflation is only global, then we need something that can be controlled at the local level, and which is meaningful at the local level. Credit or asset prices are natural candidates, certainly not inflation!

Buiter [in disagreement with Patrick Artus's assertion that inflation is only a global phenomenon, that it will only appear locally if it appears globally, which is attributed to goods mobility]   Not so. It has nothing to do with goods mobility, but inflation will become a global phenomenon if the different national fiat money bases become perfect substitutes. I agree with Alan that real things have nominal implications, just as nominal things have, at least in the short term, real implications, but this is very different from the statement that inflation has become a global phenomenon.

Increasing openness and globalization have no obvious implications for the fundamentals of what drives inflation at the national level – as long as an economy has a floating exchange rate.

Artus Take two countries, say Europe and China, with open trade between them and initially very different unit labour costs or price levels. Willem says that the exchange rate system will adjust, that we will move very quickly towards level PPP [purchasing power parity] exchange rates. In the case of China and Europe, how could this work? Unit labour costs in China are seven times lower than in Europe, and we cannot afford for the euro to depreciate by 600 per cent. So in reality we are very close to fixed exchange rates. What we see is price-level convergence with almost fixed exchange rates between these two countries, which means both an increase in the price level in China and a decrease in Europe. This is not totally consistent with theory, but it is what we see. We have seen the same before with much smaller countries, in a much less symmetrical fashion. Price-level convergence was at work when Ireland, Portugal, Greece and Spain joined the EU. This is what we have now: lower labour costs and price levels in Europe and the US, and higher price levels in China. This is not really disinflation, it is price-level convergence, but if it takes 20 years to happen, then it does seem very like disinflation during this period.

The mobility of base money is a very interesting issue. Take the US and China, for example: the US is running a very large trade deficit with China, because increasing domestic demand is being met by more imports. And this trade deficit is financed by reserve accumulation in China, which means base money growth in China. So the American consumer is being financed by base money growth in China. The mortgage market provides another illustration of the mobility of money. In the UK, for example, many people are taking out mortgages in yen; in Hungary, 90 per cent of the loans are made in euros. If we were in a world where there were very strong constraints on trade balances, an increase in domestic demand could not be met by an increase in imports. This would imply, for instance, that monetary policy would be the old-fashioned model, reacting immediately to an increase in domestic demand to stabilize the trade account. But this is not what we see. Monetary policy does not react; there are large trade deficits, which are very easily financed because of the huge mobility of capital as well as goods.

Buiter Clearly, if two countries or regions have fixed exchange rates, then their inflation rates will converge. As long as China insists on having a fixed exchange rate with the US, their inflation rates, even though we have to allow for the inflation differential in traded and non-traded goods, are going to converge. Deciding to have a floating exchange rate regime is a policy choice, and inflation is then a national monetary policy choice. This is why, for example, after the collapse of the peso–dollar currency peg, for example, inflation in Mexico was 30 per cent higher than the Chinese or American rate. So there is no issue here: with a floating exchange rate, inflation is a national monetary authority responsibility.

China's and India's entry into the world economy is certainly a monumental event. The excess capacity they create (certainly in the case of China; India is much less clear, but potentially it could have the same effect) affects global real wages, the global real rate of return to capital formation, the global risk-free interest rate, maybe even global risk premiums, but there are no mechanical implications for inflation, which is still made by national central banks. So inflation is made nationally, as long as there is a floating exchange rate.

Now, moving on to look at the implications of globalization for monetary policy. In a world with floating exchange rates, central bank coordination for normal, non-crisis monetary purposes is redundant. Globalization does not mean that greater frequency of inter-central bank meetings is desirable. It is clearly essential that there be meetings between either central banks or those in charge of financial stability to set up arrangements for dealing with global systemic risks of the 9/11 variety, and the coming credit risk crisis when it hits us. These things have to be in place, but that doesn't require regular meetings and the expenditure of large amounts of tax-payers' money for joint treasury/central bank missions to China. If there is a problem with global imbalances, for instance the unsustainable current account surplus of the rest of the world *vis-à-vis* the US, then the solution is fiscal and structural (measures to directly influence private savings and investment behaviour). Monetary policy can play a supportive role, in the adjustment of global imbalances. If it actively discourages the international relative price changes that are part of the smooth adjustment of global imbalances, this would not be helpful. Otherwise, monetary policy will play a supportive, minor role, at best, in the resolution of global imbalances.

Blinder   Let's explore the ways in which globalization might affect monetary policy. There must be a reasonable middle position between two 'non-straw men', or positions actually advocated by real people. One extreme is constituted by the position that because of globalization, all the old rules of central banking are out; everything must be learnt anew. We don't hear academics saying this, but we do hear a lot of non-academics, including some smart people in financial markets who should know better! The other extreme is that globalization has no relevance; central banks just have to carry on doing the same thing they've always done.

To argue for an intermediate position between these two extremes, we shall start with a very brief review of what monetary policy is supposed to be doing. Monetary policy is supposed to influence the paths of employment (E) and inflation (π), largely by manipulating aggregate demand and thereby the GDP gap ($y - y^*$), which it affects largely by moving the real long-term interest rate relative to its equilibrium value ($r_L - r_L^*$) (this is the modern view of monetary transmission, as opposed to the Milton Friedman view), which it does largely by moving the short-term nominal interest rate (i_S). There are already two degrees of slippage between the short-term nominal rate and the long-term real rate. So the natural questions to ask are: could globalization be affecting either the path of GDP or the path of potential GDP, how does it influence long-term real rates or the equilibrium long-term real rate, and how does it influence the link between the nominal short rate and the real long rate and/or the central bank's ability to control the nominal short rate in its own market?

First, let us look at two methodological points that economists may have learnt too well. The first is that real and nominal things are different: globalization is a real phenomenon that has to do with real trade, how the Chinese are more productive, and so on, and therefore cannot have anything to do with the nominal side of things, which fundamentally depends on the money supply. This is a perfect example of the classical dichotomy that real things cannot have nominal consequences. We as a profession should have learnt in the 1930s that that is not so. Not every real thing has a nominal consequence, but we ought not to be ruling it out of court. The second point, which we also teach our students, is that it is essential to distinguish mentally between level effects and growth rate effects, and inflation is a growth rate of something. In the real world, globalization, like most changes, is a process that has been going on for some time and will continue for some time. It is possible, conceptually, to think of a world of all closed economies and then all open economies, and the levels have changed, but this levels change takes decades, so to all intents and purposes we are dealing with growth rate changes.

Now, let us look at the idea that globalization has no effect on the way central banks actually do their business. Three arguments are put forward to disprove this:

1. Globalization should make standard *international* influences and channels more important relative to domestic ones (that is, the exchange rate affecting import prices, which in turn affect inflation, or interest rates abroad, affecting domestic interest rates).
2. A major element in globalization is the growth of the world economy through the addition of countries like China and India (and Eastern Europe, and so on) to the 'economic world'. Twenty years ago these

countries weren't in the global economy; now they are. They will become even more present over the next ten years. This might shift the global balance of aggregate demand versus aggregate supply.

3. Footloose capital may be less tolerant of inflation, and that disciplines governments in general and central banks in particular.

Let us go through these three points in more detail, starting with the idea of the added importance of international influences and channels. It is a 'fact of globalization life' that trade shares are larger than they used to be, and they're trending up all over the world. But in the rich countries, this is an evolutionary rather than a discontinuous change in history. Take the US trade share, for instance. It is not quite literally linear, but it is creeping up and up, and that will keep on happening. The trend towards increasing openness was no higher in the 1990s than it was in the 1960s: the levels are much higher, but the trend is the same. And looking more closely at the 'pass-through' channel mentioned above – whereby monetary expansion is supposed to reduce the exchange rate, currency depreciation is supposed to raise import prices, and rising import prices raises the domestic inflation rate – two strange things stand out. There is much less to it than meets the conceptual eye – it's not nearly as big a channel as it should be – and it appears to be fading, rather than increasing. One might think that as we globalize – there is more and more trade, and the countries of the world are knit more and more closely together – that there would be a stronger pass-through channel, but this is not the case. If anything, recent evidence suggests the channel is getting even weaker. Estimates of the pass-through in the US, which were always low, look like they're asymptotically going to zero as time goes by. They're tiny! This is very odd, and has yet to be explained.

The interest rate parity channel has failed miserably for decades. One might think, naively, that this is because international capital mobility wasn't quite there, and the margins weren't getting arbitraged properly. Then it would be reasonable to deduce that as you open the world to greater and more fluid electronic finance, interest rate parity should start getting closer. But once again, this does not appear to be the case at all. This is a real paradox: we know that the world is global, we know that people can sit at a computer console and move 10 billion dollars from China to New York in six milliseconds, and yet interest rate parity is just not coming close. It often doesn't even get the sign right: if you compare the two short rates in two countries, it predicts the wrong direction. This also defies all explanation.

One final channel of foreign influence concerns the influence of globalization on productivity. This is a new idea, mostly due to Rob Feenstra and Brad Jensen. When one studies the wide heterogeneity that can be found in any industry, and especially the relative productivity of different companies, plants or establishments, it turns out empirically that companies and plants that are open to trade and dealing with the international market are on average more productive than those in the closed sector. To put it in Darwinian terms, it looks like those who are forced to compete in the international market place 'run faster'.

Feenstra cites research by Mary Amiti and Shang-Jin Wei, who found that in the United States, 'over the years 1992–2000, service outsourcing can explain between 12 and 17 per cent of the total increase in productivity'. Now, if we look at how much service outsourcing there was in that period, it was negligible. The volume of service outsourcing in the USA from 2000 to 2008 will be five or ten times as much. So this percentage is actually a very high number. We can apply the methodological point made earlier, about level effects and growth rate effects, to this issue. All of these stories are about level effects on productivity, but the level is constantly getting bumped up; openness and globalization keep increasing. If each increase has a small incremental-level effect, it looks very much like a growth rate effect that may last for decades. So greater openness to trade may enhance productivity growth, for what we might call Schumpeterian reasons.

Now let us look at the second way in which globalization might affect monetary policy: the addition of new countries to the global economy. The emerging countries, especially China, appear to be adding much more to the world supply of goods and services than to world demand. What does that mean? In the Keynesian short run, more supply means more slack in the world, and this shifts the 'Phillips curve' in a favourable direction, meaning faster growth with less inflation. The potential growth rate is pushed upwards, and so monetary policy should be adjusted accordingly. In the neoclassical long run, it means a lower long-term real interest rate, and central bankers have to adjust the interest rate setting to accommodate this new environment.

The third argument in favour of the influence of globalization is that footloose capital enforces the 'Washington Consensus'. If we look at this addition of capital and labour more in terms of mobility than in terms of amounts, it's pretty clear that globalization and electronic communication have increased capital mobility much more than labour mobility. There is some labour mobility, but it's not that easy to move from China to Europe or the US. So capital mobility has increased a lot more than labour mobility, and that increases the economic or political bargaining power of capital. Now, because of the tax system, among other reasons, inflation is bad for returns to capital. That is why stock markets sag when inflation rises. So capital doesn't like inflation, and governments that make capital worry about the inflationary consequences of their policies (among other things) get punished by the world capital market. One recent example is the election of Lula in 2002, which provoked a semi-panic over Brazil; it turns out that he is actually pursuing a much more mainline economic policy, but there was great fear at the time.

So the conclusion is that increasing globalization (it must be emphasized that this is a continuous, dynamic process – it doesn't just happen overnight) ought to increase the importance of the traditional international channels mentioned above, but this doesn't seem to be the case. It might increase productivity growth for the reasons put forward by Feenstra and Jensen. It appears to be adding more to supply than to demand and therefore making the job of inflationary control easier, though I wouldn't go so far as Patrick and say that it is all down to the world money supply. Finally, it may stiffen the anti-inflationary backs of those governments and central banks which need their backs stiffening (many don't), because of the increased threat of capital withdrawal.

Friedman [from the floor]   Going back to your point, Alan, on footloose capital, was the 'bond market vigilante' idea mentioned simply as an idea that is floating around, or as something that you believe in? It appears that the bond market vigilantes have been pretty much asleep for the last 20 years. The US is running both a current account deficit and a fiscal deficit, which, in any other country, would be considered wildly irresponsible, but the bond market vigilantes aren't taking any notice whatsoever. They completely slept through the Reagan era, and even in the mid-1990s, when the speaker of the House of Representatives suggested that it might not be such a bad idea if the US government defaulted on its debt, the bond market vigilantes had their heads in the sand the entire time. And in the Asian financial crisis, there were some countries afflicted that had recognizably bad macroeconomic imbalances, while others seemed to have nothing wrong. So are these bond market vigilantes actually doing a job, and are they doing it in a way that benefits anybody?

Blinder   I very much agree with this characterization of the disappearance of the bond market vigilantes (particularly in their reactions to US markets), but I was talking about inflationary policies, and more particularly in developing countries. The US has not had an inflation problem for quite some time (unless one fixates on the decimal point – as some people are now doing!).

Solow   I would like to go back to the point made by Alan about the integration of India and China into the trading economy causing an increase in aggregate supply relative to aggregate demand. This could be sharpened.

It certainly causes an increase in the aggregate supply of labour relative to aggregate demand for labour, but in terms of the demand and supply of capital, it may be the other way round.

Question from the floor   In a world where nominal and real long interest rates are determined either by the global savings and/or interventions and policies of central banks, what are the implications for monetary policy: should it be tighter, looser or no different?

Artus   There is an interesting article by Alan Greenspan, written a couple of weeks before he left the Fed, about what we should do when long-term rates no longer react so much to short-term rates. There are two possibilities. It could be that because of credibility, the inflationary shock does not transfer to inflationary expectations, and long-term rates do not move. Central banks should not fight against that. But in reality, what we have is some kind of bizarre investor called a central bank who is buying a mountain of bonds. In many cases, the markets think that central banks are normal investors looking for returns. They are not. They have a very macroeconomic target – to stabilize a currency or to keep exporting, and so they don't care very much about returns. There have been strange discussions about whether the People's Bank of China is worried about potential capital losses on its dollars. In fact they don't care; they simply have a provision on the balance sheet, and that's it. So when we have this bizarre investor blindly buying bonds, and bond rates are not determined in the normal way (supply/demand), then central banks should be much more activist, to offset the fact that long-term rates are much more rigid than before. They probably don't dare do so; when we hear about neutral short-term rates, this doesn't mean very much. If the long-term rate no longer reacts to the short-term rate, then what is a neutral short-term rate? Probably in the contemporary world, long-term rates are very rigid, because the Chinese and others are 'blindly' buying. Normally, central banks should overreact to the disturbances to offset that, because they just control the short end of the curve.

Blinder   If you think of the People's Bank of China as an inelastic demander, then the market is getting more inelastic as China and others become bigger players. But that's no explanation for the price not moving if the demand is bouncing around. So if bond rates are moving less, it must be because supply volatility has gone down.

Buiter   Certainly, if the Chinese central bank is buying at any price, this makes it hard for national monetary authorities to conduct monetary policy which depends on the relationship between short and long rates, if the long rate is determined capriciously.

Artus A normal investor switches from bonds to cash depending on relative levels of short- and long-term rates, but central banks don't do so. That is why the reaction of the long-term rate to the short-term rate has gone down.

Issing Activism means acting before you know what your previous act has achieved. This will create such volatility in behaviour that in the end nobody can identify what your actions have achieved. So if the world is uncertain, and we don't exactly know what's going on, then activism is not the solution.

Solow Activism can be measured in two ways: by the frequency of action and by the magnitude. Bill Brainard demonstrated once that the more uncertain you are about the effects of actions, the more gently you should act.

Buiter Imagine you are standing in front of a canyon. You know it's 100 feet deep and 4 feet wide; you jump over it with a mighty leap. Now you're in front of another canyon. You know it's 100 feet deep but you don't know how wide it is. It could be 3 feet or 5 feet. Do you take a smaller leap? No, a bigger one. So uncertainty can lead to bigger actions. This is not to say that Brainard's logic was wrong, but it is important to bear in mind that uncertainty doesn't necessarily lead to caution or to modest steps.

Solow I doubt that infrequent action is the best response to uncertainty. It may depend on whether one wants to act sharply or gently, but in many ways, one response to uncertainty is exploration. Buiter had taken a case where one cannot explore. Otherwise, one solution would be to throw a pebble over that canyon.

COMMUNICATION AND TRANSPARENCY

Artus Most existing research suggests that transparency is a requirement, especially for countries pursuing inflation targeting: you have to tell the markets your opinion, how you predict inflation, what sort of models you use, why you are cutting or raising interest rates. But a lot of other research suggests quite the opposite, that transparency has negative effects. If you give more information to the markets, for example, you coordinate expectations, and this can lead to very brutal reactions. What if, to take an extreme example, the central bank says 'equity prices will collapse next year' . . . one can imagine the consequences! And the controllability of economies may be reduced if the central bank is too transparent. So do central banks need to be very transparent or not? This subject calls for more discussion. And we must not confuse transparency with predictability: they are two very different animals. A central bank can be predictable, but not transparent; people may be able to predict its actions, but if those actions are stupid or incomprehensible, the reasons behind them will not be understood.

Issing   When I joined the world of central banking in late 1990, I was not aware of what would happen in relation to the importance of communication. In the 1970s, in Germany, for example, the president of the Bundesbank gave a speech twice a year. It was extremely boring, but nobody cared about that, it was a social event! The markets did not react – there were no financial markets present. There was a monthly bulletin describing the smooth flowing of the economy or explaining problems, but the Bundesbank only accepted that there was a recession after the event. This was a time when central banks lived in a world of opacity, which they had themselves created, at least partly. It is reminiscent of the story of Lady Wilberforce, the wife of the Bishop of Worcester, who, in 1860, when she learnt about Darwin's new doctrine, is said to have exclaimed: 'Descended from the apes! Us! How awful! Let us hope that it is not true, but if it is, let us pray that it will not become generally known!'. Now the world has totally changed – and for the better, I think.

Monetary policy can only fix the short-term interest rate. The effect of policy actions on the whole yield curve depends a lot on expectations; in this context the importance of communication is obvious. We should distinguish between communication of the short-term actions of the central bank and the medium to long term. In the short term, communication mainly takes the form of code words, which create strong expectations about what will happen on the occasion of the next meeting of the committee. The longer-term view must be separated from that. Over the short term, the announcement comes close to being unconditional, because, normally, not much happens to change the situation. The longer the horizon covered by the communication, the higher the risk that conditions will change. The difference between the two is sometimes blurred, because communicating the conditionality of the announcement is an almost impossible task. This is the reason why what is seen by some as the state of the art of central bank communication, presenting the future path of central bank interest rates, is not a wise thing to do. First, it is impossible to make clear the conditionality of the announced future path of central bank interest rates. Second, if there is any change in the economic environment, such as a change in the exchange rate, it will immediately raise questions about the impact of that on the announced interest rate path. So either the central bank has to communicate permanently or there is a lot of uncertainty in the markets about the effect of the changes on the reaction function of the central bank, creating a lot of volatility. It is no accident that only central banks in small countries have gone in that direction. Few, in financial markets, care much about the communication of small central banks; it is totally different for the large central banks in the world. Third, if the decision is taken by a committee, then it is very difficult to agree about future paths of interest rates, and on top of that, if the committee members, on an individual basis, express different views, then such communication creates uncertainty and a lot of volatility in markets, having quite the opposite effect to that intended by such an approach.

A convincing strategy accompanied by a convincing track record, and thus a consistent communication policy, complement each other over the longer term and are a sign of effective monetary policy. This is the framework in which inflation expectations are anchored in a sustainable way, beyond the short term, and for that, central banks must also communicate in a way that helps the public and the markets to understand how it will react in the future to exogenous shocks, so that the reaction function is more or less evident. This is a very important condition for anchoring communication in the medium to long term.

Blinder   Twelve and a half years from now, both the ECB and the Fed will be projecting their future interest rates numerically, in some sense. According to Otmar, one of the impediments is that conditionality cannot be communicated to the markets, because people get locked into whatever the central bank says, when it was meant to be conditional on the exchange rate and many other things. If the exchange rate changes, people will expect a different monetary policy. Well they should, and they will keep this thought until the next announcement, when the ECB or the Fed or whoever will announce a different path. This won't be minute by minute, reacting to every single data point, but at each meeting or whatever the frequency is. The ECB has less of a history of openings than the Fed, because it is so new: when it opened for business it was more open than the Fed and was actually criticized a lot. It communicated more and better than the Fed. The Fed has a long history that goes back to the Dark Ages of opacity. But, as was the case with every other Fed opening, people in the Fed will end up asking: 'What were we afraid of?' and 'Why weren't we doing this five years ago?'. There has never been a negative effect of any substance from any of the Fed openings. The hard part (as has already been suggested) is that you cannot reveal what you haven't decided yourself!

Buiter   Technically, under the current constitution, an announcement of likely future rates would amount to a policy decision, so there would have to be a vote on it. To have the committee voting on contingent term structures going out for 20 or 30 years would be rather difficult. One operational way around this would be for the committee to vote on the current rate and leave the rest of the stochastic simulations of future interest rate policy to the staff (this is probably how the Norwegians do it!). I doubt whether central banks use models with forward-looking elements in them to produce inflation forecasts, but if they do, then they have to put in a reaction function at some point, just to be able to solve the model and make the prediction. So the tool kit for doing stochastic simulations and getting an interest rate fan chart in addition to inflation and output fan charts is not a deep problem – it simply has to be delegated to the staff, and therefore have a different standing from the point of view of current legislation.

Issing   On Alan's prediction of what the ECB or other central banks will do in the future, I wouldn't bet on it! We cannot just extrapolate, but there is a kind of dynamics now, in communication, and even reluctant central banks cannot afford not to join the company, not only because they would look foolish, but also they might be punished by markets. This is a good thing. By moving in the direction of increased transparency, there might, however, be events where we see transparency creating more volatility, for example, rather than delivering what is expected of it. So it cannot be excluded, but it depends on the learning process.

ACCOUNTABILITY AND INDEPENDENCE

Buiter   It's important, when talking about central bank accountability, especially with the aim of calling the ECB to account (something that is long overdue), to differentiate between formal accountability, which concerns the reporting duties of the agent or trustee to the principal or beneficiary and has to do with transparency, and substantive accountability, whereby, once this information has been provided to the principal, consequences may follow. In the case of central banks, strong operational independence, especially the kind enjoyed by the ECB (the most operationally independent central bank in the world, with the Bank of England some distance behind), means no substantive accountability: no consequences follow. You cannot fire people even for incompetence, only for gross misconduct or incapacity, and even then it can be appealed to a court. And that raises a problem. Monetary policy, narrowly defined, is best entrusted to a strongly operationally independent central bank, but this has certain implications. It follows that the reporting duties should be taken extremely seriously, so that at least the naming and shaming part of formal accountability can be done as well as possible, and this is why procedural accountability, which is singularly absent from the ECB framework – no minutes, no votes, and so on – is so important. It has to make up for the legitimacy vacuum that inevitably arises when a delegated authority is not substantively answerable or accountable.

Treating the relationship of the ECB with the European parliament as an agency–principal relationship or even a trustee–beneficiary relationship rather stretches the meaning of these constructs, because an agent that cannot be influenced (punished or rewarded) by the principal, or a trustee that has no third party sitting in judgement over him to judge whether he has acted in the best interest of the beneficiary, with all due care, is not a normal agent or trustee. The question then is: how, in a democratic system of government, can we preserve legitimacy in delegated authority to an agency that is fundamentally not answerable? One necessary condition is to restrict the domain of substantive accountability, to transform the central bank into a minimalist, operationally independent monetary authority. It should not be allowed to accumulate a host of other tasks, responsibilities and duties behind this mighty wall of untouchability that operational independence implies. In the case of the ECB, the target is clear: lexicographic price stability and subject to that, growth, employment, happiness, and so on. The instrument is also clear: the short nominal interest rate. And nothing more!

And what should the central bank not do? It should not supervise or regulate banks, financial institutions and financial markets. Clearly, that also has to be delegated, but the degree of operational independence enjoyed by a supervisor and regulator must be lower than that for a central bank, because supervising and regulating, although partly technical and expert, are also deeply political. Property rights are at stake, somebody's ox is being gored on a regular basis, so these functions cannot be put behind the same 'don't touch me' wall that independent central banks have. I would argue that even the ownership, control and management of real-time gross settlement systems (RTGS), like TARGET, could be taken from the central bank and farmed out to another agency, possibly even private. The agency, to function efficiently, would need access to an overdraft facility with the central bank, but this is different from putting the RTGS system under the central bank, and I would advocate taking it away from the ECB. Instead, the ECB (or some of its members at least) has proposed that it should not only keep RTGS, but extend it to the clearing and settlement of financial securities in general. Again, this should be entrusted to an independent agency, for the same reasons – it does not deserve and need the kind of operational independence that the central bank has. So giving it to the central bank would be a dangerous enhancement of the domain of non-accountability. And finally, I would even take the lender of last resort (LOLR) function – at least the substance of it – away from the central bank. How can we do this if we believe that central bank money does play a unique role in the resolution or prevention of liquidity crises?

Clearly, for effective addressing of the LOLR function, we need three things: a treasury with the long-term deep pockets (only the treasury can hold the promise of ultimate recapitalization), a financial regulator/supervisor (the only one with the information), and a central bank and monetary authority with the short-term deep pockets, thus the ability to create unquestioned liquidity in arbitrary amounts at no notice. The second function can of course be substantively taken away from the central bank by granting the financial regulator an unlimited overdraft facility, guaranteed by the treasury with the central bank, to discharge this function. I would recommend, in the interest of minimizing the domain of non-accountability, to give this LOLR function to such an augmented financial regulator.

Blinder First, naming and shaming *is* serious substantive accountability. Would you rather have been leaving the Fed as Arthur Burns or as Alan Greenspan? It matters. But Willem is right to say that we could do better and might want something more satisfactory. Second, there is reappointment, which is political in the US and many other countries. If you do a bad job, you can be thrown out, just like politicians can get thrown out at the next election. Third, and here I agree, it's almost impossible to do in Europe, because it's enshrined in the Treaty, but in the US (and many other countries), the Federal Reserve Act and everything in it is an Act of Congress that can be amended tomorrow morning. So *in extremis*, if the central bank really starts misbehaving and doing terrible things, Congress can take the bull by the horns – and change the bull, in absolutely any way it wants. This should be in the statutory basis of a central bank, hopefully never to be used. It has never been used in the US, at least since the Fed was restructured in 1935. So there are three ways of accountability. If we compare this to Prime Minister Tony Blair, for example: there's naming and shaming. He might or might not get reappointed by the voters, and he could lose a vote of confidence, so there is substantive accountability for the central bank.

Buiter I agree that the Fed is a lot more substantively accountable than the ECB, which is the most operationally independent central bank. But for members of the ECB, there is little substantive accountability, since there is no reappointment of the executive board (they hold office for one eight-year term), and they cannot, effectively, lose a vote of confidence, because the only way to change the legal, regulatory framework of the bank is to change the Treaty, which requires unanimity of all 25 countries, and therefore won't happen. Other operationally independent central banks like the Bank of England or the New Zealand central bank go well beyond what Alan described for the US in the form of reserve powers: the Chancellor of the Exchequer can take back the rate-fixing powers tomorrow if he wants to (subject to parliamentary approval). Many other countries have similar reserve powers, but not the ECB. All that works for the ECB in terms of substantive accountability is naming and shaming, and how effective that is depends on one's assessment of the thickness of the skin of the people involved. This is not the only mechanism one would want to rely on from the point of view of normal democratic accountability.

Friedman [from the floor]   Naming and shaming can work differently in a setting where opinions are heterogeneous. Paul Volcker is now generally thought of as an exquisite contributor to the health of the American economy, yet there was a time when people took full-page ads in both *The New York Times* and the *Wall Street Journal* to complain about how he was ruining the US economy. So in a world of heterogeneous opinions, these things can cut either way.

Issing   I have a lot of sympathy for the idea that an independent agent must be controlled somewhat by the principal. 'Public choice' people have designed punishments for such shortcomings as exceeding the inflation target. Their intention was to design a control mechanism that doesn't undermine political independence, because if the principal is the controller, one is never sure for what reasons the agent is dismissed or punished. This is a difficult issue to solve. Certainly, the broader the mandate is, the more political it is, and the more difficult it is not to interfere from the political side. If the mandate is very narrow – price stability – then it's very difficult to make the central bank responsible for something else; the discussion remains focused on how the central bank delivers on this precise objective. In principle, I follow Willem's thinking, but I'm still awaiting a convincing proposal.

Index